Viksit Bharat 2047

Possibilities, Challenges and Strategies

Chief Editor
Dr. Kaushlendra Vikram Singh

Editors
Prof. Sarita Singh
Mr. Vaish Uddin
Dr. Shweta Yadav
Dr. Laxmi Narayan

First Edition: June 2026

Made with ❤ on the Notion Press Platform

www.notionpress.com

यह पुस्तक भारत के उन नागरिकों को समर्पित है, जिनकी आकांक्षाएँ, कठोर परिश्रम और सामूहिक प्रतिबद्धता वर्ष 2047 तक एक विकसित एवं आत्मनिर्भर भारत के निर्माण का मार्ग प्रशस्त कर रही हैं।

This book is dedicated to the people of India, whose aspirations, hard work, and collective commitment are paving the way towards a developed and self-reliant India by 2047.

Contents

Foreword

The aspiration of a Viksit Bharat by 2047 represents one of the most significant national endeavors of contemporary India. As the nation advances towards the centenary of its independence, the idea of development must be understood not merely in economic terms but also through the lenses of social justice, educational excellence, technological innovation, environmental sustainability, cultural preservation, and democratic values. It is in this context that the edited volume, "Viksit Bharat 2047: Possibilities, Challenges and Strategies," assumes considerable significance.

The present volume brings together scholarly contributions that examine the multifaceted dimensions of India's developmental journey. The chapters reflect thoughtful analyses of emerging opportunities, persistent challenges, and strategic interventions required for achieving the vision of a developed nation. The contributors have addressed contemporary issues with academic rigor and a deep sense of national commitment, thereby enriching the ongoing discourse on nation-building.

Institutions of higher education play a pivotal role in generating knowledge and fostering critical engagement with issues of public importance. This publication exemplifies that role by providing a platform for meaningful academic dialogue on the future of India. I appreciate the efforts of the editors and contributors in producing a work that is both intellectually stimulating and socially relevant.

I am confident that this volume will be of immense value to scholars, researchers, students, policymakers, and all readers interested in understanding the prospects and challenges associated with the realization of Viksit Bharat. I extend my heartfelt congratulations to the editorial team and wish this publication every success.

May this work contribute meaningfully to the collective pursuit of an inclusive, prosperous, and developed India by 2047.

Prof. Mamta Pandey
Principal & Patron
Government Degree College, Hardatt nagar Girant, Jamunha, Shravasti, Uttar Pradesh
Date:16 June 2026

Preface

"Viksit Bharat 2047: Possibilities, Challenges and Strategies" is an edited volume conceived in the context of India's collective aspiration to emerge as a developed, prosperous, inclusive and self-reliant nation by the centenary of its Independence in 2047. The vision of Viksit Bharat is not confined to economic growth alone; rather, it encompasses social justice, educational excellence, scientific and technological advancement, environmental sustainability, cultural vitality and responsive governance. The present volume has been compiled with the objective of contributing to the growing academic discourse surrounding this transformative national vision.

The chapters included in this book bring together diverse scholarly perspectives on the opportunities, challenges and strategic pathways associated with India's developmental journey. Drawing upon contemporary issues and emerging concerns, the contributors have examined various dimensions of nation-building with academic rigour and intellectual engagement. The volume seeks to encourage critical reflection on the policies, institutions and social processes that will shape India's progress in the coming decades.

As institutions of higher learning continue to play a vital role in knowledge creation and public discourse, it is hoped that this publication will serve as a meaningful resource for scholars, researchers, students, policymakers and all those interested in understanding the complexities and possibilities of India's development trajectory. By fostering informed discussion and evidence-based analysis, the book aims to contribute, in its own modest way, to the realisation of the vision of a developed India by 2047.

I express my sincere gratitude to Lord Ram Ji, to my parents and to my parents-in law for their blessings. I am deeply grateful to my wife Swati, for her unwavering support, patience, and encouragement, and to my son, Kaustubh, whose presence has been a constant source of joy and inspiration. I also extend my heartfelt appreciation to to all the contributors, co-editors, and well-wishers whose support and commitment have made this publication possible. I am especially grateful to Dr Manoj Kumar, Assistant Professor-English, Dr Bhimrao Ambedkar Government Degree College, Anaugi, Kannauj, Uttar Pradesh, Dr Sanjay Kumar Gupta, Assistant Professor-Hindi, Government Degree College, Pathardeva, Deoria, Uttar Pradesh, Prof. Gagan Kumar, Professor- Economics Government Degree College Pihani Hardoi, Dr. Surendra Kumar, Associate Professor- Math, Government Degree College Mahona, Lucknow and Dr. Saurabh Kumar Assistant Professor- Chemistry L.U. for reviewing the manuscripts and offering valuable comments and suggestions. Their critical observations, academic insight and constructive feedback have substantially enhanced the scholarly quality of this volume.

I also place on record my appreciation for all those who, directly or indirectly, contributed to the successful completion of this work. Their encouragement and cooperation have been a constant source of motivation throughout the editorial process.

It is my earnest hope that this volume will stimulate further research, enrich scholarly debate and inspire constructive engagement with the challenges and opportunities that lie ahead. If this publication succeeds in contributing to the intellectual foundations of a prosperous, equitable and developed India, its purpose will have been fulfilled.

Dr. Kaushlendra Vikram Singh
Chief Editor
16 June 2026

Chapter – 1

"One Nation, One Election: Federalism and Governance Challenges for Viksit Bharat 2047"

Dr.Mamta Goutam
Assistant Professor (Political Science)
Government PG College-Noida,G. B. Nagar
mamtagoutam@gmail.com

Abstract

The concept of "One Nation, One Election" (ONOE) refers to a proposed policy to hold simultaneous elections to the Lok Sabha and all state legislative assemblies in India. The primary objective of this concept is to ensure stability in governance, reduction in election expenditure, and continuity in policymaking. It is being presented as an effective administrative reform in the vision of "Developed India 2047." However, this policy also poses several serious challenges to India's federal structure, political diversity, and constitutional balance.

This paper analyzes the potential impacts of the "One Nation, One Election" concept on India's federal structure of governance. It seeks to understand the impact of simultaneous elections for the Centre and the states on Centre-State relations, state government autonomy, and regional political representation. The study also highlights the legal and constitutional implications of this policy-specifically, discussing the need for necessary amendments to Articles 83, 85, 172, and 174 of the Constitution.

The paper further notes potential governance benefits such as policy stability, administrative efficiency, and effective resource utilization, but also warns that this could result in centralization of power and the erosion of federal diversity. Finally, it concludes that the idea of "One Nation, One Election" will be successful and democratically meaningful only if its implementation carefully balances national unity and federal diversity. This balance will determine the real direction of Developed India 2047.

Keywords:
One Nation, One Election, federalism, governance, Developed India 2047, Indian Constitution, democracy, policy, electoral reforms.

Research Objectives:

- To understand the administrative and policy rationale behind implementing ONOE in India.
- To analyze its potential impact on the federal structure.
- To review the legal challenges and the need for constitutional amendment.
- To review this topic in the context of democratic participation, political diversity, and center-state relations as we move towards a developed India 2047.

Research Methodology:
This study used qualitative methods.
- A study of available government reports, policy documents, parliamentary debates, and policy analyses.
- A comparative examination of scholars, election experts, judicial opinions, and surveys.
- A historical analysis of past and current uses of ONOE and review of state and central government policies, political party perspectives, and international precedents.

1- Introduction:

India is the world's largest and most complex democracy, where governance is based on a multi-tiered structure at the central, state, and local bodies. This federal structure fosters regular elections, which strengthen India's democratic culture, but also poses numerous administrative, financial, and policy challenges.

Under the current system, Lok Sabha, state assembly, municipal, and panchayat elections are held at different times. This results in an electoral process in some parts of the country almost every year. Frequent elections create several problems:

1- ***Administrative work*** is disrupted because the code of conduct is in effect during the election process, which delays development plans and policy decisions.

2- ***Financial burden*** increases because both the central and state governments incur significant expenditures in conducting frequent elections.

3- ***Political stability*** is affected because, in a constantly contested election environment, governments are unable to focus on long-term policies, and decisions are often made for short-term political gain.

4- ***Political division and fragmentation of public opinion:*** Holding elections at different times exposes voters to repeated political propaganda, leading to an imbalance between national and regional issues.

All these reasons led to the idea that holding simultaneous elections for the Lok Sabha and State Legislative Assemblies across the country would increase administrative efficiency, save resources, and ensure continuity of governance. This idea is called "One Nation, One Election" (ONOE).

The main objective of this concept is to ensure stability in governance, uniformity in policymaking, and savings. Its proponents believe that holding all elections simultaneously would allow governments to focus more on policy implementation throughout their tenure, accelerating the country's development. In 2024, the Central Government constituted a High-Level Committee to consider ONOE, headed by former President Ram Nath Kovind. The committee's mandate is to examine the constitutional, legal, and practical feasibility of this policy.

This initiative is also aligned with the Government of India's vision of "Developed India 2047." The goal of a developed India is not limited to economic progress, but rather a comprehensive approach towards building a stable, transparent, and accountable governance system. "One Nation, One Election" is considered a potential step to strengthen this vision, thereby providing new direction to policy continuity, administrative efficiency, and federal cooperation in India. This "One Nation, One Election" initiative is not just an effort to streamline the electoral process, but is also considered a major step towards governance reform. This idea is also highly relevant in the context of "Developed India 2047." Developed India does not simply mean economic growth, but also the establishment of a stable, accountable, and transparent governance system. From this perspective, holding simultaneous elections will not only make governance more efficient but will also accelerate policy continuity and implementation. This can also provide a new direction to administrative transparency, effective use of resources, and public participation in democratic processes.

Thus, the "One Nation, One Election" concept is not just a matter of electoral reform, but a broader issue involving federal balance, democratic diversity, and reimagining the policy system. If implemented practically in the coming years, it could prove to be a historic initiative towards making India's governance system more stable, transparent, and result-oriented. This study examines how the concept of "One Nation, One Election" may impact India's federal structure, governance system, and democratic diversity, and whether it can truly prove to be a practical and balanced step towards Developed India 2047.

2- The Concept, Background and historical context of "One Nation, One Election:

India's democracy is based on a multi-tiered and comprehensive system, in which elections are held periodically at the central, state, and local body levels. This system ensures democratic participation, but it also creates constant electoral pressure on governance, administration, and policymaking. As a solution to this problem, the concept of "One Nation, One Election" has been proposed, offering a model for bringing stability, coherence, and efficiency to India's electoral landscape.

In the early years of India's independence, elections to the Lok Sabha and state assemblies were held simultaneously. In 1952, 1957, 1962, and 1967, elections to the Lok Sabha and most state assemblies were held simultaneously. This coordinated electoral system ensured stability in governance, better utilization of administrative resources, and policy continuity.

But the situation changed during 1968–69. Some state assemblies—such as Haryana, Punjab, Bihar, and Uttar Pradesh—were dissolved prematurely, resulting in a disparity between the

Lok Sabha and state electoral cycles. From then on, central and state elections began to be held at different times, ushering India's electoral system into the "Era of Continuous Elections."

Today, elections are held in some state or local body almost every year. This causes a large part of the administrative machinery to be repeatedly engaged in election work. This has a direct impact on governance, policymaking, and development work.

Emergence and Justification of the Concept:
The concept of "One Nation, One Election" emerged with the aim of eliminating this imbalance and establishing a unified electoral cycle. Its basic principle is that—

“Elections to the Lok Sabha and all State Legislative Assemblies should be held simultaneously, so that the financial, administrative, and policy instability caused by frequent elections in the country can be eliminated.”
This proposal is being seen not only as an electoral reform, but also as a governance reform.

3- Main Objectives, Pros and Cons of “One Nation, One Election:

Proponents of "One Nation, One Election" believe that this policy could be an important step toward strengthening India's governance system, administrative efficiency, and democratic participation. Its key benefits are the following:

1- Reducing the administrative and financial burden caused by frequent elections:
Conducting frequent elections consumes a significant amount of government funds and resources. The Election Commission, security forces, teachers, administrative officers, etc., are deployed

on election duty, disrupting normal administrative work. If all elections were held simultaneously, this duplication could be eliminated and efficient use of resources could be ensured.

2- ***Maintaining Governance Continuity and Policy Stability:*** The Model Code of Conduct, which is implemented during elections, has an immediate impact on government operations. Once implemented, new schemes cannot be announced, budget approvals are halted, and ongoing projects are significantly slowed. This disrupts development work and brings administrative processes to a standstill. However, if elections are held simultaneously, the Code of Conduct will not be invoked repeatedly. This will ensure continuity in governance, ensure timely policy decisions, and ensure smoother and more effective administration.

3- Reducing disruptions to development work:

Frequent elections directly impact the implementation of development projects and policies. As soon as elections are announced in a state or region, the Model Code of Conduct comes into effect. Once implemented, the government cannot announce new schemes, budget utilization is limited, and ongoing projects are halted or significantly slowed. This delays important projects.

If "One Nation, One Election" is implemented, the Model Code of Conduct will be implemented only once and for a limited period. This will prevent repeated disruptions to project implementation. Governments will be able to continuously advance projects throughout their five-year term.

4- Enhancing political stability and decision-making:

Frequent elections lead political parties to formulate policies based on electoral gains and losses. This leads to the neglect of long-term planning. If elections are held simultaneously across the country, governments will have greater independence and stability in decision-making throughout their tenure.

5- Voter convenience and political awareness:

With a unified electoral system, there will be no need to vote at separate times for Lok Sabha and Assembly elections. Citizens will not have to travel to polling stations repeatedly, reducing voter fatigue. Holding all important elections at the same time will also make voters more mentally prepared and motivated. This could increase their participation in the electoral process and lead to a significant increase in overall voter turnout.

Related policy developments:

- The idea of "One Nation, One Election" is not new. This issue has been raised by various commissions and committees from time to time.
- The Law Commission (1999 and 2018) considered simultaneous elections practically feasible and recommended necessary amendments to the Constitution.
- The Constitution Review Commission (2002) also supported this idea, calling it a "reform that enhances governance efficiency."
- The NITI Aayog (2017) report, "One Nation, One Election: A Transformative Reform," clarified that simultaneous elections can lead to both administrative efficiency and resource savings.

The High-Level Committee constituted by the Government of India in 2024, chaired by former President Ram Nath Kovind, is a concrete initiative in this direction. The Committee is tasked with studying the constitutional, legal, administrative, and financial feasibility of this policy and presenting a practical roadmap.

The idea of "One Nation, One Election" is not just an electoral reform, but a step towards a stable, efficient, and transparent system of governance for India. Developed India 2047 aims to create an India that is politically stable, economically prosperous, and administratively accountable. If successfully implemented, this policy will strengthen governance harmony, administrative transparency, and policy continuity, which are the foundations of any developed democracy.

3- The Impact of 'One Nation, One Election' on India's Federal Structure:

The most significant impact of "One Nation, One Election" could be on India's federal structure, as it directly affects the country's center-state structure and political autonomy. The Indian Constitution grants states the right to determine the term of their legislative assemblies, their dissolution, and the holding of elections according to political circumstances. However, if all elections are held simultaneously, this constitutional autonomy of states could be limited, as they would have to follow the electoral cycle set by the center. This is likely to impact the states' independent policy-making and political decision-making capabilities.

In addition, implementing ONOE would require amendments to several key constitutional articles- such as Articles 83, 172, 174, and 356. These amendments are not only technically difficult but also politically challenging, as they require the consent of the states. At the same time, a unified electoral system could also impact India's political diversity. As national issues take center stage, local and regional issues could be overshadowed, weakening the voice of regional parties and leadership. This will have a direct impact on the country's multi-party democratic structure, where diversity and local representation are crucial elements.

This arrangement also raises some concerns regarding center-state relations. Implementing a uniform electoral schedule could lead to a more powerful role for the center in the electoral structure, while weakening the voice of the states. This could tilt the balance of power in Indian federalism toward the center, which is considered contrary to the spirit of cooperative federalism. Therefore, while ONOE may offer benefits such as governance efficiency and resource savings, a careful assessment of its long-term impact on federalism and political diversity is essential.

4- Governance Challenges in the Implementation of 'One Nation, One Election:

Implementing "One Nation, One Election" also poses several governance challenges that need to be seriously considered. The biggest challenge relates to its legal and administrative complexities. Conducting simultaneous elections across the country will require state-of-the-art IT infrastructure, a massive logistics system, secure data management systems, adequate EVM-VVPAT machines, and trained human resources. Ensuring simultaneous elections on such a large scale is not only technically challenging but also extremely costly and time-consuming.

Furthermore, opposition parties and several social groups have expressed concerns about this concept. They argue that simultaneous elections could undermine the country's democratic diversity and regional representation, as national issues dominate electoral discourse, diminishing local issues and the role of regional leadership. There are also fears that ONOE will increase the influence of national parties while shrinking the political space of smaller and regional parties.

Additionally, this system presents new challenges in terms of election campaigning and public relations. Simultaneous elections require political parties to campaign extensively across the country, potentially diminishing the focus on local candidates and regional issues. While larger parties can manage this situation, smaller parties and independent candidates may face difficulties due to a lack of resources.

The most complex question is how the electoral cycle will be maintained if a government in a state falls prematurely or the assembly is dissolved. Will an interim government be formed in that state? Will President's rule be imposed? Or will elections for the entire system be postponed or postponed? These situations are not only constitutionally complex but can also be politically contentious.

Given all these challenges, it is clear that implementing ONOE requires more than just technical or administrative preparations; it will require developing a sensitive and consensual framework that preserves democratic diversity, the constitutional structure, and the federal balance.

5- International Perspective and Comparative Insights on 'One Nation, One Election:

In many countries around the world, national and provincial elections are held simultaneously, ensuring administrative efficiency and resource savings. For example, in countries like South Africa, Sweden, Belgium, and Indonesia, elections for parliament and regional bodies are held simultaneously. In these countries, the political system is relatively simple, the population is small, and the administrative structure is uniformly organized, which allows for the smooth functioning of a joint electoral system.

However, India's democratic structure is vastly different from these countries. India is the world's largest, most diverse, and multi-level federal democracy, with 28 states, 8 union territories, thousands of local bodies, hundreds of languages, and numerous socio-political groups. This diversity means that electoral behavior and political preferences vary greatly in India. Therefore, directly applying a foreign model to India is not practical.

International examples can only be references for India, not solutions. The complexities of our federalism, state autonomy, regional identities, and political competition are factors that cannot be taken into account without implementing ONOE. India must develop a context-specific model tailored to its needs, challenges, and the spirit of the Constitution, only then will a joint electoral system be practical and acceptable.

6- Strategic Opportunities and Structural Challenges in Realizing Viksit Bharat 2047:

"One Nation, One Election" could offer India significant opportunities in moving towards the goal of Viksit Bharat 2047 as it has the potential to make governance more stable, planned, and results-oriented. The biggest opportunity relates to governance stability. Frequent elections prevent governments from consistently advancing long-term plans and projects due to the imposition of the code of conduct every few months. This stalls development work and slows down policy flow. If elections were held simultaneously and the government had the opportunity to work continuously for a full five years, more effective and timely implementation of major projects- such as infrastructure development, social welfare, education, health, and employment generation- would be possible.

The second major opportunity relates to political stability. A constant electoral environment divides governance energy, and political decisions are often based on short-term gains. However, once ONOE is implemented, political leadership will have the opportunity to focus on policies and development throughout their term. This will strengthen decision-making, ensure long-term policies are implemented with stability, and accelerate economic growth. Political stability will also have a positive impact on areas such as economic investment, industrial development, and foreign investment, further contributing to the realization of the goal of Viksit Bharat 2047.

However, these opportunities are accompanied by some serious obstacles that cannot be ignored. The first obstacle relates to India's federalism and democratic pluralism. India's political structure is based on regional diversity, with each state having its own political, social, and economic character. If elections are held simultaneously, national issues may overshadow local and regional issues, weakening regional parties, local representation, and the democratic voice of the states. This situation could go against the principles of India's pluralistic democracy and cooperative federalism.

The second obstacle is that the path to Viksit Bharat 2047 lies not only in political stability but also inclusive development, social justice, and respect for state autonomy. If the implementation of ONOE limits the autonomy of states or impacts their policymaking freedom, this reform could deviate from its original purpose.

It is therefore clear that "One Nation, One Election" can play a crucial role in accelerating Viksit Bharat 2047, provided it is ensured that its process is implemented in a balanced and respectful manner, consistent with India's federal structure, democratic diversity, and the political autonomy of the states. The balance in this equation of opportunities and constraints will determine India's true path to development.

7-Conclusion:

"One Nation, One Election" is certainly an attractive and visionary idea towards *Developed India 2047*, one that can strengthen governance stability, administrative efficiency, and policy-making continuity. It will accelerate the implementation of development plans, significantly reduce election costs, and streamline democratic processes. For these reasons, this idea offers significant opportunities for administrative reform and prudent use of economic resources.

But the success of this concept depends not only on its potential benefits, but equally on preserving India's federalism, democratic pluralism, and constitutional balance. A diverse and multi-layered country like India cannot function with a single uniform electoral structure; preserving state autonomy, regional diversity, and representation of local issues are crucial. If ONOE is implemented hastily or without adequate deliberation, it could challenge the very nature of Indian federalism, as it risks increasing the power of the center and weakening the democratic role of the states.
Therefore, the implementation of this policy will be considered practical and democratically legitimate only if-
Comprehensive constitutional amendments are made with utmost care and consensus, Participation and consent of all political parties is ensured,
and decisions are made based on extensive dialogue, transparency, and public opinion involving the public.
Ultimately, the objective of "One Nation, One Election" will be meaningful only if it is implemented while strengthening India's democratic values, constitutional ideals, and federal spirit. Only a balanced approach, cooperative federalism, and respect for democratic diversity can make this reform truly successful.

References:

- Election Commission of India. (1999). Report of the Law Commission of India on electoral reforms. Government of India.
- Election Commission of India. (2018). Reform of electoral laws: Law Commission of India—Report No. 255. Government of India.
- Government of India. (2017). One Nation, One Election: A transformative reform. NITI Aayog. https://www.niti.gov.in
- Government of India. (2024). Report of the High-Level Committee on One Nation, One Election (Chair: Ram Nath Kovind). Ministry of Law and Justice.
- Ministry of Home Affairs. (2023). Annual report on internal security and election administration. Government of India. https://www.mha.gov.in
- Ministry of Law and Justice. (2002). Report of the National Commission to Review the Working of the Constitution. Government of India.
- Ministry of Parliamentary Affairs. (2020). Handbook on election management and parliamentary procedures. Government of India.
- NITI Aayog. (2017). One Nation, One Election: A comparative analysis and framework for implementation. Government of India.
- Sharma, A., & Verma, R. (2021). Federalism and electoral reforms in India: Issues and challenges. Journal of Constitutional Studies, 12(2), 45–63.
- Singh, P. (2020). Centre–state dynamics in India: Assessing the political implications of simultaneous elections. Indian Journal of Federal Studies, 8(1), 11–29.

- United Nations Development Programme. (2022). Human development report 2022: Democracy, governance, and political participation. UNDP. https://hdr.undp.org
- World Bank. (2021). India governance report: Public administration and electoral management. https://www.worldbank.org

Chapter- 2

Political Participation in the Digital Age: Opportunities and Challenges in India's Journey to Viksit Bharat 2047

Ashutosh Singh Srinet

Research scholar, Centre for Studies in Science Policy (CSSP), School of Social Science, Jawahar Lal Nehru University (JNU), New Delhi, 110067

ashutoshshrinetsingh@gmail.com

Abstract

Political participation in the digital age has transformed the relationship between citizens and democratic institutions in India. Digital platforms, social media, and online governance initiatives have expanded opportunities for political awareness, civic engagement, public discourse, and citizen participation. These technologies enable greater access to information and strengthen democratic accountability. However, challenges such as misinformation, digital divides, privacy concerns, cyber threats, and online polarization continue to affect the quality of democratic participation. In the context of Viksit Bharat 2047, understanding these opportunities and challenges is essential for building an inclusive, transparent, and technologically empowered democracy that promotes active citizen involvement and sustainable national development.

Key Words- inclusive, government, Political participation, digital age, internet platforms

Introduction

Aristotle argues that *man is by nature a political animal* and achieves his full potential and good life (eudaimonia) only within a political community, the *polis* (city-state). If we trace the roots of our present-day democratic system, we undoubtedly find it in our ancient and time-tested texts and epics. *'Sabha'* and *'Samiti'*, as a direct participation of individuals in the decision-making body, were already present at that time as a robust framework for the better governance of the contemporary socio-political system. Over time, as population and societal complexity increased, indirect rule became essential, and societies adopted it with no suitable alternatives. In the indirect rule, citizens participate in the decision-making process of the nation through representatives they elect on their behalf for a fixed tenure.

After independence, India adopted a parliamentary democracy for which free, fair and regular (time-bound) elections are a prerequisite. The election process consists of a number of events and activities like political socialisation, electoral campaigning, narrative building and feedback, etc. During the initial period after our country's independence, people's mobilisation was confined and restricted to certain sources and manners compared to recent times. Since independence, there has been no scope for electronic or synchronous media for decades. Radio and print media were the major instruments to access information and people's mobilisation in the country. In 1959, when television was introduced in selected urban regions, a faster information proliferation took place, but still in limited strata. As far as political participation was concerned, its chance was negligible as the government had control over it and had restricted it to entertainment and educational purposes only.

In 1991, the deregulation of television networks provided the emergence of many 24/7 news channels, leading to more political engagement of the people and even facilitated opinion polls for that year's elections (Press Trust of India, 2010). Further, the internet, diffused in the 2010s, in the form of digital media platforms, transformed these scenarios in a quicker, more dynamic and subjective way and eventually became the backbone for our civic and political system. Internet, unlike the conventional means of communication like Radio, Telephone and Television, has the required potential to revolutionise the political activity because it offers the possibility of instant two-way communication, which helps both ruling elites and masses to interact more actively.

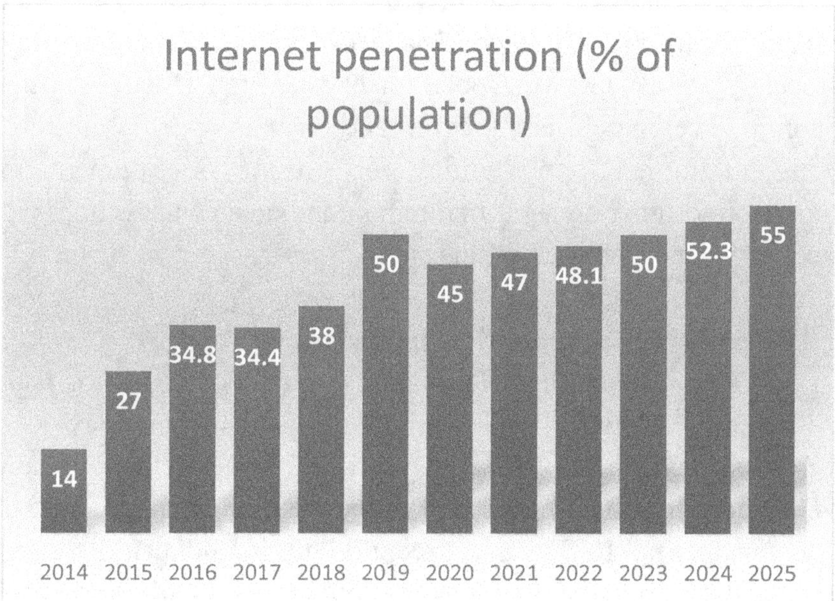

Table 1: Internet penetration rate in India from 2014 to 2025
Source- Statista (2025)

India has witnessed a massive upsurge in internet access in recent years. As per the reports published by the Telecom Regulatory Authority of India (TRAI), the number of internet subscribers has jumped from 251.6 million by March 2014 to 954.4 million in March 2024. This diffusion shows widespread smartphone adoption and cheap internet data charges- average internet data has reduced from Rs 268.97/GB in 2014 to just Rs 9.18/GB by 2024 (PIB, 2 August 2024).

This chapter intends to examine how digital media has shaped factors that influence political participation in our country. Conventional factors such as muscle and money power, local dominance, caste and religious issues, etc., are studied with special attention, whether they have become negligible or are still relevant but in another form in this digital era. The chapter includes David Easton's political system and aims to understand the role of digital media on input, output, feedback and overall environment of the political system. Growth pole theory, which suggests that economic development and growth take place in specific clusters, leading to further opportunities for greater development in comparison to other areas of that region and creates unevenness in the country, has been used in this study.

Digital democracy and political participation

Krazberg's law states that 'Technology is neither good nor bad, nor is neutral' (Melvin, 1986). Simply means the technology does not possess any inherent value in itself; the same technology can have different results after getting introduced in different contexts or circumstances. ICT is no exception to it and can be used contextually in both positive and negative ways. Cyberoptimists view it as an apparatus for faster communication, bringing people together by enabling them to have borderless access, spread and store information at their own discretion, etc. As Danah Boyd stated, "It can be a powerful tool for social justice" (Barber, 1998). Whereas pessimists see it as a tool to censor citizens by usurping their personal information, spreading misinformation to reinforce the existing power structure of the society and enhance inequality. As Evgeny Morozov has outlined, "it can be used for manipulation, surveillance, and authoritarian control" (Barber,1998) while discussing cyber utopianism.

Digital democracy refers to the enhancement, influence and transformation of democratic processes, such as political and governance deliberation, civic engagement, the manner of political campaigning, agenda setting and citizen-government networks through using ICT, especially the internet (Norris, 2001). Indeed, online forums and social media platforms provide a virtual public space with anonymity, allowing even those previously excluded/debarred by location or socio-economic status to raise their voices in debates and political discourse. According to Carole Patman (1970), democracy is strengthened when people are actively involved in decision-making processes beyond fixed and periodic elections.

Political participation refers to the behaviour and activities of individuals, groups or organisations within a society by which they try to involve themselves in the political system (Verba et al, 1995).

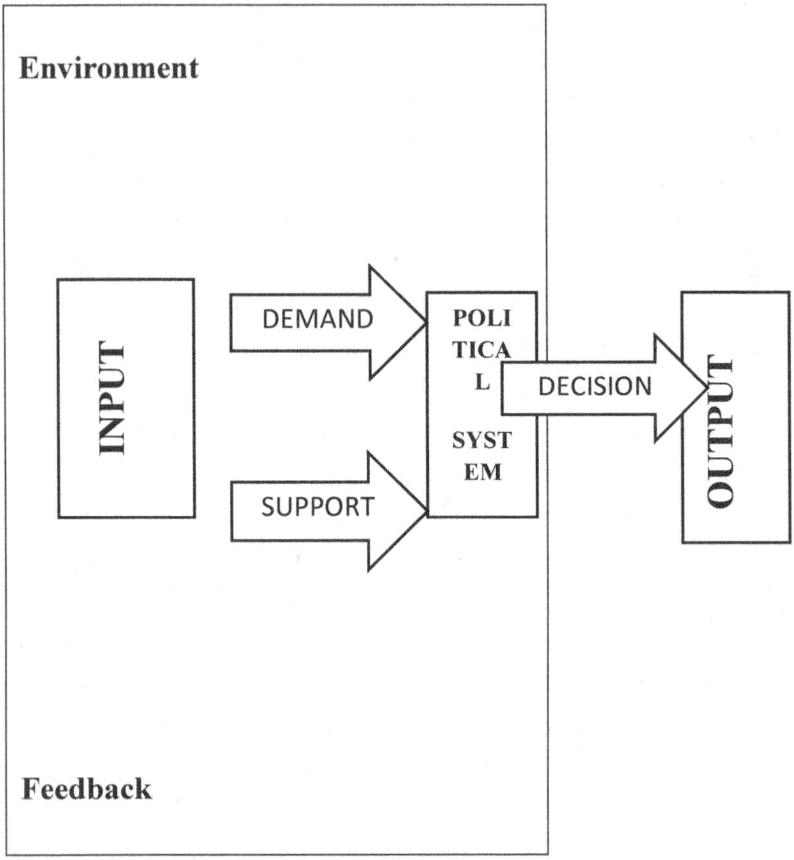

Figure 2: David Easton's Political System Analysis
Source- (Johari, 1972)

Information technology holds considerable potential to promote government accountability, foster more informed and responsible citizens, and facilitate public deliberation and political discourse within the state and civil society (Hague & Loader, 1999). ICT influences every aspect of political discourse mentioned by Johari in his political system, from the demands of the public, the government's decision on those demands, to the feedback from the citizens altogether (Dennis et al, 2019).

WhatsApp and other internet platforms are increasingly becoming important tools that political parties and candidates use to reach out to voters, particularly the younger and urban voters. By the 2019 general elections, it was dubbed by commentators as the WhatsApp election in India, with the heavy use of the messaging platform by parties to communicate their messages (Sheikh, 2024). Through digital media, citizens can criticise, provide feedback and support the public policy formulation in less time and with more intensity. Through social movements, from anti-corruption protests, the COVID-19 infodemic, the Delhi riots, to the farmer protests, social media has shown its real significance in the form of collective action (Panwar, 2023). In conventional politics, political discourse was often built and narrated by prominent personalities, but in present day scenario, digitalisation of democracy facilitates everyone with almost an equal opportunity to proliferate their opinion and dissent with others (Shirky, 2008).

Risk and Challenges

Despite the improvements and promises, India's digital democracy faces formidable challenges in the current scenario. The uneven expansion of digital access often reinforces existing social inequalities (Selwyn 2004). India Inequality Report 2022, published by Oxfam India, suggests that socioeconomic factors such as gendered social norms, geographical region and economic and social conditions are more likely to determine the ownership of devices and the affordability of internet use. Sharp unevenness in digital access may reinforce existing social inequalities. High-handedness of private companies in the matter of charging recharge fees should be capped. Although the data fee is quite low in the country in comparison with other nations, a large portion of the population has not yet borne this high amount.

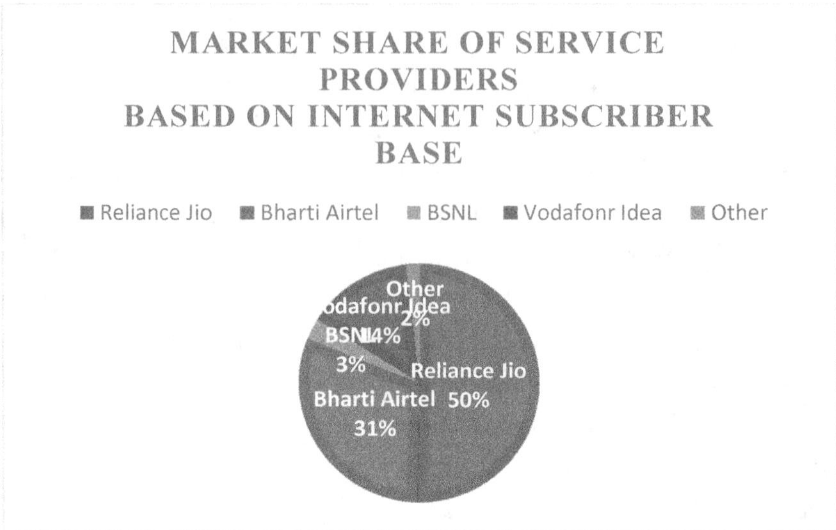

Table 2: Market share of service providers based on Internet subscribers
Source- Telecom Regulatory Authority of India (TRAI), 2024.

Political parties and public leaders routinely use data analytics, targeted messaging, and online campaigning to reach out to citizens and influence them, an innovation previously seen as an emerging trend in the 2014 general elections (Gaur, 2019). Without an unbiased formulation, explicit explanation and strict implementation, regulations to promote e-freedom may undermine democratic quality.

Digital divide and unequal political inclusion

While internet penetration has grown at a rapid pace, access remains uneven in various regions and socio-political situations. A vast segment of the rural population, dependent women, the elderly, marginalised and disabled communities, continue to experience limited and inconsistent access to digital infrastructure and resources (Wuneh & Kidanu, 2023). This imbalanced access produces asymmetric political participation, where digitally connected and having better skills enjoy more visible, vocal and influential benefits while others remain excluded (Democratic divide). This divide is becoming a privilege to the digitally literate and economically secure population because it is reinforcing existing inequalities and power hierarchies rather than eliminating them (Dijk, 2020). In the long run, it will affect political participation in a negative sense, which threatens the legitimacy of the democratic framework.

Misinformation, Disinformation and erosion of democratic trust

Other major risks associated with digital political participation are false narratives, manipulated videos, deepfake and propaganda with malicious intentions to gain political power. These practices mislead public opinion, polarise electorates and undermine the legitimacy of democratic processes. In such an ecosystem, voting behaviour may be manipulated more by misleading information, hate speech and identity-based mass mobilisation rather than multidimensional informed deliberation (Sunstein, 2017). Over time, the repetition of false and manipulated information erodes public trust in democratic institutions and electoral outcomes (Ex-Vote Chori issue) of the country.

Chilling effect, symbolic participation and democratic fragmentation

A chilling effect occurs when people self-censor or refrain from expressing their ideas and lawful activities due to fear of negative consequences, such as cyber trolling, data surveillance, legal trouble and social boycott, etc. (Penney, 2017). Digital space provides a symbolic and superficial practice with low-impact actions such as liking, sharing and hashtag activism. Contemporary youths (Gen Z) engage in political and civic mobilisation primarily through social media platforms rather than physical action (Theocharis, 2015).

Policy Recommendations

To actualise the democratic potential of this digital era for *Viksit Bharat 2047*, India needs to (a) formulate more just, inclusive and flexible but explicit policies, (b) create affordable, balanced and sustainable infrastructure, (c) implement, maintain and regulate them strictly. Below are some policies recommended for the desired goal of Viksit Bharat 2047.

1. **Institutionalising universal and equitable digital access and advancing civic education for meaningful participation-** 'Connect the unconnected'. Expand continuing such as Bharat Net, PMGDISHA, etc., subsidized internet capable devices for below poverty line (BPL) families, low-income households and the population in last-mile connectivity. Scale up digital literacy, standard skills and community training programs in the local language.
2. **Strengthening the regulatory framework for platforms accountability and citizens responsibility- there is no single** law code dedicated only to fake news and disinformation. It is fragmentarily available in various laws with no explicit explanation of it. A German is saying- "Show me the person, I will show the crime". Without a clearly stated definition and provisions, it's easy to manipulate laws by the authorities in their favour, which can lead to the distortion of democracy. Private platforms must

disclose their algorithm and should report to the Indian government routinely about their functioning.

3. Safeguarding privacy, data protection, civil liberties and combating cyberattacks to prompt trust of citizens in digital governance- Without robust safeguards, people may disengage due to concerns of surveillance and cyber trolling. Enacting a comprehensive and pro-people data protection bill is a need of the hour. Protecting privacy is not only a technical issue but a fundamental democratic right explained by the Supreme Court in case...... To combat misinformation, relying solely on punitive measure are not sufficient, but a fact-checking ecosystem should be emphasised.
4. **Building democratic resilience through adaptive and future-oriented governance-** democratic resilience in the digital age requires proactive rather than reactive policy measures. Policymakers from the multi-stakeholder entities should invest the resources in anticipatory governance, continuous research and development and institutional learning with cognitive skills to ensure that democratic norms evolve alongside technological innovation.
5. **Controlling monopoly of companies in specific sectors and fostering indigenisation (Atmanirbhar Bharat)-** Reliance Jio is controlling half of the (nearly 50%) of internet subscribers, and government-owned BSNL

encompasses merely 3%. The government should make provisions to cap the maximum and minimum fees for the recharge from which these private companies are making huge profits. Recently launched indigenous apps such as Attarai, Zoho Mail, etc., are a little but big step in this sector towards Viksit Bharat 2047.

Conclusion

Despite the progress, ensuring fair opportunities and equitable access to high-speed internet in remote and underdeveloped areas is crucial for inclusive development and Viksit Bharat 2047. Telecom and big tech companies must invest resources and develop initiatives to establish a robust mechanism for bridging the gap between '*haves*' and '*have-nots*' by creating infrastructure, maintaining privacy and protecting the personal data of users by keeping data in India only. The government should implement strict policies for the same and should impose tariffs, or others measure on such platforms who does not comply with rules. Recent developments such as e- voting, e-governance, e-complaint and e-citizen service, etc., have reshaped the political participation in an efficient way, yet the journey to Viksit Bharat 2047 requires conscious and futuristic policy choices.

If we talk about some of the most essential elements for the success of democracy, these are (a) higher participation in elections, (b) free, fair and regular elections, (c) highly connected youths, etc., India consists of all of them; it has the highest electorate, a long legacy of a stable political system through the periodic elections. The government must consider them as fuels for Viksit Bharat 2047; otherwise, these indicators could either turn into its demographic dividend or it can emerge as the biggest burden, which totally depends upon the future planning and projections. Manuel Castells, in his work 'The Information Age: Economy, Society and Culture', while discussing about the transformative impact of ICT on the fabric of society, talks about a new form of social organisation, characterised by network society. He argues that networked communication has significantly helped in penetrating the social movements and grassroots organisations to challenge the existing hierarchy of power structure.

Digital connectivity should not be considered only as a technology luxury or utility but as a democratic public good necessary for political socialisation. The coming decades of Indian democracy will be defined by the degree of activism with which common people perform their duty by asking for accountability to the government, framing policies and demanding justice, etc., through digital means.

Reference

- Castells, M. (2012). Networks of outrage and hope: Social movements in the Internet age. Polity Press.
- Chadwick, A. (2013). The hybrid media system: Politics and power. Oxford University Press.
- Diamond, L., & Morlino, L. (2005). Assessing the quality of democracy. Johns Hopkins University Press.
- Digital Empowerment Foundation. (2019). India inequality report: Digital access and inclusion. New Delhi.
- Election Commission of India. (2020). Use of social media in election campaigns. Government of India.
- Freedom House. (2023). Freedom on the Net 2023: India. Freedom House.

- Garimella, K., De Francisci Morales, G., Gionis, A., & Mathioudakis, M. (2018). Political discourse on social media: Echo chambers, gatekeepers, and the price of bipartisanship. Proceedings of the Web Conference, 913–922.
- Government of India. (2015). Digital India programme. Ministry of Electronics and Information Technology.
- Government of India. (2023). India Internet Governance Report. Ministry of Communications.
- Habermas, J. (1989). The structural transformation of the public sphere (T. Burger, Trans.). MIT Press.
- Internet and Mobile Association of India. (2022). Internet in India report. IAMAI.
- Kumar, S. (2014). Gandhi meets primetime: Globalisation and nationalism in Indian television news. University of Illinois Press.
- Loader, B. D., & Mercea, D. (2011). Networking democracy? Social media innovations and participatory politics. Information, Communication & Society, 14(6), 757–769.
- Ministry of Electronics and Information Technology. (2021). Information Technology (Intermediary Guidelines and Digital Media Ethics Code) Rules. Government of India.
- National Sample Survey Office. (2019). Key indicators of household social consumption on education and ICT. Government of India.
- Norris, P. (2001). Digital divide: Civic engagement, information poverty, and the Internet worldwide. Cambridge University Press.
- Papacharissi, Z. (2015). Affective publics: Sentiment, technology, and politics. Oxford University Press.

- Pew Research Centre. (2019). Internet, social media, and political participation in emerging economies. Pew Research Centre.
- Privacy International. (2019). Aadhaar and data protection in India. Privacy International.
- Putnam, R. D. (2000). Bowling alone: The collapse and revival of American community. Simon & Schuster.
- Shirky, C. (2011). The political power of social media. Foreign Affairs, 90(1), 28–41.
- Sunstein, C. R. (2017). #Republic: Divided democracy in the age of social media. Princeton University Press.
- Telecom Regulatory Authority of India. (2022). The Indian telecom services performance indicators. TRAI.
- Tufekci, Z. (2017). Twitter and tear gas: The power and fragility of networked protest. Yale University Press.
- Vaidhyanathan, S. (2018). Antisocial media: How Facebook disconnects us and undermines democracy. Oxford University Press.
- Verba, S., Schlozman, K. L., & Brady, H. E. (1995). Voice and equality: Civic voluntarism in American politics. Harvard University Press.
- Zuboff, S. (2019). The age of surveillance capitalism. PublicAffairs.

Chapter- 3

Financial Inclusion in India: Opportunities, Challenges and Strategic Pathways Towards Viksit Bharat 2047

"When finance reaches the last mile, development reaches the whole nation."

NARESH, Assistant Professor -Commerce, Government Degree College, Hardattnagar, Girant, Shravasti, U.P., jrfnareshkumar@gmail.com, 9891946319

Financial inclusion has become a strategic priority in India's development agenda and a necessary condition for achieving the vision of Viksit Bharat 2047. In a broad sense, financial inclusion refers to affordable, timely, and equitable access to formal financial services such as banking, savings, credit, insurance, pensions, and digital payments for all sections of society. These services are particularly important for low-income households, women, rural populations, informal workers, and micro-enterprises that have historically remained outside the organized financial system.

This chapter examines India's financial inclusion journey through six core pillars: banking access, savings mobilization, credit availability, insurance protection, pension security, and digital payments. It highlights the substantial progress made during the last decade through major policy initiatives such as Pradhan Mantri Jan Dhan Yojana, Aadhaar-enabled service delivery, Direct Benefit Transfer, expanding business correspondent networks, fintech innovation, and the rapid growth of Unified Payments Interface. These developments have significantly widened formal financial participation and improved transaction efficiency across the economy.

The chapter also identifies key challenges that continue to hinder comprehensive inclusion, including dormant accounts, inadequate financial literacy, unequal credit access, low insurance and pension penetration, gender disparities, regional inequalities, and rising digital fraud risks. It argues that the next phase of financial inclusion must move beyond account ownership toward active usage, service quality, consumer trust, and long-term financial resilience.

To address these issues, the study proposes strategic pathways such as strengthening active banking usage, promoting inclusive savings products, expanding MSME and household credit, widening insurance and pension outreach, enhancing cybersecurity frameworks, improving women-centred financial inclusion, and adopting data-driven regional policy targeting.

The chapter concludes that financial inclusion is not merely a social objective but a powerful instrument of economic transformation. A robust and inclusive financial system can stimulate entrepreneurship, improve resilience, reduce inequality, and support broad-based growth. Therefore, deepening financial inclusion across all six pillars will be critical for India's transition into an economically strong, socially inclusive, and globally competitive developed nation by 2047.

Keywords: Financial Inclusion, India, Viksit Bharat 2047, Banking, Credit, Digital Payments, Inclusive Growth, Economic Development.

1. Introduction

Financial inclusion has emerged as a critical pillar of contemporary development policy and an essential determinant of inclusive economic growth. Broadly, it refers to the provision of affordable, timely, and appropriate financial services—such as banking facilities, savings instruments, credit, insurance, pensions, and digital payment systems—to all sections of society, particularly vulnerable and underserved groups. In developing economies, financial inclusion contributes to poverty reduction, income stability, entrepreneurial expansion, and greater economic resilience (World Bank, 2022). Consequently, it is increasingly viewed not merely as a welfare objective, but as a structural requirement for sustainable development.

For India, the relevance of financial inclusion is particularly significant in the context of **Viksit Bharat 2047**, the national vision of transforming India into a developed economy by the centenary of independence. Achieving this objective requires high and sustained growth accompanied by equitable access to economic opportunities. In such a framework, an inclusive financial system enables households to save securely, smooth consumption, manage emergencies, access productive credit, and accumulate long-term assets. Likewise, enterprises—especially micro, small, and medium enterprises (MSMEs)—benefit from improved access to formal finance for investment, working capital, and business expansion.

India has made substantial progress in financial inclusion during the past decade through a combination of policy reforms, institutional innovation, and digital public infrastructure. A major milestone was the launch of Pradhan Mantri Jan Dhan Yojana in 2014, which significantly expanded account ownership among previously unbanked populations. According to the Government of India, the scheme crossed **55 crore accounts** by 2025, with a majority share held by women and a substantial proportion in rural and semi-urban areas (Government of India, 2025). This reflects an important shift toward broader demographic participation in formal finance.

Parallel to banking expansion, India has also witnessed rapid growth in digital payments. Unified Payments Interface has transformed retail transactions through instant, low-cost, and interoperable payment architecture. Monthly transaction volumes crossed historic levels in 2025, underscoring the scale of India's transition toward a digitally enabled financial ecosystem (National Payments Corporation of India, 2025). At the same time, direct benefit transfers linked to Aadhaar and bank accounts have strengthened transparency and delivery efficiency in welfare administration.

The progress of financial inclusion is also reflected in the Reserve Bank of India Financial Inclusion Index, which rose steadily to **67.0 in March 2025**, indicating improvements in access, usage, and quality dimensions of financial services (Reserve Bank of India, 2025). Nevertheless, important challenges persist, including dormant accounts, unequal credit access, low insurance and pension penetration, digital fraud risks, regional disparities, and inadequate financial literacy.

Financial inclusion is also closely linked with the achievement of the United Nations Sustainable Development Goals (SDGs) 2030. Access to affordable banking, savings, credit, insurance, and digital payment services directly contributes to multiple SDGs, particularly Goal 1 (No Poverty), Goal 5 (Gender Equality), Goal 8 (Decent Work and Economic Growth), Goal 9 (Industry, Innovation and Infrastructure), and Goal 10 (Reduced Inequalities). Inclusive finance enables poor households to build resilience, supports women's economic empowerment, improves access to productive capital for micro-enterprises, and facilitates efficient welfare delivery. India's recent progress through Pradhan Mantri Jan Dhan Yojana, Direct Benefit Transfer, and digital payment expansion demonstrates how financial inclusion can accelerate progress toward the SDG agenda by integrating vulnerable populations into formal economic systems (United Nations, 2023; World Bank, 2022).

Against this background, the present chapter examines financial inclusion in India through six interrelated pillars—banking, savings, credit, insurance, pensions, and digital payments. It evaluates recent progress, identifies persistent constraints, and proposes strategic pathways through which financial inclusion can contribute meaningfully to the realization of Viksit Bharat 2047.

2. Conceptual Framework and Dimensions of Financial Inclusion

Financial inclusion is a multidimensional concept that extends beyond the mere ownership of a bank account. Contemporary literature emphasizes that meaningful inclusion requires accessible, affordable, and appropriate financial products that are regularly used by individuals and enterprises. It encompasses not only entry into the formal financial system, but also sustained participation through savings, borrowing, risk management, retirement planning, and digital transactions (Demirgüç-Kunt et al., 2022). Therefore, financial inclusion should be understood as a continuum of financial engagement rather than a binary condition of being banked or unbanked.

Early policy approaches often equated financial inclusion with branch expansion and account opening. While these remain important, later research has demonstrated that account ownership alone may generate limited developmental impact when accounts remain dormant or disconnected from broader financial activity. Accordingly, recent frameworks, including the Reserve Bank of India Financial Inclusion Index, assess inclusion through three broad dimensions: **access**, **usage**, and **quality** (Reserve Bank of India, 2025). Access refers to the availability of financial infrastructure and services; usage concerns frequency and depth of service utilization; and quality reflects suitability, affordability, safety, and consumer experience.

For the purpose of this chapter, financial inclusion in India is analysed through six interrelated pillars that collectively shape household and enterprise participation in the formal economy.

2.1 Banking Access

Banking access represents the entry point to formal finance. It includes ownership and use of savings accounts, branch services, ATMs, mobile banking, and agent networks such as business correspondents. In India, the rapid expansion of accounts under Pradhan Mantri Jan Dhan Yojana substantially improved access among previously excluded groups (Government of India, 2025). However, effective banking inclusion requires active usage rather than passive ownership.

2.2 Savings Inclusion

Savings inclusion refers to the ability of households to deposit surplus funds securely and accumulate resources over time. Formal savings reduce reliance on cash holdings, improve resilience during income shocks, and support future investments in health, education, and housing. At the macroeconomic level, household financial savings contribute to capital formation and financial stability (World Bank, 2022).

2.3 Credit Inclusion

Credit inclusion concerns timely and affordable access to loans for consumption smoothing and productive activities. It is especially relevant for farmers, students, self-employed workers, and MSMEs. Persistent exclusion from formal credit often forces borrowers toward informal lenders charging high interest rates. Therefore, equitable credit access remains central to inclusive growth.

2.4 Insurance Inclusion

Insurance inclusion reflects protection against financial shocks arising from illness, accidents, crop losses, disability, or death. In low- and middle-income settings, uninsured shocks can reverse years of economic progress. Hence, insurance is an important pillar of financial resilience and poverty prevention (IRDAI, 2024).

2.5 Pension Inclusion

Pension inclusion focuses on long-term income security in old age. With increasing life expectancy and changing family structures, retirement security has become more important, particularly for India's large informal workforce. Micro-pension and contributory schemes can reduce future vulnerability (PFRDA, 2024).

2.6 Digital Payments Inclusion

Digital payments include mobile transfers, UPI transactions, card payments, internet banking, and Aadhaar-enabled systems. These mechanisms reduce transaction costs, improve efficiency, formalize commerce, and create digital financial histories useful for future credit assessment (BIS, 2023).

These six pillars are mutually reinforcing. A bank account facilitates savings; savings can improve creditworthiness; digital payments increase account activity; insurance reduces vulnerability; and pensions enhance long-term security. Therefore, financial inclusion should be viewed as an integrated ecosystem that supports India's transition toward a more productive, equitable, and developed economy by 2047.

3. Progress of Financial Inclusion in India: Trends, Evidence and Structural Transformation

India's financial inclusion landscape has undergone a significant transformation during the last decade. The country has moved from a model historically characterized by limited branch outreach and high cash dependence to a broader architecture based on mass account ownership, digital payments, targeted welfare transfers, and expanding social security products. This transition is widely regarded as one of the most extensive financial inclusion efforts among emerging economies (Demirgüç-Kunt et al., 2022).

A major milestone in this process was the introduction of Pradhan Mantri Jan Dhan Yojana in 2014. The scheme accelerated formal banking penetration by simplifying account opening norms and linking accounts with RuPay cards, overdraft facilities, and government benefit transfers. By 2025, total accounts opened under the programme exceeded **55 crore**, with women accounting for a majority share and a substantial concentration in rural and semi-urban regions (Government of India, 2025). This expansion indicates that previously excluded populations—particularly women and lower-income households—have entered the formal financial system at scale.

The broader improvement in financial access is also supported by global survey evidence. According to the Global Findex Database, the proportion of adults in India holding a formal financial account rose sharply over the past decade, placing India among the major contributors to global gains in account ownership (Demirgüç-Kunt et al., 2022). This suggests that policy-led expansion, when supported by digital identity and payment infrastructure, can materially reduce exclusion.

Beyond access, usage patterns have also improved. The Reserve Bank of India Financial Inclusion Index increased to **67.0 in March 2025**, compared with lower levels in earlier years, reflecting gains across access, usage, and quality dimensions (Reserve Bank of India, 2025). The rising trajectory of the index is significant because it captures a shift from basic account opening toward broader participation in financial services.

One of the most visible dimensions of progress has been the rapid rise of digital payments. Unified Payments Interface has fundamentally reshaped low-value retail transactions by enabling instant, interoperable, and low-cost transfers through mobile platforms. By 2025, monthly UPI transaction volumes crossed record levels, demonstrating both consumer acceptance and merchant integration (National Payments Corporation of India, 2025). The increasing adoption of QR-based payments among small vendors and micro-enterprises indicates that digital finance is no longer confined to urban consumers.

Another important structural development has been the success of the JAM trinity—Jan Dhan, Aadhaar, and Mobile—which enabled the expansion of Direct Benefit Transfer systems. Welfare payments deposited directly into beneficiaries' accounts have reduced leakages, improved administrative efficiency, and strengthened trust in formal banking channels (NITI Aayog, 2023). This linkage between public finance delivery and financial inclusion has been a distinctive feature of India's development model.

Progress has also extended to insurance and pension outreach. Government-backed low-premium schemes such as Pradhan Mantri Jeevan Jyoti Bima Yojana and Pradhan Mantri Suraksha Bima Yojana have broadened basic risk coverage, while Atal Pension Yojana has expanded contributory pension participation among unorganized workers (PFRDA, 2024). Although coverage remains below potential, these initiatives mark a transition from narrow banking inclusion toward wider financial security.

Institutional outreach mechanisms have also improved. Business correspondents, micro-ATMs, payment banks, and fintech platforms have reduced geographic barriers and lowered transaction costs, particularly in rural and underserved areas. These innovations have complemented traditional branch networks and improved last-mile service delivery.

Overall, India's recent experience indicates a structural shift from financial exclusion toward broader formal participation. However, progress remains uneven across regions, income groups, and service categories. Account ownership has expanded faster than productive credit, insurance depth, and retirement security. Therefore, while the achievements are substantial, the next phase must focus on deepening quality and usage if financial inclusion is to fully support Viksit Bharat 2047.

4. Opportunities of Financial Inclusion for Viksit Bharat 2047

Financial inclusion presents India with a significant opportunity to strengthen the foundations of long-term economic growth and social progress. As India aspires to become a developed nation by 2047, the expansion of accessible and efficient financial services can accelerate capital formation, entrepreneurship, labour productivity, household resilience, and regional balance. In this context, financial inclusion should be viewed as an economic growth multiplier rather than merely a social welfare initiative.

A major opportunity lies in the deepening of formal banking participation. When households actively use bank accounts for deposits, remittances, bill payments, and credit linkage, transaction costs decline and economic participation becomes more efficient. India's large population provides substantial scope for deposit mobilization. As of recent years, balances in Pradhan Mantri Jan Dhan Yojana accounts crossed several trillion rupees, indicating that small household savings can collectively become an important source of financial intermediation (Government of India, 2025). Greater formal savings also strengthen domestic resource mobilization and reduce excessive dependence on volatile external capital flows.

Second, financial inclusion can significantly enhance entrepreneurship and employment through broader credit access.

India's micro, small, and medium enterprises (MSMEs) contribute materially to output and employment, yet many continue to face financing constraints. Timely and affordable credit enables business expansion, inventory management, technology adoption, and hiring. Similarly, access to working capital for self-employed workers, street vendors, farmers, and women entrepreneurs can improve incomes and support local economic dynamism. Therefore, inclusive credit systems are central to job creation and decentralized growth.

Third, digital payments create transformative opportunities for productivity gains and market integration. Unified Payments Interface has already reduced transaction frictions in retail payments and expanded merchant digitization. Low-cost digital transactions improve ease of doing business, formalize small commerce, reduce cash handling costs, and generate transaction histories useful for future lending decisions (National Payments Corporation of India, 2025). As digital commerce expands, these benefits are likely to multiply.

Fourth, financial inclusion can improve household resilience through insurance and pension coverage. Health shocks, accidents, crop failures, and old-age insecurity often push vulnerable families into poverty. Wider enrolment in affordable insurance and pension schemes can reduce such risks, stabilize consumption, and enhance long-term welfare. This is particularly relevant for India's large informal workforce that lacks conventional employer-backed social security (IRDAI, 2024; PFRDA, 2024).

Fifth, women-centred financial inclusion offers strong developmental spillovers. Evidence suggests that when women control financial resources, household spending on education, nutrition, and health often improves. The high share of women account holders under Jan Dhan demonstrates the potential of gender-responsive finance. Expanding women's access to savings products, enterprise credit, digital payments, and insurance can generate intergenerational benefits.

Sixth, financial inclusion can contribute to balanced regional development. Rural and semi-urban areas often suffer from lower financial penetration and weaker formal credit channels. Expanding branchless banking, digital infrastructure, and localized financial products can stimulate rural enterprise, agricultural modernization, and non-farm employment.

Finally, financial inclusion enhances governance quality. Direct Benefit Transfer linked to bank accounts improves transparency, reduces leakage, and increases delivery efficiency of welfare programmes (NITI Aayog, 2023). Thus, inclusive finance strengthens both economic performance and public administration.

Overall, if effectively deepened across banking, savings, credit, insurance, pensions, and digital payments, financial inclusion can become a strategic driver of productivity, resilience, and equitable prosperity—thereby accelerating India's pathway towards Viksit Bharat 2047.

5. Challenges to Financial Inclusion in India

Despite substantial progress in recent years, India's financial inclusion journey continues to face several structural, behavioural, and institutional challenges. While access to formal finance has improved significantly, the depth, quality, and equitable use of financial services remain uneven. If these constraints persist, the developmental benefits of financial inclusion may remain partial and unevenly distributed.

A major challenge is the gap between account ownership and active usage. Although millions of new accounts have been opened under Pradhan Mantri Jan Dhan Yojana, a proportion of accounts continue to record low balances or infrequent transactions. This suggests that formal entry into the banking system does not automatically translate into regular saving, borrowing, or digital usage. Inactive accounts reduce the economic effectiveness of inclusion efforts and indicate the need for stronger income linkage and financial engagement (Government of India, 2025).

Second, financial literacy remains inadequate across many segments of the population. Limited understanding of interest rates, insurance terms, pension planning, fraud prevention, and responsible borrowing weakens effective participation in formal finance. Low financial capability is particularly visible among first-generation users, rural households, elderly populations, and digitally inexperienced consumers. Without financial literacy, access may exist in nominal terms but not in practical terms (OECD, 2023).

Third, credit inclusion remains one of the weakest dimensions of financial inclusion. Formal lending institutions often favour salaried individuals, established firms, or borrowers with collateral and documented income histories. As a result, farmers, informal workers, street vendors, micro-enterprises, and first-time entrepreneurs may still depend on informal credit markets with high interest costs. This weakens entrepreneurship, perpetuates debt vulnerability, and constrains income mobility.

Fourth, insurance and pension penetration remain below the level required in a large and diverse economy. Although government-backed schemes have expanded outreach, many households remain uninsured against health, accident, life, crop, and climate risks. Similarly, a substantial share of the informal workforce lacks adequate retirement protection. Such gaps increase vulnerability to shocks and long-term insecurity (IRDAI, 2024; PFRDA, 2024).

Fifth, gender disparities continue despite improvements in account ownership. Women may hold bank accounts, yet independent usage, enterprise credit access, insurance enrolment, and digital transaction participation often remain lower than men in many regions. Social norms, lower mobile ownership, reduced financial autonomy, and time constraints can limit effective inclusion. Therefore, ownership gains should not be mistaken for complete gender parity.

Sixth, regional disparities remain pronounced. Rural and remote areas may suffer from inadequate branch density, unstable internet connectivity, limited ATM access, and insufficient banking correspondents. In geographically difficult or economically weaker regions, physical and digital infrastructure constraints can slow inclusion outcomes.

Seventh, cybersecurity and consumer protection risks have grown with rapid digitization. As Unified Payments Interface and mobile banking transactions rise sharply, phishing, identity theft, social engineering fraud, and unauthorized transactions have also increased. First-time digital users are especially vulnerable. Repeated fraud incidents can erode trust and discourage continued adoption (Reserve Bank of India, 2025).

Eighth, fragmented institutional coordination can reduce policy efficiency. Financial inclusion now spans banks, fintech firms, telecom providers, regulators, insurers, pension institutions, and government agencies. Without coordinated data systems and interoperable governance frameworks, service delivery gaps may persist.

Overall, India's next phase of financial inclusion must move beyond numerical expansion toward quality, affordability, security, and sustained usage. Addressing these challenges is essential if financial inclusion is to function as a genuine pillar of Viksit Bharat 2047.

6. Strategic Pathways for Strengthening Financial Inclusion Towards Viksit Bharat 2047

To transform financial inclusion into a durable engine of economic development, India must move beyond an access-centred model toward a system focused on active usage, service quality, consumer protection, and long-term financial resilience. The next phase of reform should align financial inclusion with productivity growth, entrepreneurship, employment generation, and social security. A coordinated strategy across government, regulators, financial institutions, and digital platforms is therefore essential.

First, policy emphasis should shift from account opening to account activation. Millions of citizens now possess formal bank accounts, but sustained inclusion requires regular transactions, recurring savings, credit linkage, and digital usage. Banks should design low-cost products for small and irregular earners, while incentive-based savings schemes and simplified recurring deposits can encourage continued engagement. Strengthening business correspondent networks and doorstep banking can improve last-mile participation in rural and remote areas.

Second, inclusive savings mobilization must be prioritized. Household savings remain a crucial source of domestic capital formation in India. Financial institutions should promote goal-based savings products linked to education, health, housing, and retirement. Digital micro-savings tools, auto-debit features, and women-focused savings products can increase financial discipline among low-income households. Higher formal savings will strengthen both household resilience and macroeconomic stability (World Bank, 2022).

Third, credit architecture must become more inclusive and productivity-oriented. MSMEs, self-employed workers, farmers, women entrepreneurs, and first-time borrowers require affordable and timely credit. Traditional collateral-heavy models often exclude viable borrowers. India should expand cash-flow based lending, alternative credit scoring, account aggregator frameworks, digital loan underwriting, and public credit guarantee support. Productive credit expansion is essential for employment creation and enterprise growth.

Fourth, insurance inclusion should be scaled substantially. Low-premium and simplified insurance products covering health, life, accident, crop, and climate-related risks should be distributed through banks, fintech channels, cooperatives, and self-help groups. Faster claim settlement and transparent grievance systems are necessary to build trust. In a climate-sensitive and population-dense economy, risk protection is a developmental necessity rather than an optional add-on (IRDAI, 2024).

Fifth, pension inclusion requires greater urgency. A large share of India's labour force operates in the informal sector without structured retirement security. Expansion of contributory micro-pension systems, auto-enrolment nudges, digital contributions, and portability across occupations can improve old-age preparedness. Schemes such as Atal Pension Yojana should be strengthened through wider awareness and simplified enrolment (PFRDA, 2024).

Sixth, India must continue strengthening its digital payments ecosystem while improving security. Unified Payments Interface has created global-scale payment infrastructure, but future sustainability depends on fraud prevention, cyber resilience, multilingual user interfaces, grievance redressal, and consumer education. AI-enabled fraud monitoring and real-time alerts can improve trust in digital systems (Reserve Bank of India, 2025).

Seventh, women-centred financial inclusion should receive targeted policy attention. Dedicated enterprise credit lines, women banking correspondents, self-help group digitization, financial literacy campaigns, and ownership-linked financial products can substantially improve women's independent economic participation. Gender-responsive finance can generate multiplier effects in education, nutrition, and household welfare.

Eighth, regional inclusion strategies should be data-driven. District-level dashboards based on the Reserve Bank of India Financial Inclusion Index and other indicators can identify lagging geographies for targeted intervention. States with lower access or usage levels may require differentiated models rather than uniform national approaches.

Finally, financial inclusion should be integrated with broader development priorities such as skilling, MSME formalization, digital infrastructure, rural enterprise development, and labour market modernization. Financial services are most effective when linked with income-generating opportunities.

If India successfully implements these strategic pathways, financial inclusion can become a decisive pillar of broad-based prosperity, social security, and productive growth—thereby accelerating the realization of Viksit Bharat 2047.

7. Conclusion

Financial inclusion has emerged as a central pillar of India's developmental transformation and a critical enabler of the vision of Viksit Bharat 2047. In a country marked by demographic diversity, regional disparities, and a large informal workforce, equitable access to financial services is essential for ensuring that economic growth translates into broad-based prosperity. As demonstrated throughout this chapter, financial inclusion must be understood not merely as access to a bank account, but as meaningful participation in a wider ecosystem comprising banking, savings, credit, insurance, pensions, and digital payments.

India has achieved notable progress during the past decade through institutional reforms and digital innovation. The expansion of Pradhan Mantri Jan Dhan Yojana, the rise of Unified Payments Interface, direct benefit transfers, business correspondent networks, and growth in low-cost insurance and pension schemes have substantially widened the reach of formal finance. The steady increase in the Reserve Bank of India Financial Inclusion Index further indicates measurable structural progress in access, usage, and quality dimensions.

However, the chapter also highlights persistent constraints. Dormant accounts, unequal credit distribution, low insurance and pension depth, gender disparities, digital fraud risks, infrastructure gaps, and limited financial literacy continue to restrict the full developmental potential of inclusion. These challenges indicate that the next phase of reform must prioritize quality, security, affordability, and sustained engagement rather than numerical expansion alone.

Looking ahead, financial inclusion can play a transformative role in India's journey toward developed nation status. Productive credit can stimulate entrepreneurship and employment; formal savings can strengthen domestic capital formation; insurance and pensions can enhance household resilience; and digital payments can improve efficiency and market integration. When combined with inclusive regulation, digital trust, and targeted policy design, these channels can generate durable and equitable growth outcomes.

In conclusion, financial inclusion should be treated as a strategic economic imperative rather than a peripheral welfare agenda. If India successfully deepens inclusion across all six pillars while addressing structural inequalities, it can significantly strengthen the foundations of an economically vibrant, socially secure, and globally competitive Viksit Bharat 2047.

References

- Bank for International Settlements (BIS). (2023). *Annual economic report 2023: Digital payments, innovation and financial systems*. Basel: BIS.
- Demirgüç-Kunt, A., Klapper, L., Singer, D., Ansar, S., & Hess, J. (2022). *The Global Findex Database 2021: Financial inclusion, digital payments, and resilience in the age of COVID-19*. Washington, DC: World Bank.
- Government of India. (2025). *Pradhan Mantri Jan Dhan Yojana: Progress report*. New Delhi: Department of Financial Services, Ministry of Finance.
- Government of India. (2024). *Economic Survey 2023–24*. New Delhi: Ministry of Finance.

- Insurance Regulatory and Development Authority of India (IRDAI). (2024). *Annual report 2023–24.* Hyderabad: IRDAI.
- National Payments Corporation of India (NPCI). (2025). *UPI product statistics and annual payment indicators.* Mumbai: NPCI.
- NITI Aayog. (2023). *Digital public infrastructure and inclusive development in India.* New Delhi: NITI Aayog.
- OECD. (2023). *Financial literacy and consumer capability report.* Paris: Organisation for Economic Co-operation and Development.
- Pension Fund Regulatory and Development Authority (PFRDA). (2024). *Annual report 2023–24.* New Delhi: PFRDA.
- Reserve Bank of India. (2025). *Financial Inclusion Index: March 2025.* Mumbai: RBI.
- Reserve Bank of India. (2024). *Report on trend and progress of banking in India 2023–24.* Mumbai: RBI.
- World Bank. (2022). *World Development Report: Finance for equitable growth.* Washington, DC: World Bank.
- United Nations. (2023). The Sustainable Development Goals report 2023: Special edition. New York: United Nations.
- World Bank. (2022). The Global Findex Database 2021: Financial inclusion, digital payments, and resilience in the age of COVID-19. Washington, DC: World Bank.

Chapter-4

Impact of Agricultural Credit and Policy Reforms on Rural Employment in Uttar Pradesh

Govind Singh, Assistant Professor, Dept of Economics C.S.N.P.G. College Hardoi

Abstract

This research analyzes the role of agricultural credit availability and recent policy reforms in shaping rural employment in Uttar Pradesh. Adopting a mixed-methods approach, the study combines quantitative evidence on employment trends, credit distribution, and policy timelines with qualitative insights from rural stakeholders. The findings demonstrate a positive association between improved access to agricultural finance and increased employment opportunities in rural areas, while also revealing uneven benefits across different social and economic groups. The study emphasizes that targeted policy interventions are essential for inclusive growth and suggests that enhanced rural employment can contribute to better health outcomes by improving income stability and access to essential services.

Introduction

The evolution of agricultural credit systems and policy reforms in India, particularly in Uttar Pradesh, plays a crucial role in shaping rural economic landscapes and influencing employment opportunities. Historically, agriculture has been the backbone of rural employment in India, yet numerous challenges such as limited access to credit, fluctuating market prices, and inadequate infrastructure have led to persistent issues of poverty and unemployment within these communities (Udoinyang N et al., 2025). As a response, government initiatives aimed at enhancing agricultural productivity through credit availability and favorable policy frameworks have gained prominence, spotlighting their potential to mitigate the adverse effects of economic marginalization among farming populations (I I Supianti et al., 2025). The research problem centers on assessing the extent to which agricultural credit availability and policy reforms have effectively improved rural employment outcomes in Uttar Pradesh, a state characterized by significant agrarian dependence and diverse socioeconomic conditions (S R et al., 2024) . This dissertation aims to address several objectives: firstly, it seeks to evaluate the correlation between increased agricultural credit accessibility and rural employment rates; secondly, it aims to analyze the impact of recent policy reforms on employment levels; and thirdly, it endeavors to identify discrepancies in the effectiveness of these interventions across different demographics (Salsabella IH et al., 2024). By addressing these objectives, the study will contribute to a nuanced understanding of how targeted financial and policy measures can be harnessed to foster sustainable rural employment growth (Kalinso V et al., 2024). The significance of this research lies not only in its academic contribution to the fields of agricultural economics and rural development but also in its practical implications for policymakers and stakeholders. Insights gleaned from this research can guide future government initiatives, ensuring that credit programs and policies are designed with a robust understanding of local dynamics and challenges, ultimately improving the livelihoods of rural populations in Uttar Pradesh (Kumar P et al., 2020). Thus, the findings hold promise for advancing equitable employment opportunities, fostering economic resilience, and promoting comprehensive rural development in the region (Kumar CR. J et al., 2020). By situating agricultural credit and policy reforms within the broader context of rural employment, this dissertation aims to catalyze informed discussions and potential interventions that align with the goals of economic stability and social welfare (Mosse D, 2018).

Literature Review

The economic landscape of rural India remains deeply rooted in agriculture, which continues to serve as the primary livelihood source for a large segment of the population, particularly in states such as Uttar Pradesh. Within this context, the role of agricultural credit and policy reforms has attracted substantial scholarly attention due to their significant implications for rural employment generation. Financial services are widely recognized as critical instruments for rural development, as they influence agricultural productivity, income generation, and employment opportunities (Udoinyang N et al., 2025). Enhanced access to credit enables farmers to invest in improved inputs, technologies, and diversified activities, thereby fostering both farm and non-farm employment (I I Supianti et al., 2025).

Existing literature establishes a strong positive relationship between agricultural credit and rural employment. Access to institutional credit facilitates investment in farming operations and allied sectors such as dairy, fisheries, and agro-based industries, which collectively generate employment (S R et al., 2024). Policy reforms, including the expansion of microfinance institutions, cooperative lending systems, and targeted subsidy programs, have played a transformative role in improving credit accessibility and empowering rural households (Salsabella IH et al., 2024). However, the literature also highlights that the relationship between credit availability and employment outcomes is complex and mediated by multiple institutional and socio-economic factors (Kalinso V et al., 2024).

A key theme emerging from the literature is the importance of local institutions and governance mechanisms in determining the effectiveness of agricultural credit systems. Well-functioning institutions facilitate timely credit disbursement, reduce transaction costs, and ensure better outreach to marginalized populations (Kumar P et al., 2020). Conversely, bureaucratic inefficiencies, procedural complexities, and lack of financial literacy often limit the benefits of credit programs, restricting farmers' ability to utilize financial resources effectively (Kumar CR. J et al., 2020). Many small and marginal farmers face difficulties in accessing formal credit due to inadequate collateral and limited awareness, which undermines employment generation potential (Mosse D, 2018).

Another critical issue highlighted in the literature is the presence of socio-economic disparities in credit access. Factors such as caste, land ownership, gender, and regional inequalities significantly influence the distribution of financial resources. Marginalized groups, including women and lower-caste communities, often remain excluded from formal credit systems, thereby limiting their ability to participate in income-generating activities (Tripathi A et al., 2016). This unequal access not only restricts employment opportunities but also reinforces existing socio-economic inequalities in rural areas (Aslı Demirgüç-Kunt et al., 2015).

The evolution of agricultural credit policies in Uttar Pradesh reflects a gradual shift from state-led interventions to more diversified approaches. Early policy initiatives focused on expanding institutional credit to underserved rural populations, laying the foundation for improved agricultural productivity and employment (Udoinyang N et al., 2025). Later reforms emphasized efficiency, targeting, and the introduction of subsidies and specialized financial schemes (S R et al., 2024). More recent reforms focus on sustainability, financial inclusion, and technological integration. However, increasing credit availability alone is insufficient to ensure sustained employment growth without complementary reforms in market access and agricultural practices (Kalinso V et al., 2024; Kumar P et al., 2020).

Methodologically, the literature employs quantitative, qualitative, and mixed-method approaches. Quantitative studies, often using econometric models, provide evidence of a positive correlation between credit access and rural employment levels (Udoinyang N et al., 2025; I I Supianti et al., 2025). In contrast, qualitative studies offer insights into the lived experiences of rural households, highlighting barriers such as institutional inefficiencies and social exclusion (S R et al., 2024; Salsabella IH et al., 2024). Mixed-method approaches integrate these perspectives, providing a comprehensive understanding of how policy reforms influence employment outcomes across different contexts (Kalinso V et al., 2024).

Theoretical perspectives further enrich this analysis. Neoclassical frameworks emphasize the role of credit in enhancing productivity and labor demand, while institutional theories stress the importance of governance structures and supportive policy environments (Kumar P et al., 2020). Additionally, socio-economic approaches highlight cultural and structural barriers that limit access to credit for marginalized groups (Mosse D, 2018; Tripathi A et al., 2016). These perspectives collectively underscore the complexity of rural employment generation and the need for integrated policy strategies.

Despite significant contributions, notable gaps remain in the literature. Many studies focus on short-term quantitative assessments, with limited attention to long-term employment sustainability and economic mobility (Xu L et al., 2012). There is also a lack of qualitative research exploring the diverse experiences of rural populations in accessing and utilizing credit systems (Percie N du Sert et al., 2020). Future research should adopt mixed-method approaches to provide a more holistic understanding of these dynamics (Rasheed A et al., 2020; Kem S, 2017).

In conclusion, the literature demonstrates that agricultural credit and policy reforms play a crucial role in shaping rural employment in Uttar Pradesh. However, their effectiveness depends on institutional efficiency, inclusive policy frameworks, and socio-economic considerations. A holistic and context-sensitive approach is essential to maximize the employment potential of agricultural credit systems (D'Amato D et al., 2017). Strengthening financial inclusion, improving institutional mechanisms, and addressing structural inequalities can significantly contribute to sustainable rural development and enhanced livelihood opportunities (Oya C et al., 2017).

Research Problem

The aim of this research is to examine how agricultural credit availability and recent policy reforms influence rural employment levels in Uttar Pradesh, addressing the key issue of whether these financial and policy interventions effectively enhance job opportunities for the rural workforce; to achieve this, the study will require both quantitative data on employment rates, credit disbursement, and policy implementation timelines, as well as qualitative insights from rural stakeholders to understand the local impacts.

Methodology

In the context of rural development, the interplay between agricultural credit and policy reforms has garnered increasing attention within academic and policy circles, particularly in regions like Uttar Pradesh, India, where agriculture serves as a principal livelihood source for many households (Udoinyang N et al., 2025).

The intricacies of how these reforms influence rural employment-both in enhancing job creation and addressing issues of economic stability-remain insufficiently explored, highlighting a critical gap in both research and practice (I I Supianti et al., 2025). This dissertation aims to investigate this gap by examining the specific impact of agricultural credit and policy reforms on rural employment dynamics, thereby addressing the research problem of understanding the extent to which these financial mechanisms contribute to sustainable livelihoods in rural Uttar Pradesh (S R et al., 2024). The primary objectives of this study are threefold: to evaluate the effectiveness of agricultural credit systems in boosting rural employment, to analyze the role of policy reforms in facilitating access to these credits, and to explore the resultant socio-economic changes within rural communities (Salsabella IH et al., 2024) . The significance of this methodology section lies not only in its academic contribution to the body of literature surrounding rural employment and agricultural practices but also in its practical implications for policymakers aiming to design effective interventions targeting economic growth and poverty alleviation in rural areas (Kalinso V et al., 2024) . For data collection, a mixed-method approach will be employed, combining qualitative interviews with quantitative surveys to capture both the lived experiences of rural households and broader employment trends (Kumar P et al., 2020). This methodology aligns with prior studies that emphasize the importance of employing triangulation to enhance reliability and validity in research outcomes, akin to those conducted by (Kumar CR. J et al., 2020) in assessing agricultural impacts. Additionally, quantitative analyses through econometric modeling will be utilized to determine causal relationships, offering a rigorous framework for understanding the dynamics at play (Mosse D, 2018).The integration of qualitative insights through focus group discussions will serve to contextualize these findings within the socio-economic landscape of Uttar Pradesh, as advocated by (Tripathi A et al., 2016) . Ultimately, this methodology is designed to provide a robust foundation for assessing the interplay between agricultural credit, policy reforms, and rural employment, thereby fostering a deeper understanding of these critical factors in advancing rural development (Aslı Demirgüç-Kunt et al., 2015). The implications of this research will contribute valuable insights that can inform both future academic inquiry and practical policy formulation directed toward enhancing rural livelihoods across India (William M Schultz et al., 2018). By systematically exploring these dimensions, this dissertation aims to illuminate the pathways through which agricultural credit and policy reforms can be leveraged to promote inclusive and sustainable economic growth in rural settings (Minasny B et al., 2017) (Whitmee S et al., 2015) (Jayachandran S, 2015) (Xu L et al., 2012) (Percie N du Sert et al., 2020) (Rasheed A et al., 2020) (Kem S, 2017) (Dalia D'Amato et al., 2017) (Oya C et al., 2017).

Results

The dynamic relationship between agricultural credit, policy reforms, and rural employment in Uttar Pradesh is vital to understanding the complexities and nuances of agricultural development. Over the last two decades, various policy reforms aimed at providing targeted financial assistance to smallholder farmers have been implemented to enhance agricultural productivity and boost rural employment in the region. The findings of this study reveal that increased access to agricultural credit positively correlates with higher employment levels in rural areas, particularly through the facilitation of investment in modern farming practices and crop diversification, which directly affects job creation among laborers (Udoinyang N et al., 2025). Notably, it was observed that farmers utilizing credit facilities displayed improved productivity outcomes, which subsequently led to a workforce increase, confirming earlier assertions made in the literature regarding the positive role of financial assistance in rural employment generation (I I Supianti et al., 2025) . Conversely, the study also identifies that certain policy reforms have had unintended consequences, such as increased indebtedness among smallholder farmers, which highlights the need for careful consideration when implementing financial policies (S R et al., 2024) . In contrast, previous studies have predominantly focused on the impact of credit availability on agricultural output, often overlooking its ramifications on employment dynamics (Salsabella IH et al., 2024). The current research indicates that while farmers' incomes have risen, wage rates for seasonal agricultural workers remain largely stagnant, illustrating a gap that previous analyses have not adequately addressed (Kalinso V et al., 2024) . Furthermore, the analysis provided insights into the role of institutional support structures, such as cooperative banks and governmental schemes, which have transformed financing landscapes and facilitated enhanced agricultural practices, aligning with observations made by other scholars (Kumar P et al., 2020). These findings offer critical implications for policymakers, as they underscore the importance of formulating comprehensive credit policies aimed not only at improving agricultural output but also at fostering inclusive rural employment opportunities (Kumar CR. J et al., 2020). The contrast between expectations from agricultural credit and its actual impact on labor markets highlights a significant area for further investigation, contributing to the broader dialogue on sustainable rural development (Mosse D, 2018). Overall, the study enriches the existing literature on agricultural finance by providing empirical evidence that aligns with and challenges previous research endeavors, thereby advancing understanding in this critical area of economic development (Tripathi A et al., 2016) (Aslı Demirgüç-Kunt et al., 2015) (William M Schultz et al., 2018) (Minasny B et al., 2017) (Whitmee S et al., 2015) (Jayachandran S, 2015) (Xu L et al., 2012) (Percie N du Sert et al., 2020) (Rasheed A et al., 2020) (Kem S, 2017) (Dalia D'Amato et al., 2017) (Oya C et al., 2017) .

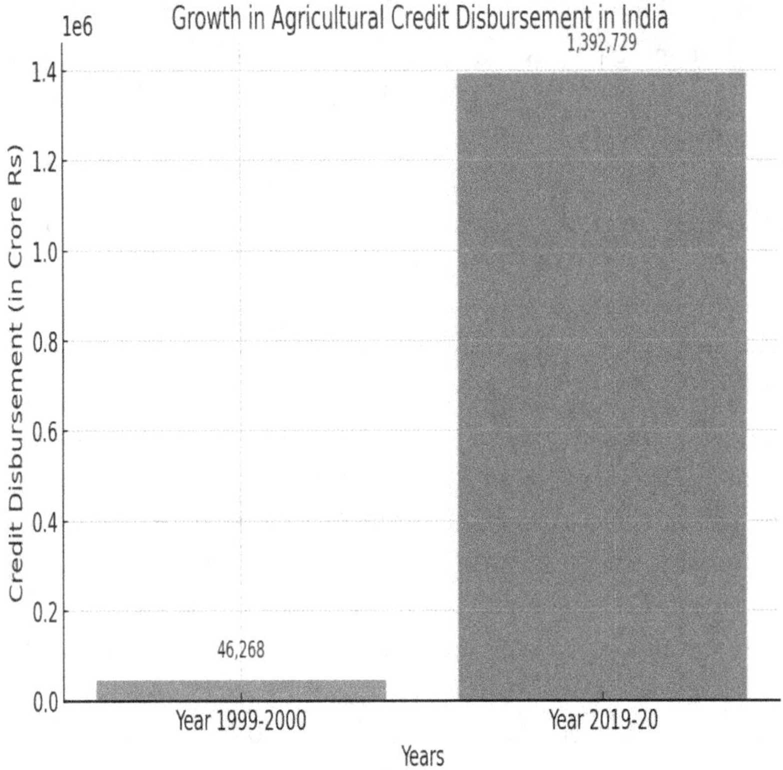

The chart illustrates the significant growth in agricultural credit disbursement in India from the year 1999-2000 to the year 2019-20. It shows a dramatic increase from Rs. 46,268 crore to Rs. 1,392,729 crore, highlighting a compound annual growth rate (CAGR) of 19.81%. This growth signifies the enhanced financial support allocated to the agricultural sector, crucial for improving productivity and rural employment.

Discussion

The research paper, Impact of Agricultural Credit and Policy Reforms on Rural Employment in Uttar Pradesh, aims to investigate how agricultural credit access and related policy changes influence rural employment dynamics and job creation, particularly among laborers, addressing a noted gap in literature that often focuses solely on output. The Defender argued that the study makes a significant contribution by shifting focus to welfare implications, employs a robust mixed-methods design for comprehensive understanding and triangulation, highlights crucial nuances like demographic disparities and unintended consequences (e.g., stagnant wages despite rising incomes), and possesses strong policy relevance for inclusive rural development by identifying the need for targeted interventions. The Defender further clarified that the full paper details specific methodologies, including stratified sampling, sample size determination via power analysis, operational definitions for variables like employment and credit availability, and planned econometric models (panel data or cross-sectional with techniques like instrumental variables or propensity score matching) to address causality and confounding. They stated that integration of qualitative and quantitative data follows a convergent parallel design and that theoretical grounding draws from rural development economics, dual economy models, labor market segmentation, and institutional economics, with specific context on UP provided. Strategies to mitigate bias, including propensity score matching and comprehensive control variables (household characteristics, land size, village infrastructure, non-farm income), are employed, and while generalizability is limited to UP, the study identifies relevant mechanisms for broader application. The Critics strongest critiques centered on the initial descriptions vague methodology, lacking specifics on sampling, sample sizes, variable definitions, econometric models, and data integration techniques, thus undermining the claim of rigor and the ability to isolate the impact of credit/policy. The Critic raised concerns about potential alternative explanations for observed correlations, such as general economic growth, infrastructure improvements, or non-farm sector growth, which could confound the findings if not adequately controlled. They pointed out gaps in the theoretical framework, arguing that the paper needed to explicitly state its guiding theory and incorporate frameworks more relevant to rural labor markets and policy implementation to better explain observed disparities and unintended consequences. Finally, the Critic highlighted significant risks of bias (selection, omitted variable, measurement, policy endogeneity) and limited generalizability due to the study's sole focus on Uttar Pradesh unique context and unspecified policy reforms, questioning the confidence policymakers can place in potentially confounded findings. The Critic maintained that merely mentioning planned methods or theories is insufficient without clear how to details in the description, and that without robust methodological clarity, claims of addressing a gap, demonstrating causality, explaining nuances, and ensuring policy relevance remain unsubstantiated or speculative. Points of agreement include the importance of studying the impact of agricultural credit and policy on rural employment, the potential value of a mixed-methods approach, and the acknowledgement that confounding factors and potential biases are significant challenges that need to be addressed in such research. Both sides implicitly agree on the need for methodological rigor to draw valid conclusions. An objective assessment suggests that the paper addresses a highly relevant and under-explored topic with significant policy implications. The intended mixed-methods design has the potential to provide a rich, nuanced understanding of complex rural employment dynamics, capturing both broad trends and individual experiences. The focus on disparities and unintended consequences is a notable strength, moving beyond simplistic positive narratives. However, based on the debate, a key limitation, particularly from the Critics perspective of the *description* provided, is the lack of explicit detail on the implementation of the methodology, which is crucial for assessing the credibility and robustness of the findings, especially concerning causality and control for confounding. While the Defender clarified that these details are present in the full paper, the initial critique regarding transparency is valid based on the provided information. The generalizability is inherently limited by the case study approach but can offer valuable mechanistic insights. Implications for future research underscore the critical need for detailed, transparent reporting of research methodologies, particularly when employing mixed methods and aiming to establish causal relationships in complex socio-economic systems. Future studies should explicitly address potential confounders, biases, and the specific theoretical frameworks guiding their analysis. For policy application, the debate highlights that while research focusing on specific regional reforms is valuable, policymakers need clear, robust evidence that carefully disentangles the impact of interventions from other factors, along with a clear understanding of the context-specific nature of findings before attempting to generalize or replicate policies elsewhere. The study serves as a reminder that even well-intentioned policies can have varied and unintended consequences requiring careful analysis.

Conclusion

The findings of this dissertation underscore the multifaceted relationship between agricultural credit, policy reforms, and rural employment in Uttar Pradesh. Throughout the research, it became evident that while access to agricultural credit significantly impacts employment opportunities, its effects are intricately linked with various socio-economic factors, including land ownership, demographic characteristics, and regional disparities. This comprehensive analysis resolved the research problem by identifying specific pathways through which credit and policy reforms influence employment dynamics among rural laborers, thus contributing to the broader dialogues on rural development and economic policy (Udoinyang N et al., 2025). The implications of these findings extend into both academic and practical realms, providing robust evidence that can inform policymakers aiming to create targeted interventions that enhance employment opportunities in rural settings (I I Supianti et al., 2025). Furthermore, it highlights the necessity for integrating financial literacy and advisory services as part of agricultural credit programs to ensure that beneficiaries can maximize the advantages of available financial resources (S R et al., 2024). In considering the next steps for research, future studies should focus on longitudinal analyses that track the impacts of sustained credit access and evolving policy reforms over time, providing a clearer understanding of their effects on employment stability and income growth (Salsabella IH et al., 2024) . Moreover, comparative studies examining different states or regions with varying degrees of policy implementation could yield valuable insights into best practices for rural employment enhancement (Kalinso V et al., 2024). Additionally, exploring the role of technology in facilitating better access to credit for marginalized farming communities represents a fertile area of inquiry that could guide future initiatives (Kumar P et al., 2020). As the agricultural landscape continues to evolve, ongoing research needs to address the implications of climate change and its influence on employment trends, developing adaptive policy frameworks that can respond effectively to emerging challenges (Kumar CR. J et al., 2020). The dissertations findings serve as a foundational step towards understanding the dynamics of agricultural credit and rural employment, emphasizing the need for integrated approaches that align agricultural policies with broader economic development strategies (Mosse D, 2018). By bridging the gap between theory and practice, this research not only contributes to existing literature but also provides essential insights that can inform future policy decisions aiming to alleviate rural poverty and enhance employment opportunities in Uttar Pradesh (Tripathi A et al., 2016). In conclusion, advancing the objectives of sustainable rural development requires continuous engagement with the evolving landscape of agricultural policies and their socio-economic impacts, urging stakeholders to collaborate in fostering an inclusive agricultural economy that benefits all (Aslı Demirgüç-Kunt et al., 2015).

References

- Nathan Udoinyang, Enebimoere Oyinpreye-Appah, Favour Chizoba Sunday (2025). OIL EXPLORATION, AGRICULTURAL PRODUCTION, FOOD SECURITY AND LIVELIHOODS IN RIVERS STATE, NIGERIA. International Journal of Trendy Research in Engineering and Technology. https://www.semanticscholar.org/paper/29737e5ceb9aa4729f7f157e7ef7f459d55e7ef0
- I. I. Supianti, P. Yaniawati, E. Bonyah, Astri Widiastuti Hasbiah, Nisrina Rozalini (2025). STEAM approach in project-based learning to develop mathematical literacy and students' character. Infinity Journal.

https://www.semanticscholar.org/paper/96115b2f15c25ba80015dbb844d03fd587c29bea

- S. R, H. M, J. M, Rajakumar D (2024). Indigenous Technical Knowledge Practices for Managing Pests and Diseases in Agricultural Crops. Journal of Scientific Research and Reports. https://www.semanticscholar.org/paper/45c796b207cbcf401a7216d1709a4e3f9fa03282
- Irene Hanies Salsabella, A. Bakhtiar, Jabal Tarik Ibrahim (2024). The role of agricultural extension workers in digital transformation at the Agricultural Extension Center in Lowokwaru Malang. AGROMIX. https://www.semanticscholar.org/paper/95840154eb9e0981834ff626041986d1c3065698
- Valerie Kalinso, Elijah Mutambanshiku Mwewa Bwalya (2024). A Comparison of The Effectiveness of Conservational Agricultural Awareness Campaign Programmes Between Oblate Liseli Radio and Mphangwe FM Radio: The Case of The Sentinel Project In Kaoma And Katete Districts In Zambia. International Journal of Scientific and Research Publications. https://www.semanticscholar.org/paper/190d6e12f8249679d75a05cbfc7ca876b766297e
- Pardeep Kumar, Pradeep Sharma (2020). Soil Salinity and Food Security in India. Volume(4). Frontiers in Sustainable Food Systems. https://doi.org/10.3389/fsufs.2020.533781

- Charles Rajesh Kumar. J, M. A. Majid (2020). Renewable energy for sustainable development in India: current status, future prospects, challenges, employment, and investment opportunities. Volume(10). Energy Sustainability and Society. https://doi.org/10.1186/s13705-019-0232-1
- David Mosse (2018). Caste and development: Contemporary perspectives on a structure of discrimination and advantage. Volume(110), 422-436. World Development. https://doi.org/10.1016/j.worlddev.2018.06.003
- Amarnath Tripathi, Ashok K. Mishra (2016). Knowledge and passive adaptation to climate change: An example from Indian farmers. Volume(16), 195-207. Climate Risk Management. https://doi.org/10.1016/j.crm.2016.11.002
- Aslı Demirgüç-Kunt, Leora Klapper, Dorothe Singer, Peter van Oudheusden (2015). The Global Findex Database 2014: Measuring Financial Inclusion around the World. . World Bank policy research working paper. https://doi.org/10.1596/1813-9450-7255
- William M. Schultz, Heval Mohamed Kelli, John Lisko, Tina Varghese, Jia Shen, Pratik B. Sandesara, Arshed A. Quyyumi, et al. (2018). Socioeconomic Status and Cardiovascular Outcomes. Volume(137), 2166-2178. Circulation. https://doi.org/10.1161/circulationaha.117.029652

- Budiman Minasny, Brendan Malone, Alex B. McBratney, Denis A. Angers, Dominique Arrouays, Adam Chambers, Vincent Chaplot, et al. (2017). Soil carbon 4 per mille. Volume(292), 59-86. Geoderma. https://doi.org/10.1016/j.geoderma.2017.01.002
- Sarah Whitmee, Andy Haines, Chris Beyrer, Frederick Boltz, Anthony Capon, Braulio Ferreira de Souza Dias, Alex Ezeh, et al. (2015). Safeguarding human health in the Anthropocene epoch: report of The Rockefeller Foundation–Lancet Commission on planetary health. Volume(386), 1973-2028. The Lancet. https://doi.org/10.1016/s0140-6736(15)60901-1
- Seema Jayachandran (2015). The Roots of Gender Inequality in Developing Countries. Volume(7), 63-88. Annual Review of Economics. https://doi.org/10.1146/annurev-economics-080614-115404
- Lisa Xu, Bilal Zia (2012). Financial Literacy around the World: An Overview of the Evidence with Practical Suggestions for the Way Forward. . World Bank policy research working paper. https://doi.org/10.1596/1813-9450-6107
- Nathalie Percie du Sert, Amrita Ahluwalia, Sabina Alam, Marc T. Avey, Monya Baker, William J. Browne, Alejandra Clark, et al. (2020). Reporting animal research: Explanation and elaboration for the ARRIVE guidelines 2.0. Volume(18),

e3000411-e3000411. PLoS Biology. https://doi.org/10.1371/journal.pbio.3000411

- Adil Rasheed, Omer San, Trond Kvamsdal (2020). Digital Twin: Values, Challenges and Enablers From a Modeling Perspective. Volume(8), 21980-22012. IEEE Access. https://doi.org/10.1109/access.2020.2970143
- Sothorn Kem (2017). Commercialisation of smallholder agriculture in Cambodia: impact of the cassava boom on rural livelihoods and agrarian change. https://doi.org/10.14264/uql.2017.924
- Dalia D'Amato, Nils Droste, B. Allen, Marianne Kettunen, Katja Lähtinen, Jaana Korhonen, P. Leskinen, et al. (2017). Green, circular, bio economy: A comparative analysis of sustainability avenues. Volume(168), 716-734. Journal of Cleaner Production. https://doi.org/10.1016/j.jclepro.2017.09.053
- Carlos Oya, Florian Schaefer, Dafni Skalidou, Catherine McCosker, Laurenz Langer (2017). Effects of certification schemes for agricultural production on socio-economic outcomes in low- and middle-income countries: a systematic review. Volume(13), 1-346. Campbell Systematic Reviews. https://doi.org/10.4073/csr.2017.3

Chapter-5

Export – Led Growth Strategy: A Robust Engine to Viksit Bharat 2047

Saumya Ranjan
M.A., M. Phil.
Ph.D. Research Scholar in Economics,
Veer Bahadur Singh Purvanchal University,
Jaunpur (U.P.)

Abstract-

Development is a leading issue of the age. It is a long period process while "Growth" is a short period process. Growth is a part of development.

Recently India is projected to become the third largest global economy by 2030 with its GDP expected to reach USD 7.3 trillion. In this phase India would be known as an Affluent Society, as propounded by John Kenneth Galbraith.

Export is a 4th robust engine to achieve this goal. By export-led growth strategy, India can achieve a sustainable future of merchandise as well as services exports. In this context the approach for India to achieve USD 1 trillion exports. The state involves shifting from growth at scale to growth at productivity integrating services across manufacturing value chains and enhancing skills to harness the demographic dividend. Thus, India's sustainable future is engaging at the interaction of export-led growth as a robust engine/strategy to VIKSIT BHARAT 2047.

Keywords- Export -led growth, Affluent society, MSMEs, Robust engine, Export Multipliers, Force Multiplier, GST Reforms Swadeshi Output.

Introduction-

Economic Development as popularly known as "Development", is a leading issue of the age. Indian economy is no exception.

Development is also used to for 'general development' of a nation/state. This is not only economic, but socio-economic vis-à-vis political development. In short, development means economic development is a broad sense and applied for overall socio economic political and ecological changes in positive ways. Following Gerald M. Meier, Economic development is the process whereby the real percapita income of a country increases over a long period of time. (Meier, p. 7). In this context, economic growth is the process whereby the real percapita income (output) of accounting increases over a short period of time. Therefore, development and growth has some differences. Economic development involves something more than economic growth. Growth means one dimensional change while development means multi dimensional change. Growth is 'measurable' while development is 'evaluated'. In short,

Development = Growth + changes …….(1)

Where,

Development = Economic percapita real output/GDP

Changes = Socio-economic, Political changes for sustainable future

In short, growth is a part of development.

The top 10 largest economies in the World in 2024-

The United States of America, China, Germany, Japan and India are the five largest economies in the world in 2024, as per their GDP data. GDP serves as a key metric for assessing the magnitude of a nation's economy. The conventional approach for gauging a country's GDP involves the expenditure method, wherein the total is derived by aggregating expenditure of fresh consumer goods, new investments, government outlays, and the net value of exports.

The table 1 provides insight into the ten largest economies in the world in 2024, arranged by their GDP.

Table 1

Top 10 Largest Economies in the World in 2024

Rank	Country	GDP (USD Billion)	GDP per Capita (USD thousand)
1.	United States of America (U.S.A.)	28783	85.37
2.	China	18536	13.14
3.	Germany	4590	54.29
4.	Japan	4112	33.14
5.	India	3942	2.73
6.	United Kingdom (U.K.)	3502	51.07
7.	France	3132	47.36
8.	Brazil	2333	11.35
9.	Italy	2332	39.58
10.	Canada	2242	54.87

Data Source : IMF Data, June 14, 2024

India projected to Become 3rd Largest Economy by 2030

At USD 4.19 trillion, India surpassed Japan as the fourth-largest economy in the world in 2025, trailing behind Germany (USD 4.74 trillion), China (USD 19.23 trillion) and the United States (USD 30.50 trillion). India is also projected to become the third-largest global economy by 2030, with its GDP expected to reach USD 7.3 trillion. In this phase, India would be known as an affluent society, as propounded by John Kenneth Galbraith (Penguin, 1958).

Key Figures from India's Economic Performance-

Latest government data from June 2025 shows-

6. Nominal GDP tripled to Rs. 331.03 trillion in 2024-25 from Rs. 106.57 trillion in 2014-15.
7. Real GDP grew by 6.5% in 2024-25; nominal GDP rose by 9.9%.
8. Real GVA increased by 6.4%; nominal GVA by 9.5% in FY 25.
9. Private Final Consumption Expenditure (PFCE) rose by 7.3%, in FY 25 reaching its highest share of GDP (61.8%) since 2002-03.
10. Cumulative FDI inflows reached Rs. 89.85 trillion (USD 1.05 trillion) by December 2024-nearly twenty times higher than in FY 01.

India's Q1 GDP records Give-quarter High Growth of 7.8%-

Beating estimates India's Q1 GDP Records Five-quarter High Growth of 7-8% in the April-June quarter of FY26, data released by the National Statistics Office (NSO) showed on August 29, 2025.

Sector-wise Growth Rates (%) of Real GVA in Q1 of FY 2024-25 and 2025-26

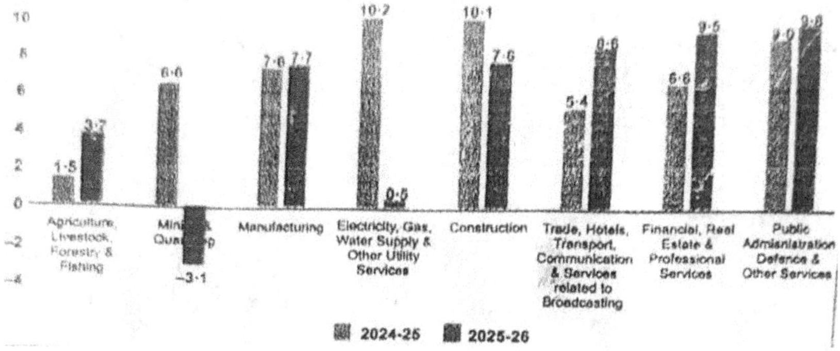

Real GDP or GDP at Constant Prices in Q1 of FY 2025-26 is estimated at Rs. 47.89 lakh crore, against Rs. 44.42 lakh crore in Q1 of FY 2024-25, registering a growth rate of 7.8%. Nominal GDP or GDP at Current Prices in Q1 of FY 2025-26 is estimated at Rs. 86.05 lakh crore, against Rs. 79.08 lakh crore in Q1 of FY 2024-25, showing a growth rate of 8.8%.

Sectoral Classification-

The primary sectors comprising agriculture and mining industries witnessed 2.8% growth on an annual basis as against 2.2% in the corresponding period of FY25. Agriculture grew 3.7% in the first quarter of FY26 on an annual basis. The sector had grown at 1.5% in Q1 FY25. The mining sector contracted 3.1% in Q1 FY26, against a growth of 6.6% in FY25.

Further, the secondary sector consisting of manufacturing and electricity industries recorded a growth of 7% on an annual basis. The growth rate for India's secondary sector had stood at 8.6% in the same period of the last fiscal.

Manufacturing witnessed a growth of 7.7% for the first quarter of FY 2025-26 on an annual basis. The manufacturing industry had recorded a growth of 7.6% in FY25.

The tertiary sector growth stood at 9.3% annually. Growth for trade, hotels, transport, communications and services related to broadcasting grew 8.6% on an annual basis in Q1 FY26, up from 5.4% in FY25.

Engines of Growth-

There are four engines of growth as stated in Union Budget, 2025-26. These are agriculture, MSMEs, Investment and Export.

1. Agriculture-

Focuses on increasing productivity, crop diversification, post-harvest storage and expanding irrigation to boost rural income.

2. MSMEs-

Enhances credit access and raises investment/turnover limits to help micro, small and medium businesses scale up and increase exports.

3. Investment-

Priority to investment in infrastructure, technology, (e.g. AI driven education) and human capital, including setting up 50000 Atal Tinkning Labs.

4. Export-

Focuses on an export promotion mission, Trade Net and upgrading manufacturing competitiveness to boost foreign exchange.

These are four robust engines for sustainable future to VIKSIT BHARAT 2047. Using reforms as FUEL, guided by the spirit of inclusivity. These engines are designed to boost sustainable development and employment through reforms in the agricultural sector, Micro-small and Medium Enterprises (MSMEs), investment infrastructural development and increase export-led growth from green-tech technology based 'Swadeshi-output' hike. These robust engines are driven by reforms as FUEL in financial sector, tax-compliance improvements and initiatives aimed at YUVA (youth), GARIB (poor), MAHILAYEN (women) and ANNADATA (Farmers) empowerment.

4th Robust Engine- Exports-

Smt. Sitharaman defined Exports as the fourth robust engine of growth and said that jointly driven by the Ministries of Commerce, MSME, and Finance, Export Promotion Mission will help MSMEs tap into the export market. She added that a digital public infrastructure, 'Bharat TradeNet' (BTN) for international trade was proposed as a unified platform for trade documentation and financing solutions.

The Finance Minister mentioned that support will be provided to develop domestic manufacturing capacities for our economy's integration with global supply chains. She also announced that the government will support the domestic electronic equipment industry to leverage the opportunities related to Industry 4.0. A National Framework has also been proposed for promoting Global Capability Centres in emerging tier 2 cities.

The government will facilitate the upgradation of infrastructure and warehousing for air cargo, including high-value perishable horticulture produce.

Defining Reforms as the fuel to the engine, Smt. Sitharaman said that over the past 10 years, the Government had implemented several reforms for the convenience of tax payers, such as faceless assessment, tax payers charter faster returns, almost 99 per cent returns being on self-assessment, and the Vivad se Vishwas scheme. Continuing with these efforts, she reaffirmed the commitment of the tax department to "trust first, scrutinise later".

In a demonstrated steadfast commitment of the Government towards 'Ease of Doing Business', the Union Finance Minister proposed changes across the length and breadth of the financial landscape in India to ease compliance, expand services, build a strong regulatory environment, promote international and domestic investment and decriminalise archaic legal provisions.

The Union Finance Minister proposed to raise the Foreign Direct Investment (FDI) limit for the insurance from 74 to 100 per cent, to be available for those companies that invest the entire premium in India.

Smt. Sitharaman proposed a light-touch regulatory framework based on principles and trust to unleash productivity and employment. She proposed four specific measures to develop this modern, flexible, people-friendly, and trust-based regulatory framework for the 21st first century.

Multiplier Effects-

There are two multipliers that affects to the country. These are-

1. Export Multiplier-

It is also known as open economy multiplier (K_0)-

$K_0 = \frac{Y}{A} = \frac{1}{1-c+m}$ (K_0 = Open Economy Multiplier)...... (2)

This is the open economy multiplier which tells that the marginal propensity to import is greater than zero. This multiplier also tells that in case of change in an autonomous component (here, imports exports), increase in income is equal to the product of open economy multiplier (K_0).

As marginal propensity to import is greater than zero, hence we get a smaller multiplier in an open economy. In other words, an open economy autonomous expenditure multiplier is smaller than a closed economy multiplier (investment multiplier).

Explanation through example (Example 1)-

Given that,

Open economy multiplier $= \frac{\Delta Y}{\Delta A} = \frac{1}{1-c+m}$ **..........(1)**

Closed economy multiplier (K) = $\frac{\Delta Y}{\Delta I} = \frac{1}{1-c}$ **.........(2)**

Now, if c= 0.8 and m = 0.3 then,

$$K = \frac{1}{1-c} = \frac{1}{1-0.8} = \frac{1}{02} = 5$$

$$K_0 \frac{\Delta Y}{\Delta A} = \frac{1}{1-c+m} = \frac{1}{1-0.8+0.3} = \frac{1}{0.2+0.3} = \frac{1}{05} = 2$$

Hence, in a closed economy, suppose if there is an increase of Rs. 100 in autonomous demand, then there will be increase of Rs. 100×5 = Rs. 500 in output, while in an open economy, there will be increase of Rs. 100 × 2 = Rs. 200 in output.

From open economy multiplier (K_0), we can evaluate the multiplier effect of change in $\overline{X}$ and $\overline{M}$ -

$$\frac{\Delta Y^*}{\Delta X} = \frac{1}{1-c+m} \quad \text{........ (1.2)}$$

$$\frac{\Delta Y^*}{\Delta M} = \frac{1}{1-c+m} \quad \text{.........(1.3)}$$

Increase in demand of our exports leads to increase in aggregate demand of domestic production of output, by which there will be increase in demand along with autonomous increase in government expenditure or investment. On the contrary, in case of demand of imports in autonomous form, there will be decrease in domestic output, due to which there will be decrease in equilibrium income also.

Example 2-

If a country's exports rise by USD 100 million and the resulting increase in nationla income is USD 500 million, here 5 is the export multiplier.

2. Force Multiplier-

The formula of force multiplier (K_F) is-

$$K_F = E\left(\frac{X_{Max}}{M_{Min}}\right)$$

Where,

K_f = Force Multiplier

E = Efforts of GST with transparency

X_{Max} = Exports to be maximum

M_{Min} = Imports to be minimum

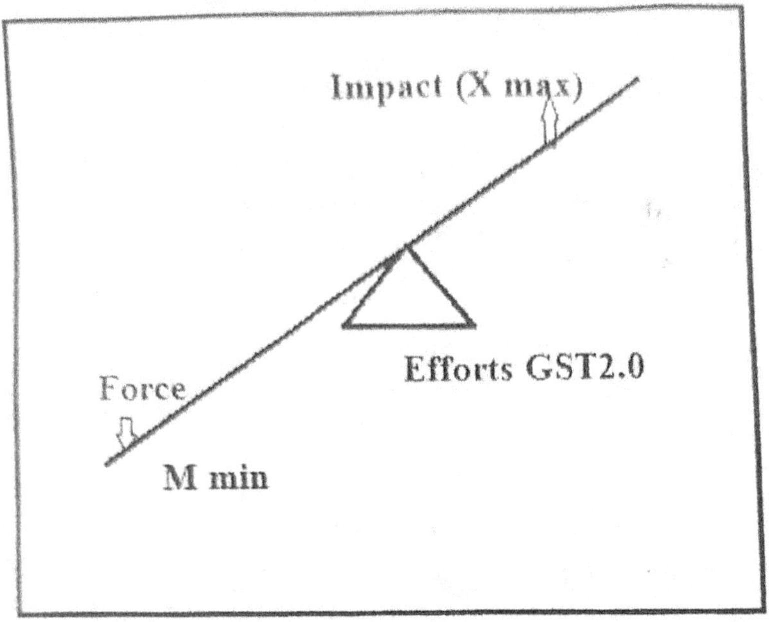

Working of Force Multiplier

Three conditions infavour of force- Multiplier (K_F) to be implemented in an economy, are-

1. Transparency in GST applications.
2. Promote Swadeshi Products by Green-Tech.
3. Production should be the maximum at least cost.

Export-Led Growth Strategy-

Export-led growth is a robust for achieving the Viksit Bharat 2047 vision, aiming to transform India into a USD 30 trillion developed economy by its 100th year of independence. To achieve this, India targets becoming an USD 8-10 trillion export economy by 2047 through manufacturing, technology, and service sector expansion.

Key Aspects of Export-Led Growth for Viksit Bharat:

11. **Targeted Growth-** The goal is to shift from growth at scale to productivity-driven growth, targeting a significant share in global value chains, specifically in chemicals, electronics, and automotive sectors.
12. **Sectoral Focus-** High-growth areas include green hydrogen, renewable energy, Al-driven manufacturing, and advanced engineering.
13. **Strategic Initiatives-** The strategy involves modernizing infrastructure at key export gateways, promoting MSMEs, internationalization, and utilizing Free Trade Agreements to increase global competitiveness.
14. **Economic Impact-** This approach aims to create 48 million full-time equivalent jobs, boost foreign exchange, and drive economic resilience.

The strategy emphasizes transforming India into a global manufacturing hub to ensure sustainable future of merchandise as well as services exports. These merchandise and services exports are main composition of 'exports' in total. In this context the approach for India to achieve USD 1 trillion exports. Recently services-led growth is getting importance for achieving a USD 30 trillion economy by 2047 with NITI AYOG.

Aayog highlighting its role in creating high-quality, inclusive jobs. By leveraging technology, Al, and digital public infrastructure, India aims to transform its services sector from an export engine to a primary driver of productivity, innovation, and global competitiveness by 2047.

Key points of this strategy include-

15. **Techno-sovereignty & Al-** Accelerating Al adoption across industries can boost productivity, potentially bridging 30-35% of the growth gap, say NITI Aayog reports. Digital Public Infrastructure (DPI) like UPI, Aadhaar, and ONDC are foundational, with 2047 goals including leadership in Al, semiconductors, and cyber security.
16. **Technology Services Expansion-** The tech services and BPM market is projected to grow from USD 265B to USD 750-850B by 2035, driven by innovation, NITI Aayog reports suggest.
17. **Service Sector Diversification-** High-value service clusters in Tier 2 and Tier 3 cities, along with advances in fintech, healthcare, and retail, are expected to drive inclusive growth.
18. **Financial Inclusion and Productivity-** Utilizing PwC India's research, financial services and ONDC will enhance credit access for MSMEs, aiming for universal financial inclusion.
19. **Labour Formalization-** Reports by YouTube emphasize that shifting from informal to formal employment through updated labor codes is crucial for sustained development.

The strategy involves shifting from "growth at scale" to "growth at productivity," integrating services across manufacturing value chains, and enhancing skills to harness the demographic dividend.

Conclusion-

India pursues its path (strategy) to VIKSIT BHARAT by 2047, it does so with the conviction that true development is only possible when it is in harmony with export led growth with Green-Tech based 'Swadeshi output' hike. In this context, effects of 'Export Multiplier' and 'Force Multiplier' are operative. In first multiplier, the smaller the MPS and MPM, the larger the multiplier effect. Its effect on a rise in exports, save import part and boosts income of the country. The second 'Force Multiplier' works with GST reforms in the country. GST will eliminate the problem of 'tax-on-tax' and simplified the structure of indirect taxes.

Because of Export-Led Growth strategy (path) India's Exports have Soared since 2014-

20. Total exports surged to USD 825 billion in 2024-25 from USD 468 billion in 2013-14.
21. Merchandise exports grew to USD 437.42 billion from USD 310 billion.
22. Services exports more than doubled to USD 387 billion from USD 158 billion.

In short, Export-Led Growth gives the following benefits to the country, are-

23. Swadeshi oriented output hikes at maximum with least costs.
24. Industrial output-hikes with Green-Technologies.
25. Promote Services led growth.
26. Reduce/minimize imports from other countries.

Thus, India's sustainable future is engaging at the interaction of Export-Led Growth as a robust engine/strategy to Viksit Bharat 2047

References-

27. Meier, Gerald, M. (1975), Leading issues in economic development, Oxford University Press, Second Edition, Hongkong.
28. Kapila, Uma (2025-26), Indian Economy since Independence, Academic Foundation, New Delhi.
29. Galbraith, J. K. (1958), The Affluent Society, Penguin Books, U.K.
30. Mehta, J. K. (1967), Rhyme, Rhythm and Truth in Economics, Asia Publishing House, Bombay.
31. Ojha, Ruby (2014), Export-Led Growth stragy : A policy choice for development in India, Himalaya Publishing House, Mumbai.
32. Raychaudhuri, et. al.(2012), International Trade in Services in India, Oxford University Press, New Delhi.
33. Das, K., et al. (Oct.-Dec. 2007), Export-Led Growth in South Asia, The Indian Economic Journal, Vol. 55, No. 3.

Chapter-6

Role of Education and Skill Development in The Making of Education Viksit Bharat 2047

Tahreem Siddiqui
Research Scholar, Department of Sociology, DDU Gorakhpur University

Abstract

Education and skill development are fundamental pillars in realizing the vision of Viksit Bharat 2047. Quality education fosters knowledge, critical thinking, innovation, and social responsibility, while skill development enhances employability and productivity. Together, they empower individuals to contribute effectively to economic growth, technological advancement, and social transformation. By bridging educational and skill gaps, India can build a competent workforce capable of meeting global challenges. Strengthening these sectors will ensure inclusive development, sustainable progress, and national prosperity by 2047.

Key Words: Education, Education, Skill, Economic, sustainable growth

''Where the mind is without fear and the head is held high
Where knowledge is free
Where the world has not been broken up into fragments
By narrow domestic walls...

Into that heaven of freedom, my Father, let my country awake.''- (Tagore, 1912, p. 35)

The above lines are from the poem, 'Where the Mind is Without Fear' by Rabindranath Tagore, from the book 'Gitanjali' (1912). It was written when India was still in the control of the British empire. The text gave the description of an ideal society or a nation where people are free to explore and express themselves without any fear, where knowledge is available to everyone, where unity and peace lie among people, where honesty and truthfulness is the core of communication, where people work for growth and development of the nation, where reason is the soul guide to actions. Tagore's idea and noble vision is the core of 21st century India.

India's journey in development has been a complex process. It is on the evolving path, being a 'Third World Country' where it has passed many socio-economic and political barriers and still working on to get the status of 'Developed Country'. India's rich intellectual tradition has evolved over history, the evolution from spiritually rooted and holistic Vedic education to interdisciplinary Modern education. Several sociologists like S.C. Dubey (1971), M. N. Srinivas (1966), A.R. Desai (1959,) etc., have focused on the importance of education in the process of social change and modernization. Sociologist Yogendra Singh in the book, 'Essays on Modernization in India' (1977) explained, Modernization is a complex concept, as it depends on the path or the ideologies chosen. It is related to the concept of development, growth, evolution and progress. Countries like India which is still developing traditional values, culture and identity play the major role. This journey involved systematic changes in the social, political, and economical systems of India. The social reformers like Raja Ram Mohan Roy, Dayanand Saraswati, Ishwar Chandra Vidhyasagar and many more have contributed in eradicating social evils and inculcating the importance of education among the masses.

G. S. Ghurye, in the book 'Caste, Class, and Occupation' (1961), highlighted the role of education in modernization of India. He believed that education helped in cultural integration by uniting groups in postcolonial India. Ram Ahuja in his book, 'Society in India', gave five goals for the reconstruction of education, in which first goal was 'to make education relevant to the country's development needs and expectations of society'. This will be done by providing the employment and vocational training. Other goals highlighted by Ahuja focused on reducing inequality of opportunity, strengthening infrastructure, content of science and technology.

The year 1947, marked the crucial change in the history of India due to the end of colonial rule. In the chaos of political, economic, socio-demographical and administrative crisis, as an aftermath India gained the golden opportunity to frame its own course for growth and development. The implementation of Five-year plan, Land reforms, Economic Liberalization of 1991, Globalization and FDI, India started blooming. The economic growth and development were seen in every sector.

"I and you, we should all encourage people for a Viksit Bharat. We should motivate especially young minds to realize this dream."- Prime Minister Shri Narendra Modi

Viksit Bharat 2047 is our government's vision to transform India into a developed nation by year 2047, 100th anniversary of its independence. The vision tagline "Sabka Saath, Sabka Vikas, Sabka Vishwas, Sabka Prayas" which is emphasizing upon the collective efforts, development for all leaving no one behind. To become Viksit and to achieve economic, social and sustainable growth India has to focus on education, healthcare, infrastructure and innovation which is dependent on four pillars- Youth, Poor, Women and Farmers. The Vision include transforming India into a developed nation with the economic ambition of $30 trillion economy.

According to IMF and NITI Aayog, India's nominal GDP projects approximately $4.187 trillion, which makes India fourth largest economy in the world. According to UNFPA 2025, State of World Population Report, India has become the world's most populous country, with the population 1.46 billion people. The countries population becomes an asset through investment in human capital. Unlike any physical capital it is not something that can be bought, but it is rather cultivated through investments in education, healthcare, training and skill development.

"Development has to be more concerned with enhancing the lives we lead and the freedoms we enjoy." - Amartya Sen, Development as Freedom (1999)

Viksit Bharat 2047 focus on investment in human capital as a core strategy. Through various national missions, initiatives and policies Indian government aims to enhance the employability of youth, to enhance the market – relevant skills, to foster the innovation and entrepreneurship and to create a productive population which contribute in the growth and development of the country.

According to the Periodic Labour Force Survey (PLFS) Annual Report 2023–24, conducted by the National Sample Survey Office (NSSO) under the Ministry of Statistics and Programme Implementation (MoSPI), literacy rate among people aged 7 and above is 80,9%. Earlier in 2017-18 it was 77.7%, this shows a significant progress in education attainment. According to Global Innovation Index (GII), India is ranked 38th among 139 economies, (published annually by World Intellectual Property Organization). It lags behind leading countries like Switzerland, Sweden, USA, South Korea and China, though it is top performer in Central and Southern Asia. With the support of policies, investment and initiatives like Digital India, Start-up India (2016), Atal Innovation Mission (2016), and its talent pool, India will emerge as a powerhouse of innovation not only among developing economies but also globally.

India allocated 4.6% of its GDP to Education in its budget for financial year 2025, if we compare it with US and China it is 6% and 6.13% respectively. The NEP 2020 aims to increase investment in education to 6% of GDP gradually.

In a paper published by Tahir Hussain Ansari and Mohd Azam Khan in 2018, Each year, approximately 12 million young individuals in India enter the job market with inadequate education and minimal job skills. If these young people remain unemployed due to skill shortages, it could lead to significant social unrest. In summary, for India's socio-economic and demographic progress, enhancing skill development is essential. Specifically, to advance into a knowledge-driven economy, foster industrial growth, and attain substantial economic progress, it needs to boost its investment in education and training for youth, ensuring a proper balance between the two.

According to UNICEF, India has largest youth population in the world. The report highlights, the necessity of investing in education, health and infrastructure which is important for demographic dividend. It makes up 27-29% of India's total population. As India is moving towards the path of development, an article 'Shaping the future: Education and Skill Development for Viksit Bharat 2047' by Hafzal, Gayathri and Shet (2024) gave the insight of problem faced by India today. Even with significant advancements in access to education and skill-building, India still faces a number of problems. Despite its vast scope, the educational system is frequently criticised for its out-of-date curriculum, lack of focus on critical thinking, and incompatibility with its needs. There are also notable differences in access to high-quality education, particularly in underserved and rural communities. Even if programs like Skill India have achieved remarkable progress, bridging the skills gap in a nation of more than a billion people is still a difficult task. With the conclusion, India can ensure that its citizens are prepared for the evolving world by tackling issues related to access, quality, and relevance in education by building a strong skill development ecosystem.

Education is vital to society and prepares workers for advancement, whereas skill development accelerates it. Beyond imparting knowledge, education promotes critical thinking, creativity, and a love of learning. High-quality, fundamental education drives a nation's intellectual resources (Singh, 2010). The relationship between skill development and knowledge acquisition in India is to maximize the nation's human resources, the declaration emphasizes a comprehensive approach, teamwork, and creativity. India can overcome difficulties, capitalize on opportunities, and adopt technological advancements to achieve unprecedented levels of achievement and affluence with a skilled and educated populace. (Patel, Fernandes, 2024)

Review of literature

Education and skills development the role of education and skills development in enhancing employability in India, Ankit Chaurasia and Dr. Rupali Saini

This paper explored various initiative the government and its organization took to improve the quality of education and development of skills. This research paper examines the role of education and skill development in enhancing employability in India. It highlights the importance of continuous learning and up skilling in today's fast changing world. The study used quantitative research design. Secondary data was collected from review of existing literature, books, articles, reports and surveys. The detailed analysis of schemes such as Jan Shikshan Sansthan, DDU Gramin Kaushal Yojna and PMKVY gave a clear insight.

The Significance of Skill Development and Education in India, 2024, Dr. Anita Patel, Dr. Jacksan Judan Fernandes

The paper examined how the skill development initiatives is helpful in lowering the 'skill gap' which is barrier in employability. Exclusive skill development and education will empower the youth and will be helpful in societal growth and nation's development. This paper also highlights the impact of technology on education and acquisition of skills.

Akhil Bhartiya Shiksha Samagam, Report on Creating a Synergy between Education and Skilling – Future of work (2023), Government of India.

The report emphasizes on the need of aligning education with the demands of the workforce, (the synergy of education and skill training). The report discusses about evolving technology and its relation with skilled workforce, employment retention. Various suggestions like development of new age curriculum, investing on upskilling of youth, reskilling as the new age technologies like AI, robotics and automation is in great demand. It also discusses about the sustainable energy, self-reliance of Indian Manufacturing. The stakeholders from public, private and academic sectors gave their perspective on working together.

Women Empowerment through Skills Development and Vocational Education, (2016) T. Ahamad, A Sinha.

This paper focuses on women empowerment through skill development, vocational education and improving employability and income – earning opportunities for women. Skill is the bridge between job and workforce. It explains how the skill development and vocational training (Pradhan Mantri Kaushal Vikas Yojna, National Skill Development Mission and Vocational Education Program) of women will serve as an agent in promoting the women's employment. Ministry of Skill Development and Entrepreneurship and its missions like Skill India and Make in

India will come in exercise only when all the stakeholders will work hand-in-hand in a structured format.

Objectives and Data Collection

The main objective is to highlight the importance of education and skill development in the making of Viksit Bharat by 2047. The study also highlights the government schemes and initiatives such as Skill India Mission, Pradhan Mantri Kaushal Vikas Yojana (PMKVY). The study is done by the secondary data gathered by books, published reports, academic papers, articles and press information.

Historical Orientation: From Colonial Education to Making India a Global Education Hub

India owned to title of 'Vishwa Guru' (in English) World Teacher or Land of Great Wealth and Knowledge by renowned travelers like Xuanzang, a 7th century Chinese Buddhist monk and scholar who wrote about India's rich culture and about Nalanda University, one of the world's earliest residential universities, in his work 'The Great Tang Records on the Western Regions'. Al-Biruni, a 11th century scholar from Persia wrote a book named, Kitab-ul-Hind praising the achievements in mathematics, astronomy and philosophy and the intellectual skills of Indian scholars. Leaders like Swami Vivekananda visioned India as a global leader, his huge faith in youth for the transformation globally by innovation and ethical values which was rooted in the ancient Indian knowledge system. Indian knowledge system was crucial foundation for numerous scientific and philosophical foundation. Who would not know about the text like 'Surya Siddhanta' and 'Aryabhatiya' which introduced the basics of trigonometry and 'Sushruta Samhita' and 'Charaka Samhita' for detailed surgical procedures and medicine? Renowned educational institutions like Takshashila, Nalanda, Vallabhi, Vikramshila,

Mithila and other universities attracted scholars from all around the world, as it served as a global hub of wisdom and knowledge. It was truly the golden age of India.

Before British rule India had village level schools known as Pathshalas and Madrasas, which was supported and maintained by local communities financially, though the literacy rates were not up to mark, but relatively higher than during the colonial period. Education at the time of colonial period was served to teach western education, to propagate Christianity, and to serve as interpreters between British rulers and natives. To create a class of people who are "Indian in blood and color, but English in taste..." Macaulay's Minutes (1835) was passed with a 'Filtration Theory'. Various acts, dispatch, schemes and commissions laid the foundation of Modern education. In the year 1854, Wood's Dispatch which is also known as Magna Carta of English Education in India, laid the revolutionary foundation and establishment of universities with the promotion of female education. It created a structured system from primary to university level. In 1882, Indian Education Act was passed by the recommendation of Hunter commission to establish free and compulsory primary education. The Universities Act of 1904 established universities in major cities Calcutta, Bombay, and Madras on British model. After the independence, Government of India took various steps to improve the education system and promote the higher education. This time the aim was future oriented, it was for the development of its citizens and economic development of nation itself. Concept of 'Nai Talim' or Basic Education was introduced in the year 1937, Wardha Scheme. Main principle of this scheme was "Learning by doing".

"By education, I mean an all-round drawing out of the best in the child and man—body, mind, and spirit." - Mahatma Gandhi, Harijan, 1937

Gandhi's Nai Talim focused on the development of the child – body, mind, and sprit. it lies in the philosophy of self-reliance, holistic education, and skill development. Gandhi's modal of education and training was village-centric, as he promoted the handcraft skills, spinning, weaving, agriculture, and small- scale industries.

Dr. Sarvepalli Radhakrishnan, one of India's greatest educationists and philosophers, believed that education is directly linked to economic change and social progress, as it enhances the productivity, rational thinking and innovation of citizens. He chaired the University Education Commission (1948-49), which suggested the establishment of UGC. This commission also gave emphasis on technical and vocational training to deal with the need of country's developing economy.

"The end-product of education should be a free, creative man, who can battle against historical circumstances and adversities of nature."- Dr. S. Radhakrishnan, Report of the University Education Commission, 1948–49

National Education Policy, 1968 which was the first intensive policy on education which gave equal access to education to all. After few decades in 1986, National Education Policy came into effect with the focus on improvement in the quality of education and eliminating the disparities. Initiatives like Sarva Shiksha Abhiyan (2001) to universalize primary education, Right to Education Act (RTE), 2009, which ensures that every child aged 6-14 years gets free and compulsory education. Mid-Day Meal which is now known as PM-POSHAN Scheme aims to provide nutrition and encouraging attendance. Aligning with the Goal-4 of Sustainable Development Goals (SDG) for Agenda 2030, India launched its third education policy NEP 2020 with the aim to make India a 'global knowledge superpower'. This 5+3+3+4 structure has holistic objective of multidisciplinary education, skill-based learning and emphasis on research.

"Education is the foundation for human development, and skills are the bridge to productive employment, innovation, and inclusive growth." - UNESCO, Education for Sustainable Development: Towards Achieving the SDGs (2021)

Integrated Vision and its Framework

"When the youth of the country are skilled, educated, and innovative, the country will become self-reliant and developed." - Prime Minister Narendra Modi, Atmanirbhar Bharat Address, May 2020

Various Initiatives in the domain of Education, Skill Development and Research/Innovation are launched by government under the leadership of our Prime Minister such as Rashtriya Uchchatar Shiksha Abhiyan (RUSA) 2014, Skill India Mission launched; and its flagship scheme Pradhan Mantri Kaushal Vikas Yojana (PMKVY) 2015, Pradhan Mantri National Apprenticeship Promotion Scheme (NAPS) 2016, Udaan and Pragati Schemes 2016, Samagra Shiksha Abhiyan 2018, PM POSHAN Scheme 2021, PM eVIDYA Programme 2021. Skill India Digital Platform 2023, PM Kaushal Vikas Yojana 4.0, 2023–24, National Research Foundation (NRF) 2023, Atal Innovation Mission 2.0 2022, National Quantum Mission 2023.

Skill India Mission is bridging 'the skill gap' by making the way for Aatmanirbhar (Self- reliant and Viksit Bharat. Various flagship schemes like Pradhan Mantri Kaushal Vikas Yojana (PMKVY), Pradhan Mantri National Apprenticeship Promotion Scheme (PM-NAPS) and Jan Shikshan Sansthan (JSS) scheme are now under the same Central Scheme of 'Skill India Programme'.

Pradhan Mantri Kaushal Vikas Yojana (PMKVY)

The Pradhan Mantri Kaushal Vikas Yojana (PMKVY) was launched in 2015 by the Ministry of Skill Development and Entrepreneurship (MSDE) under the leadership of our Prime Minister Narendra Modi. It was launched in 4 phases till now with different objectives and focuses. The foundation phase of PMKVY introduced Recognition of Prior Learning (RPL) which formalized traditional and informal skills. According to PIB, during its pilot phase around 19.85 lakh candidates were trained. In 2022, Ministry of Skill Development and Entrepreneurship stated that total of 1,36,61,011 candidates has been trained by June 2022 out of which 24,16,610 candidates have been placed under STT component, and 54,18,524 have been certified under RPL component. Currently PMKVY 4.0 (2023-2026) is aiming to train youth for Industrial technologies like Artificial Intelligence (AI), 3D printing, robotics, drone technology. It is integrated with Skill India Digital Platform, which provide skill learning, certification and job search online. In this scheme three types of training for different target group are projected. It emphasizes on re-skilling and up-skilling to deal with the current dynamic job market where rapid technological advancement is taking place. Under this scheme around 25 lakh candidates have been trained, in which women, marginalized groups and youth are involved in traditional crafts and upskilling, special projects targeting tribes and marginalized groups, vocational training aligning with NEP 2020. It also integrates skill training with the Academic Bank of Credits (ABC), which enables it for transfer in credits between formal education and skill. Total of 1.6 crore candidates have been trained over last ten years and out of which 1.29 crore has been certified by June 2025.

India is working on skilling it workforce for making it future ready. These grassroot initiatives has positive outcome for the youth and nation as it will contribute in the overall development and growth of India. Various Rozgar Melas are organised in different parts of country to establish active interaction between employer and skilled candidates. As per the report by Ministry of Skill Development and Entrepreneurship, 94% of employers hire trained candidates under PMKVY. As per the evaluation done by Indian Institute of Public Administration (IIPA), 70.5% of candidates received the desired placement.

Conclusion

The journey of Viksit Bharat 2047 will lead India towards Developed, innovative and knowledge driven society. The role of education and skill development serves as the foundation for the nation building, linking the human capital with the sustainable economic development. The paradigm shifted from literacy to life-long learning, from degrees to employability, from academic knowledge to skill and innovation. The education system and skill development can work better when stakeholders work together. The link between Education ➡ Skill ➡ Employment ➡ Innovation ➡ Development represents the path of human progress. With the educated, skilled, and innovative citizens the vision of Viksit Bharat can be achieved. Modern programs like Pradhan Mantri Kaushal Vikas Yojna (PMKVY) and Skill India Mission (SIM) align with the Gandhian philosophy, as it links learning with livelihood. The purpose of skills is to contribute in the economic building of nation. The education, skill building and innovation by research will act as an investment in the human capital, as it is the greatest resource which the country owns.

References-

- Government of India. (2020). National Education Policy 2020.Ministry of Education, New Delhi.
- Ministry of Skill Development and Entrepreneurship (MSDE). (2024). Annual Report 2023–24. Government of India.

- NITI Aayog. (2018). Strategy for New India @75. Government of India.
- National Sample Survey Office (NSSO). (2024). Periodic Labour Force Survey (PLFS) Annual Report 2023–24. Ministry of Statistics and Programme Implementation (MoSPI), Government of India.
- Press Information Bureau (PIB). (2023). PMKVY 4.0 Launched to Focus on Industry 4.0 Skills for Viksit Bharat 2047.Government of India.
- National Skill Development Corporation (NSDC). (2023). Skill India Digital Platform: Empowering India's Workforce.New Delhi.
- UNDP India. (2022). Human Development Report: Education, Employment and Skills for Sustainable Growth.
- World Bank. (2020). Skilling India: No Time to Lose. Washington, D.C.
- Sen, Amartya. (1999). Development as Freedom. Oxford University Press.
- Radhakrishnan, S. (1948–49). Report of the University Education Commission. Ministry of Education, Government of India.
- Planning Commission of India. (2013). Twelfth Five Year Plan (2012–17): Faster, More Inclusive and Sustainable Growth. Government of India.
- UNESCO. (2023). Global Education Monitoring Report 2023: Technology in Education. Paris: UNESCO Publishing.
- Ministry of Education. (2023). Viksit Bharat@2047: Vision Document – Roadmap for Developed India. Government of India.
- International Labour Organization (ILO). (2023). Skills and Jobs in the Post-Pandemic World: The Indian Experience.

- Hussain, A, T. (2018) "Role of Education and Skill Development to Promote Employment in India."
- Hafzal. M, Gayathri. B J, and Shet. (2024) "Shaping the Future: Education and Skill Development for Viksit Bharat @ 2047"
- T. Ahamad, A. Sinha, and R. K. Shastri, "Women empowerment through skills development & vocational education,"
- Government of India Report, Akhil Bhartiya Shiksha Samagam.(2023) "Report on Creating a Synergy between Education and Skilling – Future of work"
- Ghurye, G. S. (1961). Caste, Class and Occupation.
- Singh, Y. (1973). Modernization of Indian Tradition. Thomson Press.
- Ahuja, R. (2014). Social Problems in India. Rawat Publications.
- Ahuja, R. (1999). Society in India.
- Gandhi, M. K. (1937). Harijan.
- Tagore, R. (1912). Where the mind is without fear. In Gitanjali: Song offerings (pp. 35–36).

Chapter- 7

The North - South Divide On Climate Efforts Continues Post – Cop 28

By: Rashmi Singh

Abstract

In the lead up to the 28th Conference of Parties (COP28) meeting could have been a key moment, reflecting on its Paris Agreement incarnation Garland figures. This machine development has a purpose: at its core is to assess overall progress so far and stimulate yet more ambitious climate change measures. This in turn has given rise to almost certain speculation that there will be no real commitment fostering change away from fossil fuels at the global convention. However, a close look at the real situation demonstrates that there is still a built in North-South division within the outcomes, obstructive of any significant new global cooperation. This paper analyzes these divergent positions and priorities, using the four nations of India, South Africa, Germany and the United States as examples. It puts forward the notion that the Global Stocktake and the ultimate agreement of fossil fuel switching it embodies b represent procedural advances rather than addressing basic structural inequalities. Developed countries still take technology and private finance as theirs for the asking, while for developing nations subjects of immediate climate disasters which they did not cause, relieving climate change debts requires concessional finance which should not exceed its repayment burden or technology transfer without a bill attached. The paper concludes that without proper means of distributing finance, technology and historical responsibility, things like aspirations toward the Paris Agreement may just end up as empty talk for governments an ever-widening gulf between what diplomats say and the hard realities on ground.

Keywords:
Climate Finance, North South Cooperation, COP28, Global Stocktake, Energy Transition, Climate Justice, Nationally Determined Contributions (NDCs)

Introduction -

The physical realities of climate change, once a chatting point threat, is now an active crisis that will only become more urgent. Increasing global temperatures, erratic weather patterns, and increasing frequency of extreme events from catastrophic floods in Pakistan that displaced millions to crop failures across sub-Saharan Africa highlight the relative vulnerability of populations in Global South; Tol (2009), Vivier-Desjardins (2022), Osaka (2024) This dilemma is highlighted by a stark inequity: the countries least responsible for the past build-up of greenhouse gas emissions are suffering the worst effects. Industrialization in the Global North was based on two centuries of unimpeded fossil fuel use, while developing economies such as India and South Africa are now forced to plot their development trajectories under the yoke of a climate crisis they didn't cause.

The annual Conference of the Parties (COP) summits have been the main venue for multilateral climate negotiations for almost 30 years. In a world where these agreements, declarations or voluntary pledging have multiplied, however, global emissions continue to rise and the generative implementation gap between political statement-making and action remains high (Lawson 2016).The Paris Agreement's bottom up architecture of Nationally Determined Contributions (NDCs) was a diplomatic success, but intentionally avoided any binding enforcement mechanisms that had previously caused problems for the Kyoto Protocol (Aichele & Felbermayr, 2013; Seo, 2017).

Set against this backdrop, COP28 in Dubai was framed as a turning point, heralding the first Global Stocktake [a process that is supposed to assess collective progress towards the Paris Agreement's long-term goals and inform subsequent NDC targets (United Nations, 2023)]. The expectation was a strong signal on the move away from fossil fuels. This paper examines whether COP28 was a meaningful rupture with the status quo or simply another round in longstanding North-South conflicts. By tracing the fault lines, especially when it comes to finance, technology and what counts as a climate commitment, of India, South Africa, Germany and the United States whose positions tend to dominate the global political landscape this analysis examines how tensions that continue to exist are still holding back an equitable and feasible global response.

Instituted as a periodic process, the Global Stocktake (GST) provides countries an opportunity to assess collective progress in achieving the purpose and long-term goals of the Paris Agreement. Its findings aim to guide parties in updating and enhancing their climate actions and support. But the first GST at COP28 revealed a large disconnect between the aspirational goals of the agreement and what is presently on track to occur around the globe. The scientific consensus established in the stocktake process was clear. The UN Environment Programme's Emissions Gap Report 2023 stated that current policies are taking the world on a disastrous course towards an average rise in temperature of between 2.4 to 2.9°C by the end of the century, which is well above Paris Agreement's goal of limiting warming to (UNEP, 2023). To keep up with the 1.5°C target, global greenhouse gas emissions must fall by 43% by 2030 this requires a major and severe transformation of worldwide energy systems, industries processes, and land use. (United Nations[23], 2023).

In response to this urgent finding, the decision text from COP28 essentially invited parties to "phase out fossil fuels in energy systems, in a just, orderly and equitable manner." Though linguistically notable as the first explicit mention of fossil fuels in a COP decision, the GST outcome was couched as options to be considered and encouraged rather than enforced. Countries were called on to "contribute" to global efforts, but no legally binding obligations were created. This fate exemplifies the systemic flaws of the Paris Agreement, its dependence on voluntary state commitments and lack of a strong enforcement regime (Aidam, 2024). The GST thus runs the risk of emerging as a glorified exercise in gap analysis that lacks the enforceable and accountable governmental machinery to actually close the gaps that it identifies dooming it to repeat the loss of ambition record of international climate policy going back to failures in key regards with respect to how shall we say Kyoto Protocols.

We found this discrepancy in the responses to the GST's findings, and indeed to climate action more broadly, can be explained by structural realities across the North-South divide. Such an unstitching is not just geographical, but carries with it discrete historical responsibilities, development status and economic capabilities that underlie the contributions made to climate talks.

Southern NDCs Are Contingent -

Developing countries climate action is always closely associated with energy access, poverty alleviation and sustainable development imperatives. In nations such as India and South Africa, where large segments of society still lack consistent access to electricity, the energy transition is not merely a problem in terms of technological substitution but instead a multifaceted socioeconomic challenge. Their economies are often structurally reliant on fossil fuels for jobs, revenue and basic energy security.

Their NDCs explicitly reflect this reality. India's Long-Term Low-Carbon Development Strategy, for example, lays out that many of its targets are conditional on international climate finance and technology transfer (Government of India 2022). Not a negotiating tactic but rather a pragmatic acknowledgment of resource constraints. This presents a national challenge because it is estimated that the scale of investment required to both decarbonize and meet development goals far exceeds domestic financial capacities over $2.5 trillion for India by 2030. (Government of India, 2021)

Likewise, through the idea of a "Just Transition," South Africa brings attention to both the need for rapid decarbonization and its profound social implications. If coal mines and power plants are closed too early without proper social safety nets, retraining programs, and alternative economic development there is a risk of creating widespread job loss in communities that will collapse while deepening poverty for the very people who need decent jobs to forge sustainable social stability (Government of South Africa 2021). Climate policy is a matter of survival and equitable development for these nations and in rich countries such as Germany and America, climate policy is largely seen as a problem of technological innovation and market efficiency. Its strategies centre on encouraging investment in renewables, driving private-sector innovation via incentives and carbon pricing, and developing market structures for clean energy rollout (Federal Republic of Germany, 2023). This way, although it works in their cases, presupposes strong institutional capacity and matured financial markets "and the fiscal space needed to absorb transition costs" things that are largely missing in Global South.

The Eternal Stalemate of Climate Finance-

Finance is the most concrete and controversial expression of the North-South divide. It was a landmark commitment that developed countries made in 2009 to mobilize $100 billion annually by 2020 for developing countries (OECD, 2021), but one where meetings were missed years in a row, and whose adequacy is now widely questioned and the target of $100 billion a year, even if met regularly, is dwarfed by the scale of need. Moreover, a vital element which is often neglected the composition of this finance. A large fraction of this aid comes in the form of loans rather than grants, exacerbating debt burdens on developing countries (Chowdhury & Jomo 2022). This effectively asks countries already facing a disaster they did not trigger to finance their own amelioration and adaptation, adding yet another layer of indebtedness reminiscent of colonial and neo-colonial economic arrangements that have prevailed for the last several centuries. This demand from the Global South stems less from needing more money, than new, additional and concessional finance that will not weaken their fiscal sovereignty or development opportunities.

The Unfulfilled Promise of Technology Transfer-

The Paris Agreement also enshrined technology development and transfer as an important means of support for actions by developing countries. The idea was to allow countries to leapfrog over the carbon-intensive development trajectory of the Global North by providing access to leading edge clean technologies. But this vision has been mired in the inflexibilities of the global intellectual property (IP) regime.

Many developing countries claim that prohibitive costs and strict patent protections for technologies such as advanced solar PV, battery storage, and green hydrogen effectively exclude them from the clean energy transition (Government of South Africa, 2020). They call for a more flexible framework of IP, including mechanisms like compulsory licensing or patent pools that could enable access. Countries that comprise the market for this technology, where the companies holding these patents are based, argue that strong IP protection is critical to fueling the innovation required to find new climate solutions. Both positions have merit, but the absence of pragmatic compromise creates a "technology gap" preventing[...] diffusion of solutions at the speed and scale demanded by the climate crisis.

Energy Transition: Rhetoric vs. Structural Reality-

That COP28 agreement to "transition away from fossil fuels" is a big step on the way there, if only in rhetoric. For the first time, fossil fuels were specifically mentioned as the main driver of climate change in a final COP text. But there is an important gap between these kinds of declarative statements and the structural realities of the global energy system. While "net-zero" emissions are scientifically necessary, the idea can obscure a need for absolute cuts. It enables the continued use of fossil fuels, but on conditions of future deployment (at scale) of largely unproven technologies to capture and sequester carbon dioxide or nature-based offsets which can postpone urgently needed mitigation action (Fankhauser et al., 2022).This uncertainty is embedded in the unabated infrastructural buildup of fossil fuel across most industrialized countries while they proclaim to be aligning society with their renewable energy pushers (Ordonez et al., 2010). The simultaneous expansion of wind and solar at the same time as oil and gas production hitting record levels in countries such as the United States illustrates this structural contradiction.

Furthermore, the social costs of the transition are not evenly distributed. As evidenced by the experience of coal-mining communities in Appalachia, without robust and intentional just transition policies, the decline of fossil fuel industries (and other dirty energy) can produce profoundly destabilizing economic shockwaves as well as social dislocation and public health emergencies (Young et al., 2023).In many developing nations that depend significantly on fossil fuel revenue or employment, the push to transition without adequate financial and technical support for economy diversification is not just unrealistic but threatens to reproduce and amplify these social harms on a much larger scale.

The Enforcement Deficit and Paths Forward

The international climate regime has a core weakness in its dependence on a system of "name and shame," rather than enforced rules. There is no European, American or other supranational body able to force a sovereign state to fulfill its climate pledges. The key mechanisms of influence are diplomatic pressure, reputational risk and domestic political accountability (Roberts 2011). This is a toothless enforcement mechanism that has clearly and demonstrably failed to change the pace of change necessary. This voluntarist framework can be left behind in order to bridge the implementation gap and bring about real global cooperation, which calls for a much more structured and equitable system. Main priorities for action include:

Operationalizing Mandates: The goals of the Global Stocktake need to be translated into timebound, measurable mandates with clear reporting requirements that progress from voluntary "contributions" to more structured commitments.

A higher financial floor: reforming climate finance. Critically, this finance must consist of grants and highly concessional loans far more overwhelmingly than at present, while new mechanisms for debt relief/restructuring in the context of climate action should be considered (Chowdhury & Jomo, 2022).

Enabling Technology Access: It is imperative to have a practical global architecture for the transfer of technology. This might include publicly funded R&D collaborations, patent pools for climate-friendly technologies and differentiated pricing models that enable developing countries to access essential innovations.

Ensuring Transparency and Accountability: The strong and transparent monitoring, reporting, and verification systems are a prerequisite for building trust that will allow civil society and the public to scrutinize actions taken with MRV creating conditions necessary for political accountability leading stronger action.

Conclusion

COP28 and the inaugural Global Stocktake were major procedural landmarks in the long-term development of the international climate regime. That the need for this transition away from fossil fuels is so explicit in the statement represents a significant step forward in political discourse. That North-South divide is the great fault line. In the Global North, climate action is increasingly portrayed as an opportunity for technological leadership and green growth. For the Global South, it is a battle for climate justice and survival, as well as for equitable development. So long as the international community does not fill this abyss with more than words morphing climate finance into something truly transformative, unblocking technology transfer and making real the principle of common but differentiated responsibilities and respective capabilities then promises around the Paris Agreement will stay at risk. The world cannot wait any longer for a diplomacy that puts procedural consensus ahead of the concrete action demanded by the growing climate crisis.

References

- Aidam, K. (2024). COP28 and the Global Stocktake: Farce of Climate Action? Frontiers in Sustainability, 5, 1388266.

- Aichele, R., & Felbermayr, G. (2013) Carbon Emissions and The Kyoto Protocol. Journal of Policy Analysis and Management, 32(4), 731–757.

- Conference of the Food & Agriculture Organization. Chowdhury, A., & Jomo, K. S., (2022).
  The climate finance conundrum. Development, 65, 29-41.

- Fankhauser, S., Smith, S., Allen, M., Axelsson, K., Hale, T. Hepburn, C. & Wetzer, T. (2022). What net-zero emissions is and why it matters Nature Climate Change, 12, 15-21.

- Federal Republic of Germany. (2023). Eighth National Communication and Fifth Biennial Report under the UNFCCC.

- Government of India. (2021). India's Third Biennial Update Report to the United Nations Framework Convention on Climate Change (UNFCCC). Ministry of Environment, Forest and Climate Change.

- Government of India. (2022). India's Long-Term Low-Carbon Development Strategy. Environment, Forest and Climate Change Ministry

- Government of South Africa. (2020). Technology Needs Assessment for Climate Change South Africa Department of Science and Innovation.

- Government of South Africa. (2021). Paris agreement First Nationally Determined Contribution Department of Forestry, Fisheries and Environmental.

- Lawson, E. T. (2016). Negotiating the participation of Stakeholders in the Ghana national climate change policy: the politics. International Journal of Climate Change Strategies and Management, Vol. 8 No. 3, pp. 399–417.

- OECD. (2021). Climate finance delivered and mobilised by developed countries for 20132019. OECD Publishing.

- Ordonez, J., Jadraque, E., Alegre, J. & Martinez, G. (2010). It provides an analysis of the photovoltaic solar energy potential of house roofs in the Andalusia region. Renewable and Sustainable Energy Reviews, 14(8), 2122–2130.

- Osaka, S. (2024). Earth hit a dreaded level of warming over the past year. The Washington Post.

- Roberts, A. (2011). Comparative international law? The application of international law by domestic courts International and Comparative Law Quarterly 60, 57–92.

- Seo, S. N. (2017). Climate Policy Negotiations Beyond the Paris Agreement. Regional Science Policy & Practice, 9, pp. 121-140.

- United Nations. (2023). First Global Stocktake of the Paris Agreement UNFCCC.

- Young, T., et al. (2023). Mined, lost, and forlorn: Energy transitions and opioid use in an Appalachian coal community Energy Research & Social Science, 99, 103046.

Chapter- 8

From Rural Reconstruction to Developed India: A Study of Social Justice in the Novels of Bhabani Bhattacharya

Dr Sandeep Kumar Gupta
Assistant Professor (Dept of English)
Govt Degree College, Kanth, Moradabad

Bhabani Bhattacharya is rightly regarded one of the greatest thinkers of twentieth century. His contribution to literature and philosophy has been accepted by all. As a writer, he emphasizes the importance of noble family, intellectual culture, cultural environment, high intelligence, learning wisdom, financial security, sincere friendship, philosophical insight etc. He is an imitator of Vivekananda, Tagore and Gandhi, Pt Nehru etc. Like Tagore, Bhabani Bhattacharya believed that God is the creator of this universe. He accepted Togore's contribution in the field of education, politics, literature, economics and social institutions. The novelist also analyzed various social and economic problems and suggested ways and means for rural construction and regeneration of mankind.

Almost all Gandhian principles influenced Bhabani Bhattacharya very much. Like many Indian politician, he accepted him as a living presence. The practical side of the Gandhian principles have been described by him in *Shadow from Ladakh.* For him, Gandhi is a practical Idealist, a yogi and a man of action. He always regarded him the follower of the principles of universal brotherhood and religious tolerance. In his autobiography *My Experiments with Truth* Gandhi accepted the influence of *The Gita. The Ramayana. The Mahabharata, Theory of Utility, Plea for*

Vegetarianism, Civil Disobedience. Unto the Last, The *Bible*, *Vision and Religion*, etc. Bhabani Bhattacharya also felt tempted to study the above-mentioned books. In 1969, Bhabani Bhattacharya became popular for his book *Gandhi The Writer: The Image as it Grew*. Not only this, he accepted his indebtedness to Gandhi in Mahatma Gandhi (1977). Here he asserted the practical aspect of Gandhism for the welfare of Indian masses and the world at large. *Shadow from Ladakh* confirms above mentioned opinion. Like Gandhi, Bhabani Bhattacharya also accepts that there is no politics devoid of religion with politics. Hence, he asserts the need of adopting good means to achieve noble ends. He emphasized. the intimate relationship of aims and means. Then he spoke in favour of universal religion. As a matter of fact, his religion can be grasped by heart. Same is the case with Devata in *So Many Hungers*! It has got to be accepted that Gandhi was not a rigid and traditional Hindu. His religion transcends Hinduism. He believed in the disinterested search after truth which purifies one's heart and transforms all life. Religion consists in serving the poor and the needy. In A Goddess Named Gold Atmaram too wanted to establish the kingdom of peace, social justice and truth. Devata spoke in favour of equality of all religions.

Gandhiji asserted that society based on non-violence can only consist of groups settled in villages in which the country co-operation is the condition of dignified and peaceful existence. Once he said that the new social order would be determined by the people according to their mental, moral and cultural development. Since he gave importance to individual freedom, he did not trust the unlimited authority of the state. He accepted the concept of village Panchayat. Let every village have the freedom to manage its own affairs. For this he admired the policy of decentralization. Then he advocated the concept of small-scale industries in lieu of large industries. In such an economic structure all the professions will be equal. People will not be greedy. As he was opposed to imperialism and capitalism, he advocated the system of Trusteeship. He regarded Satyagraha the weapon of the brave. Like Thoreau. he accepted the concept of civil disobedience. Like Milton he spoke in favour of peace and condemned war. He gave his own conception of education for the regeneration of village life.

Bhabani Bhattacharya approves all these principles of Gandhi in *Shadow from Ladakh* and *He Who Rides A Tiger*. It is an accepted fact that the Gandhian approach to life can be noticed in each of his first five novels. So Many Hungers! discusses Gandhi's influence on Indian Freedom Struggle. *Music for Mohini* pleads for rural uplift, social re-construction and adult education as preached and practiced by Gandhi in his life. He Who Rides A Tiger fosters the cause of the poor and the downtrodden for whom Gandhi fought undauntedly and untiringly. Raja Rao, R.K. Narayan, Arun Joshi etc. came under the influence of Gandhiji as inspired by him, they turned towards the depiction of the life of the common man, the poor and the illiterate, particularly on he villages.

In 1949 Bhabani Bhattacharya went to Washington D.C. to serve as Press Attaché. Embassy of India. During his stay in U.S.A. he studied the works of Ralph Waldo Emerson and Henry David Thoreau. He regarded both of them great scholars of 19th century. They never felt restless due to their poverty and thanked God for His moderate goodness. Both of them followed the voice of their conscience. Like Christ. they always looked within their heart and got inner strength. Like Gandhiji, Bhabani Bhattacharya accepted their contribution to humanity. Emerson's essays The American Scholar, The Over-Soul, Nature, Self-Reliance, Intellect. Prudence etc., left a deep mark on the mind of Bhabani Bhattacharya. having visited England Emerson remarked that everything is Roman in Great Britain. Sarcastically he said that he found the Ruins' of Rome there. Emerson wanted that the new America should have her own culture.

Bhabani Bhattacharya accepted Emerson and Thoreau, great moral teachers mainly because they practiced themselves whatever they taught others. Like Thoreau, Bhabani Bhattacharya wanted to be thought-free and hated to be dictated mentally. He learnt from Thoreau that he must have high moral sense and should not be prepared to serve the devil at any cost. This is the reason that he wrote novels with a mission and that mission was to draw the seeds of sincerity, simplicity, faith, innocence, and friendliness. Through certain characters he inspired his readers to get rid of lust, violence, possessiveness, avarice, selfishness, temptation, meanness, anxieties, restlessness etc. In Shadow from Ladakh and So Many Hunger! he describes the horrors of poverty in real colours. But he adopts the approach of Swami Vivekananda who inspired people to work hard to improve themselves in every field.

Bhabani Bhattacharya regarded Swami Vivekananda one of the architects of modern India and the most powerful spiritual ambassador to foreign land. Swamiji believed that God had given him the mission to communicate the message of Vedantic philosophy to the people of the world. Since he was a graduate of the Calcutta University, he had studied the thought of Spenser, Mill, Kant, Fichte Hegel etc. When he visited U.S.A. U.K. and other European countries, he admired the progress of the West. There was a pain in his heart mainly because Indians were poor, orthodox, superstitious and hungry. Vivekananda had been admired by Bhabani Bhattacharva because the former tried his level best to make an effective synthesis of Hindu spirituality and western science. It is true that he had gone to the West to propagate the Vedantic philosophy. It is also true that he wanted the reconstruction of India as a whole on new pattern. Vivekananda had strong belief in the existence of God and told people that it is possible for everyone to realize Him. Bhabani Bhattacharya had respect for this great Yogi because the latter believed the essential unity of all religion. Even in the Parliament of Religions, he asserted the need of universal religion as that was the only way to remove misery of humanity. Before meeting Shri Ramakrishna Paramhansa, Swami Vivekananda, he had many doubts in his mind. He loved philosophical discussion and would not accept anything on the authority of others. He had the feeling that purity of body and soul is a spiritual force whose fire penetrates into every aspect of life, but is extinguished by the slightest defilement'. He had accepted Brahmoism at one stage but had abandoned its theism after a reading of Mill's essay on Religion. He was thus in a skeptical frame of mind when he met Sri Ramakrishna. He had a lot of knowledge of Vedanta and of Western Philosophy, and could have become an impressive professor of Philosophy; but in order to become Swami Vivekananda itwas necessary for him to have the spiritual experience of which Vedanta is an intellectual exposition.

He also thought of the present and the future, and then the idea as to what he should do to relieve the misery of the masses dawned upon his mind. From 1888 to 1893 he wandered all over the country, mostly on foot, and often had to face starvation and was sometimes in great peril of his life. But undaunted by hardships and dangers, he led the life of a true Sanyassin. He had the opportunity of seeing the real face of India, observing on the one side the grinding poverty of millions and millions of his poor country men living in their huts, and on the other, the luxurious and ostentatious life of the rich in their palaces. The idea dawned upon him that the first duty of a truly religious person was to take care of the poor and raise them.

This approach of Vivekananda touched the inner heart of Bhabani Bhattacharya. Like Vivekananda Bhabani Bhattacharya had full faith in the spiritual treasures of India. His novels teach the principles of Vedanta though his medium is different from Vivekananda's. Bhabani Bhattacharya told the members of East-West center and the students of university of Hawaii that Swami Vivekananda impressed Max Muller too much. Swamiji stayed in U.S.A. for three years after the Parliament of Religions was over. Throughout his stay, he never forgot his mission which included giving to the West the spiritual achievements in the treasures of India and to take to India what appeared admirable in Western civilization scientific, economic and industrial spheres, its social welfare activities, and above all its apparent democratic equality in contrast to which the inequality of the Indian caste system seemed all the more brutal.

The novel *Shadow from Ladakh* confirms the view that Bhabani Bhattacharya admires Pt. Nehru's contribution to world politics. He accepted him as the maker of modern India and apostle of peace. He knew that Nehru's democratic socialism was a philosophy of life with a cosmopolitan outlook and an international perspective. Moreover, his socialism was another facet of his humanism. Like Gandhi and Patel, he was a fighter for the bright future of his country. There is no denying the fact that he fought against Colonialism and Imperialism. The working of U.N.O. appealed him, as he loved peace and friendship among all the nations of the world. He believed in speeding up productive activity and tremendous growth in the field of science and technology. Through Bhaskar, Bhattacharya expressed his faith in Nehru's ideology. Bhattacharya accepted Nehru's view that Tagore and Gandhi were complementary to each other. Like Bhaskar, Nehru regarded steel very essential for the economic progress of the country.

Gandhiji rightly said that the new economic policies should inspire the villagers to stay in their villages for jobs. Why should they run towards cities for employment? Power-fed heavy machines failed to attract him. Of course, heavy machines could be established in the country if there was no other alternative. Spinning wheel was regarded by him as the best solution of various economic problems. He presented his own Charkha to Satyajit and the latter was proud of it. The author says:

> ...His hands plied the spinning wheel an everyday chore in all the twenty years past, a Gandhian inheritance. The wheel that turned cotton into yarn had been in Gandhi's hand an instrument of social philosophy and so it was still in Satyajit's reckoning. The wheel was the common man's answer to power-fed machines. It was an emblem of unity between all classes of the people; the manual effort of plying the wheel was an obligation for all. And in the days before freedom, alien authority had looked upon the wheel with immense dread and hatred.

He regards Kama the first product of the mind. As a matter of fact, Dharma, Arth, Kama and Moksha are the four fundamental values of Indian philosophy and equal importance has been attached to each one of them by our ancestors. Everybody should perform his duty (Dharma) righteously. He has to earn some money for his living. Karma is essential for health, wealth and procreation. But the ultimate aim of life is liberation i.e. Moksha. Since Bhabani Bhattacharya was keenly interested in Indian philosophy, he described the importance of Kama through Nishi in *A Dream in Hawaii*. Bhattacharya is not averse to the depiction of sex in the novel. Sex can be a powerful subject matter for fiction since it constitutes an integral part of human life. There should not be any impositions or restrains regarding sex in literature. Since the novel as a creative art is finally concerned with the "human scene", sex as a theme cannot be omitted, as its omission will limit the vision of the novelist whose "final business" is to reveal the "truth" of life in a realistic way.

In his novels, Bhabani Bhattacharya succeeds in rising above the limited sphere of Indian culture and attained the universal level. For example, In *A Dream in Hawaii*, he mentions the clash of values between the East and the West. Of course, he does not reach the conclusion that 'East is East and West is West' and no efforts should be made for the harmony between the two'. Like E.M. Forster, he makes efforts to understand the differences that exist among the people of different races and nationalities.

Thus, Bhabani Bhattacharya presents the contemporary Indian problems in true colours and at the same time, feels his duty to present a solution. It is true that he had lived out of India for a long time yet he could depict the various miseries of his fellow beings. While reading So Many Hungers! And He Who Rides A Tiger, every reader feels himself to be witnessing the famine of Bengal with his own eyes. The disgusting scenes of famine-hit-Bengal touch human heart and yet Bhabani Bhattacharya has got to be admired for his positive vision of life. Like G.B. Shaw and John Galsworthy, he was always conscious of social purpose of his art. The realities may be hard and bitter but Bhabani Bhattacharya draws the attention of the readers towards them. Similarly, the various movements started by Mahatama Gandhi to achieve national freedom, took a tragic turn. Bhabani Bhattacharya could portray the same tragedies of freedom struggle as he has witnessed the same himself. Hence, Bhabani Bhattacharya describes poverty, corruption, ignorance, exploitation, the gap between the Haves and Have Nots, greedy and lustful people and yet does not lose his interest in life. He hopes that good sense will prevail among the people and his country will also be a part of brave new world.

REFERENCES

- Bhabani Bhattacharya: *Gandhi The Writer: The Image as It Grew*, New Delhi: National Book Trust, 1969.
- Dr. K.K. Sharma Bhabani Bhattacharya: *His Vision and Themes*; Publications), 1979, New Delhi : Abhinav Publications, 1979.
- Bhabani Bhattacharya: *A Dream in Hawaii*; Delhi: Macmillan Co. of India, 1978,
- Balram S. Sorot : *The Novels of Bhabani Bhattacharya*; New Delhi: Prestige Books, 1991.
- Bhabani Bhattacharya: *Shadow from Ladakh*; Delhi, Hind Pocket Books, 1966.

Chapter-9

भारतीय संस्कृति विविधता एवं एकता

डॉ0 सत्येन्द्र नाथ तिवारी
असिस्टेन्ट प्रोफसर–संस्कृत
श्यामेश्वर महाविद्यालय सिकरीगंज, गोरखपुर

प्रस्तावना–

भारतीय संस्कृति के विषय पर विचार करने के पूर्व हमें भारतीय संस्कृति के कतिपय अवधारणाओं को समझना समीचीन प्रतीत होता है। ये अवधाणाऐं– राष्ट्रीय एकता, अनेकता, बहुलता और एकीकरण की है। भारतीय समाज की सांस्कृतिक विरासत बहुत ही विशाल है। जिसमें कई जीवन समुदाय एवं जीवन पद्धतियाँ निहित हैं। भारतीय संस्कृति विभिन्न प्रकार की प्रजातियों, धर्मो तथा आस्थाओं का मिश्रण है। यह भारतीय संस्कृति चारों तरफ से विविधतापूर्ण प्रतीत होता है, परन्तु इसकी अखण्डता अक्षुण्ण है। किसी भी संस्कृति में एकता और विविधता का सिंहावलोकन करने के लिए उसकी सांस्कृति विशेषता का अध्ययन अनिवार्य होता है। फलस्वरुप जब हम भारतीय संस्कृति को देखते हैं, तो ज्ञात होता है कि भारतीय संस्कृति की मूल विशेषता उसकी सहिष्णुता व ग्रहणशीलता और गत्यात्मक प्रकृति है। जिसका निदर्शन हमें समय–समय पर आये भारतीय समाज में आर्य, अनार्य, द्रविड, शक, हूण, पुर्तगाली फ्रांसिसी, मंगोल, पारसी आदि अनेक आक्रान्ताओं के लोग समय समय पर यहॉ आये, एवं यहाँ की संस्कृति के रंग में रंगते हुए राष्ट्रीय धारा में समा गये। इतना ही नहीं भारतीय संस्कृति विश्व की विभिन्न संस्कृतियों विचारों, दर्शनों, धर्मो, भाषाओं आदि के प्रति सहनशीलता का परिचय देते हुए उन्हें अपने में समाहित किया है। फलतः भारतीय संस्कृति विभिन्नताओं में एकता की एक लीला भूमि बन गयी है। जिसका प्रमाण बृहदारण्यकोषनिषद ये पंक्तियाँ हैं, जो सभी के कल्याण, सुख, शान्ति की कामना करती दिखती हैं।

"सर्वे भवन्तु सुखिनः सर्वे सन्तु निरामयाः।।
सर्वे भद्राणि पश्चयन्तु मा कश्चिद दुःख भाग् भवेत।।

ऊँ शान्तिः शान्तिः शान्तिः"[1]

यद्यपि भारतीय संस्कृति का बाह्य स्वरुप अनेक विभिन्नताओं का पुंज है, किन्तु इसका आन्तरिक स्वरुप एक है, जो अखण्ड एवं मौलिक है। इस क्रम में हम देखने का प्रयास करेंगे कि भारतीय संस्कृति का आन्तरिक स्वरुप कितना विविधतापूर्ण इसके लिए हम देखते है कि भारतीय संस्कृति अति प्राचीन तथा गौरवपूर्ण है। आजकल का युग आर्थिक महत्व का है, एवं मनुष्य का एक ही उद्देश्य है, धन कमाना किन्तु हमें यह भी स्मरण रखना चाहिए कि सांस्कृतिक कार्य भी कल्पवृक्ष की भांति फलदायी होते हैं। विश्वा में अलग–अलग स्थान की अलग–अलग संस्कृतियाँ है, जिनमें विभिन्नता देखने को मिलती है। ऐसे में भारतीय संस्कृति एवं समाज अपनी अलग ही अहमियत रखता है। जो सहस्रों शताब्दियों उपरान्त भी अक्षुण्ण बना हुआ है। भारतीय संस्कृति ने जीवन एवं जगत के प्रति "सर्व–भूत–हिते–रता" होना ही अपना परम लक्ष्य समझा। फलस्वरूय भारतीय संस्कृति का मुख्य उद्देश्य सम्पूर्ण मानवधर्म का विकास करना है और इसी लक्ष्य की पूर्ति के लिए भारत ने वसुधैव कुटुम्बकम' की भावना अपने अन्तरस्वरूप में समाये हुए आज भी विद्यमान है। भारतीय संस्कृति की प्राचीनता, सर्वांगीणता, विशालता, उदारता एवं सहिष्णुता की समता अन्य कोई संस्कृति नहीं रख सकती। राष्ट्रीयता, शान्ति, अहिंसा एवं विश्वबन्धुत्व का संदेश समता भारतीय संस्कृति ने मानवता का विकास किया है व्यक्ति के मन शरीर तथा आत्मा से सम्बद्ध नैसर्गिक शक्तियाँ संस्कृति से ही परिवर्तित एवं परिस्कृत होती हैं।

इस प्रकार हमारी उदात्त संस्कृति के विषय में और भी अन्य जिज्ञासाएँ होने पर हम लोगों को यह ज्ञात होता है कि संस्कृति शब्द की व्यूत्पत्ति सम् उपसर्ग पूर्वक कृ धातु से निष्पन्न होता है, जिसका अर्थ परिष्कृत अथवा परिमार्जित करने के भाव का सूचक है। संस्कृति शब्द मनुष्य की सहज प्रवृत्तियों, नैसर्गिक शक्तियों तथा उसके परिष्कार का द्योतक है। साथ ही साथ यह मनुष्य के भूत, वर्तमान तथा भावी जीवन का सर्वांगीण विकास है एवं जीवन के नानाविध रूपों का समुदाय ही संस्कृति है।

---

[1] *बृहदारण्यकोपनिषद–01.04.14*

यद्यपि संस्कृति की अनेक परिभाषाएँ भारतीय समाज में प्रचलित हैं, जिससे भारतीय संस्कृति की विष्टिता एवं विशालता का परिचय सहज ही मिल जाता है तथापि कतिपय विद्वानों की परिभाषाओं पर विमर्श अभीष्ट है। इस क्रम में सर्वप्रथम डॉ0 सम्पूर्णानन्द की यह परिभाषा द्रष्टव्य है–

डॉ0 सम्पूर्णानन्द के मत में "मानव का प्रत्येक विचार प्रत्येक संस्कृति नहीं है, पर जिन कामों से किसी देश विशेष के समस्त समाज पर कोई अमिट छाप पड़े, वही स्थायी प्रभाव ही संस्कृति है। संस्कृति वह आधारशिला है, जिसके आश्रय से जाति समाज व देश का विशाल भव्य प्रसाद निर्मित होता है।"[2]

डॉ0 व्हाइटहेड के मत में–'संस्कृति मानसिक प्रयास, सौन्दर्य और मानवता की अनुभूति है।[3]

गिलिन के मत में, "प्रत्येक समूह तथा समाज में व्यवहार के ऐसे प्रतिमान होते हैं, जो एक पीढ़ी से दूसरे पीढ़ी को हस्तान्तरित होते हैं, तथा बच्चों को सिखलाये जाते हैं, जिनमें निरन्तर परिवर्तन की सम्भावना रहती है।[4]

रामधारी सिंह दिनकर के मत में–"संस्कृति एक ऐसा गुण हैं, जो हमारे जीवन में छाया हुआ है। यह एक आत्मिक गुण है, जो मनुष्य के स्वभाव में उसी तरह व्याप्त हुआ है, जिस प्रकार फूलों में सुगन्ध और दूध में मक्खन इसका निर्माण एक दो दिन में नहीं होता है, अपितु युग–युगान्तर में होता है।[5]

ग्रीन के मत में– "संस्कृति ज्ञान व्यवहार, विश्वास की उन पद्धतियों को तथा ज्ञान व्यवहार से उत्पन्न हुए साधनों की व्यवस्था को जो कि समय के साथ परिवर्तित होती है, कहते हैं, जो सामाजिक रुप से एक पीढ़ी से दूसरी पीढ़ी को दी जाती है।[6]

इस प्रकार विभिन्न विद्वानों ने किसी विशेष समूह, देश, जाति या कलात्मक एवं बौद्धिक विकास के रुप को देखते हुए संस्कृति की परिभाषा

---

[2] *भारतीय संस्कृति और हमारा भविष्य–डॉ0 सम्पूर्णानन्द*

[3] *डॉ0 व्हाइटहेड प्रकाशन 19वीं शती में जॉन मुहर द्वारा हुआ।*

[4] *गिलिन Culture Sociology प्रकाशन–1942*

[5] *रामधारी सिंह दिनकर संस्कृति के चार अध्याय, लोकभारती प्रकाशन संसकरण (1955ई0)*

[6] *ग्रीन, भारतीय संस्कृति की मुख्य विशेषताएँ, JVBI लाडन द्वारा प्रकाशित PDF पेज नं0–5*

दी गई है। या यूँ कह सकते हैं कि सभ्यता के सूक्ष्म, शुद्ध और उदात तत्वों के रचनात्मक विकास और पल्लवन का नाम कि संस्कृति है। साथ ही साथ संस्कृति वह जीवन पद्धति है, जिसकी स्थापना मानव व्यक्ति तथा समूह के रुप में करता है, वह उन आविष्कारों का संग्रह है जिनकी खोज मानव ने अपने जीवन को सफल बनाने के लिए की है।

संस्कृति एवं सभ्यता में अन्तर–

प्रकृति के विविध तत्वों का ज्ञान प्राप्त कर मनुष्य अपनी भौतिक आवश्यकताओं को पूर्ण करता है। वह अपने जीवन को अधिक सरस और सैन्दर्यमय बनाने का प्रयत्न करता है। इस प्रकार ''मनुष्य अपनी बुद्धि का प्रयोग कर विचार और कम के क्षेत्र में जो सृजन करता है, उसी को संस्कृति कहते हैं।

एवं प्रकृति द्वारा प्रदत्त पदार्थो, तत्वों और शक्तियों का उपयोग कर मनुष्य ने भौतिक क्षेत्र में जो असाधारण उन्नति की एवं निरन्तर उन्नति कर रहा है, इसी उन्नति को हम सभ्यता कह सकते हैं।

निष्कर्ष रुपेणः– यह कहा जा सकता है, कि जहाँ संस्कृति बिम्ब रुप है, तो वहीं सभ्यता उसका प्रतिबिम्ब रुप है। संस्कृति कारण है, तो सभ्यता उसका कार्य एवं संस्कृति ही सभ्यता की जननी है तथा दोनों में जन्यजनक भाव है।

भारतीय संस्कृति की विशेषताएँ :–

इस प्रकार भारतीय समाज के इन विविध आयामों पर दृष्ट्यालोचनोपरान्त अब हमें भारतीय संस्कृति की विशेषताओं पर भी विचार–विमर्श समीचीन होता है।

प्राचीन ,वं स्थायित्वः– भारत की संस्कृति वि"व की प्राचीनतम् संस्कृतियों ,वं समाज व्यवस्थाओं में से ,क है। समय के साथ–साथ मिश्र, सीरिया, यूनान, रोम आदि की प्राचीन संस्कृतियाँ नष्ट हो गईं एवं उसके अवशेष मात्र ही शेष बचे हैं, किन्तु हजारों वर्ष बीत जाने पर भी भारत की आदि संस्कृति व समाज व्यवस्था आज भी जीवित है, जिसका समर्थन मो0 इकबाल की ये लाइनें करती दिखती हैं–

''यूनान–ओ–मिस्र,–ओ रुमा सब मिट गये जहाँ से,
अब तक मगर है बाकी नाम ओ निशाँ हमारा,
कुछ बात है कि हस्ती मिटती नहीं हमारी

सदियों रहा है, दुश्मन दौरे जहाँ हमारा................।[7]

आज भी हम भारत में वैदिक धर्म को मानते हैं, पवित्र वैदिक मंत्रों का यज्ञ भी समाज में जीवन्त है। भारतीय समाज में आज भी विवाह रीति वैदिक मन्त्रों से सम्पन्न किये जा रहे हैं, साथ ही साथ ग्राम–पंचायत, जाति–प्रथा, संयुक्त परिवार प्रणाली, लोक परम्पराएँ आदि भी निर्वमान दिख रही हैं। गीता, बुद्ध महावीर के उपदेश आदि भी भारतीय संस्कृति में जाग्रत हैं।

समन्यवादी दृष्टिकोण–भारतीय समाज एवं संस्कृति की जो अपनी दूसरी विशिष्टता है, वह उसकी अपनी समन्वयवादी दृष्टिकोण ही है, जिसका निदर्शन हमें इस समाज में स्थित जनजातीय, हिन्दू, मुस्लिम, शक्, हूण ईसाई आदि सभी संस्कृतियों के प्रभाव से यहाँ का समाज एवं संस्कृति नष्ट नहीं हुई वरन उनसे समन्वय एवं एकात्म स्थापित कर लिया। जिसका उदाहरण मुस्लमानों के सम्पर्क से दीनलाई धर्म पनपा। इसी प्रकार अनकों समन्यवादी दृष्टिकोण निरन्तर गतिमान रही है, जो आज भी विद्यमान दिखती है।

आध्यात्मवाद एवं धर्म की प्रधानता–धर्म एवं आध्यात्मिकता भारतीय समाज एवं संस्कृति की आत्मा है, जिसकी झलक हमें मनुस्मृति में धर्म की ऐसे विशद लक्षण को देखकर ही मिल जाती है–

'धृतिक्षमादमोऽस्तेयं शौचमिन्द्रिय निग्रहः।
धीर्विद्यासत्यमक्रोधो दशकं धर्म् लक्षणम्''।[8]

एवं महाकवि तुलसीदास जी के रामचरित मानस में बड़े सरल एवं निष्कर्ष रुप में भी दिख जाती है–

परहित सरिस धर्म नहिं भाई''[9] पर पीड़ा सम नहिं अधमाई''।।

इसी प्रकार अष्टादश पुराणकार महर्षि वेदव्यास भी धर्म को इस प्रकार व्याख्यायित करते है–

''अष्टादशपुराणेषु व्यासस्य वचनद्वयम्।
परोपकराये पुण्याय पापाय परपीडनम्''[10]।।

---

[7] *मो0 इकबाल की कविता ''तराना–ए–हिन्दी'' या सोर–जहाँ से अच्छा न्दिोस्ताँ हमारा''*
[8] *मनुस्मृति, अध्याय–06, श्लोक–92।*
[9] *श्रीरामचरितमानस उत्तराखण्ड–7.41*
[10] *स्कन्दपुराण वर्ष 1972, अध्याय–36, श्लोक 3*

सहिष्णुता–भारतीय समाज एवं संस्कृति की एक महान विशेषता इसकी सहिष्णुता है। भारत में सभी धर्मों, जातियों, प्रजातियों एवं सम्प्रदायों के प्रति उदारता, सहिष्णुता एवं प्रेमभाव पाया जाता है। हमारे यहाँ समय–समय पर अनेकों विदेशी संस्कृतियों का आगमन हुआ, और सभी संस्कृतियों को फलने–फूलने का अवसर दिया गया।

समायोजन की सामर्थ्य–भारतीय समाज एवं संस्कृति को अमर बनाने में इसकी अनुकूलनशील प्रवृत्ति का महान योगदान है। हमारी संस्कृति अपने दीर्घ जीवन के लिए समय चक्र और परिस्थितियों के अनुसार सदैव समाज के साथ सामंजस्य करती रही है, जिसके परिणामस्वरुप यह आज तक बनी रही है। जिसका समर्थन करते कतिपय विचारक द्रष्टव्य हैं–

महात्मा गाँधी के मत में –अनुकूलनशीलता नकल नहीं है, इसका अर्थ है, प्रतिरोध और आत्मसात करने की शक्ति है।''

काकूजो ओकाकुरा के मत में–"जीवन की कला अपने परिवेश के साथ निरन्तर सामंजस्य स्थापित करने में निहित है।''

जेसिका हेगेडॉर्न के मत में–"जीवन जीने का सरल रहस्य अनुकूलनशीलता में निहित है।''

जार्ज वनार्ड शा के मत में–''समझदार व्यक्ति स्वयं को संसार के अनुरुप ढाल लेता है, जबकि नामसझ व्यक्ति संसार को अपने अनुरुप ढालने का प्रयास करता रहता है।''

विचार और आदर्शः–भारतीय समाज के प्राणतत्व भारतीय संस्कृति में कुछ ऐसे तत्व हैं, जो युग–युगान्तर एक व्यक्ति के अस्तित्व के आधार होते हैं। 'सादा–जीवन उच्च विचार' का सिद्धान्त अपरिग्रह को श्रेष्ठता प्रदान करते हैं। जिसकी झलक इन लाइनों में स्पष्ट दिख रही है–

"अयं निजः परोवेति गणना लघु चेतसा, उदार चरितानां तु वसुधैव कुटुम्बकम्''[11]
आत्मनः प्रति कुलानि परेषाम् न समाचरेत्।[12]

---

[11] *महोपनिषद, अध्याय 4, श्लोक 71*

आत्मवत् सर्वभूतेषु यः पश्यंति सः पण्डितः।[13]
शठे शाठ्यम समाचरेत्।[14]

इस प्रकार यह समाज 'वसुधैव कुटुम्बकम्' का संदेश समग्र विश्व को सहज ही सिखाता है। भारतीय समाज और संस्कृति के ऐसे आदर्श और विचार सदैव एकता को बनाये रखने का प्रयन्त करते हैं।

वर्णाश्रम—प्राचीन भारतीय संस्कृति की उल्लेखनीय व्यवस्था है,वर्ण एवं आश्रमों की व्यवस्था। भारतीय समाज में चार वर्णों की व्यवस्था उल्लिखित है—ब्राह्मण, क्षत्रिय वैश्यएवं शूद्र। जिसकी घोषणा श्रीमद्भगवद्गीता में भगवान श्रीकृष्ण स्वयं करते हैं—

"चातुर्वर्ण्यम मया सृष्टम गुण कर्म विभागशः[15]

अर्थात् गुण एवं कर्म के प्राधान्य से ही भारतीयसमाज एवं संस्कृति में चार वर्णों की व्यवस्था की गयी है। ब्राह्मण बुद्धि एवं शिक्षा के प्राधान्य के प्रतीक,क्षत्रिय शक्ति के, वैश्य भरण—पोषण (व्यापार निपुणता) के प्रतीक, एवं शूद्र समाज सेवक के प्रतीक थे। साथ ही साथ समाज में मनुष्यों की न्यूनतम आयु 100 वर्ष निर्धारित मानते हुए भारतीय मनीषियों द्वारा सम्पूर्ण जीवन को 4 आश्रमों में विभक्त किया गया—प्रथम आश्रम ब्रम्हचर्य, विद्याध्ययन हेतु, द्वितीय आश्रम गृहस्थ आश्रम, विवाह आदि सांसारिक दायित्त्वों एवं पितृऋण से मुक्ति हेतु, तृतीय आश्रम वानप्रस्थ आश्रम, सांसारिक गतिविधियों के सम्पन्न कर संसार से बिरक्ति के अभ्यास हेतु, तथा चतुर्थ आश्रम संन्यास आश्रम, परलोक की सिध्दि (सांसारिक मुक्ति) हेतु निर्धारित थे। सम्प्रति भारतीय समाज में इसकी अवस्थिति विद्यमान नहीं मिलती है।फिर भी इसकी यह विशिष्टता इसे विश्व इतिहास में इसे अद्वितीय बनाती है।

कर्म एवं पुनर्जन्म का सिद्धान्त—

भारतीय संस्कृति में कर्म को अत्यधिक महत्व दिया गया है। यह माना जाता है कि, अच्छे कर्मों का फल अच्छा और बुरे कर्मों का फल बुरा मिलता है। श्रेष्ठ कर्म करने वाले को उत्तम योनि में जन्म

---

[12] *अध्याय 4, श्लोक—71।*
[13] *हिनोपादेश, मित्रलाभ, श्लोक—14।*
[14] *महाभारत, उद्योगपर्व, विदुरनीति।*
[15] *श्रीमद्भगवद्गीता, अध्याय—4, श्लोक—13*

और सुखी जीवन व्यतीत करने का अवसर मिलता है, जबकि बुरे कर्म करने वाले को मनुष्येतर योनि में जन्म लेना होता है तथा नाना प्रकार के कष्ट उठाने पड़ते हैं। फलस्वरूप भारतीय समाज एवं संस्कृति की यह विशिष्टता भारतीयों को अनुचित कर्म प्रबृत्ति से रोकता है, तथा सदाचरण में सदैवप्रबृत्ति कराता है।

सर्वांगणीता–

भारतीय समाज तथा संस्कृति की एक विशिष्टता यह भी है, इसका सम्बन्ध किसी एक जाति, वर्ण, धर्म या किसी व्यक्ति विशेष से नहीं होकर समाज के सभी पक्षों से है और इसके निर्माण एवं विकास में राजा, किसान, मजदूर, शिक्षित, शूद्र, ब्राह्मण आदि सभी का का योगदान रहा है। जैसा कि इसके मूल में भी यही सन्निहित है– "सर्वे भवन्तु सुखिनः,सर्वे सन्तु निरामयाः इस प्रकार भारतीय समाज और संस्कृति के ऐसे आदर्श और विचार सदैव एकता को बनाये रखने का प्रयत्न करते हैं।

विश्वकल्याण एवं विशिष्टता विश्वबन्धुत्व की भावना–भारतीय संस्कृति की सबसे बड़ी विशिष्टता यह है, कि यह समग्र विश्व में बन्धुता का प्रसार करती है। जिसके समर्थन में इस संस्कृति का यह नारा द्रष्टव्य है–

"सर्वे भवन्तु सुखिनः सर्वे सन्तु निरामयः।
सर्वे भद्राणि पश्चयन्तु मा कश्चित दुःख भाग् भवेत्।।[16]

अर्थात् सब सुखी हो तथा सभी स्वस्थ रहें, इस प्रकार का मन्तव्य भारतीय संस्कृति की विशेषता रही है। भारतीय संसकृति इस प्रकार के अनेकानेक विशिष्टताओं से समन्वित रहते हुए, अनेकता में एकता को संजोये हुए मनुष्य, जीव मात्र की सहायता करना रक्षा करना एवं कल्याण करने को विशेष महत्व दिया है। इस संस्कृति में केवल मनुष्य ही नहीं, अपितु पशु–पक्षियों तक के निरन्तर कल्याण की दृष्टि से पश्चयज्ञों में भूतयज्ञ भी सम्मिलित किया गया। जिससे प्रतिदिन पशु पक्षियों के प्रति भी मनुष्य सहृदय बना रहे और उनका पोषण करता रहे। इस प्रकार सभी जीवों के कल्याण की कामना के

[16] *बृहदारण्यकोपनिषद–1.4.14*

साथ–साथ सभी में परस्पर सौहार्द्र एवं बन्धुत्व का प्रतिपादन भी भारतीय संस्कृति ने किया है, जिसके पोषण में यह उद्धरण प्रस्तुत है–

''अयं निजः परो व्रेति गणना लघुचेतसाम्।
उदारचरितानां तु वसुधैव कुटुम्बकम्।।[17]

भारतीय संस्कृति ने सदैव संकुचित विचारधारा और स्वार्थों से ऊपर उठकर विश्वकल्याण एवं सम्पूर्ण मानवता की सेवा पर बल दिया। भारतीय संस्कृति ने सदैव संकुचित विधारधारा और स्वार्थो से ऊपर उठकर विश्वकल्याण एवं सम्पूर्ण मानवता की सेवा पर बल दिया।

त्यागभाव–भारतीय संस्कृति की एक अन्य विशेषता है–त्याग भावना। आज विश्व में अन्य जितनी संस्कृतियाँ परिलक्षित होती हैं, उनमें त्याग भावना को वह समादर प्राप्त नहीं हो सका, जो भारतीय संस्कृति में प्राप्त हुआ। इस संस्कृति में यह स्पष्ट किया गया है कि, मनुष्य मात्र में स्वार्थ की प्रवृत्ति जितनी सहज है, संग्रह की लालसा भी उतनी ही स्वाभाविक है। यह नैतिक मूल्य को अधिक श्रेष्ठता देती है, बजाय अर्थ की प्रचुरता के। जिसका प्रदर्शन यह श्लोक भी करता दिखता है–

"मातृवत् पर दारेषु, पर द्रष्येषु लोष्ठवत।
आत्मवत् सर्वभूतेषु यः पश्यति सः पश्यति।।[18]

अर्थात् हमें दूसरे की पत्नी को माता के समान एवं दूसरे के धन को मिट्ओी के समान एवं सभी प्राणियों को अपनी आत्मा जैसे मानने की शिक्षा द्वारा भारतीय संस्कृति अपनी त्याग भावना को ही पूर्णरुपेण प्रदर्शित करती है।

निष्कर्षः– इस प्रकार भारतीय समाज एवं संस्कृति मानव समाज की एक अमूल्य निधि है। यदि संसार की कोई संस्कृति अमर कहीं जा सकती है, तो निःसन्देह वह भारतीय संस्कृति ही है जो अपनी समस्त आभा और प्रतिभा के सभा चिरकाल से स्थायी है। अपने सुदीर्घ इतिहास में भारतवासियों ने एक ऐसी समाज व्यवस्था एवं संस्कृति का विकास किया जो अपने आप में मौलिक, अनूठी और विश्व की अन्य संस्कृतियों एवं समाज व्यवस्थाओं से भिन्न है। इस देश के महापुरुष, तीर्थस्थानः प्राचीन

---

[17] महापनिषद, अध्याय–4, श्लोक–71
[18] चाणक्य नीति, गीता प्रेस प्रकाशन

कलाकृतियों, धर्म, दर्शन और सामाजिक संस्थाएँ भारतीय समाज एवं संस्कृति के सजग प्रहरी रहे हैं। अब हम यहाँ भारतीय संस्कृति की उन विशेषताओं का उल्लेख करेंगे, जिनके कारण हजारों साल बीत जाने पर भी वह आज जीवित है।

सन्दर्भ ग्रन्थ सूची

- *बृहदारण्यकोपनिषद–01.04.14*
- *भारतीय संस्कृति और हमारा भविष्य–डॉ0 सम्पूर्णानन्द*
- *डॉ0 व्हाइटहेड प्रकाशन 19वीं शती में जॉन मुहर द्वारा हुआ।*
- *गिलिन Culture Sociology प्रकाशन–1942*
- *रामधारी सिंह दिनकर संस्कृति के चार अध्याय, लोकभारती प्रकाशन संसकरण (1955ई0)*
- *ग्रीन, भारतीय संस्कृति की मुख्य विशेषताएँ, JVBI लाडन द्वारा प्रकाशित PDF पेज नं0–5*
- *मो0 इकबाल की कविता "तराना–ए–हिन्दी" या सोर–जहाँ से अच्छा न्दिोस्ताँ हमारा"*
- *मनुस्मृति, अध्याय–06, श्लोक–92।*
- *श्रीरामचरितमानस उत्तराखण्ड–7.41*
- *स्कन्दपुराण वर्ष 1972, अध्याय–36, श्लोक 3*
- *महोपनिषद, अध्याय 4, श्लोक 71*
- *अध्याय 4, श्लोक–71।*
- *हिनोपादेश, मित्रलाभ, श्लोक–14।*
- *महाभारत, उद्योगपर्व, विदुरनीति।*
- *श्रीमद्भगवद्गीता, अध्याय–4, श्लोक–13*
- *बृहदारण्यकोपनिषद–1.4.14*
- *महापनिषद, अध्याय–4, श्लोक–71*
- *चाणक्य नीति, गीता प्रेस प्रकाशन*

Chapter- 10

भारतीय संस्कृति, विविधता और राष्ट्रीय एकता: विकसित भारत 2047 के विशेष सन्दर्भ में

वैश उद्दीन
सहायक आचार्य, समाजशास्त्र विभाग श्यामेश्वर महाविद्यालय , सिकरीगंज, गोरखपुर

भारतीय संस्कृति अपनी ऐतिहासिक जड़ों, जीवनदर्शन और मानवीय मूल्यों के कारण विश्व की सबसे प्राचीन एवं समृद्ध संस्कृतियों में गिनी जाती है जिसमें निरंतरता और परिवर्तन दोनों का अद्‌भुत समन्वय है । यह संस्कृति सिर्फ रीति–रिवाजों, त्योहारों और परंपराओं तक सीमित नहीं है, बल्कि जीवन के प्रत्येक क्षेत्र भाषा, भोजन, कला, साहित्य, दर्शन, धर्म और सामाजिक व्यवहार में विविधता को आत्मसात करते हुए एक व्यापक सांस्कृतिक चेतना का निर्माण करती है जहाँ अनेक धर्म, पंथ, जातियाँ, जनजातियाँ और भाषाई समुदाय सह–अस्तित्व की भावना के साथ रहते आए हैं। भारत की यह सांस्कृतिक विविधता उसकी सबसे बड़ी शक्ति है क्योंकि उत्तर से दक्षिण और पूर्व से पश्चिम तक खान–पान, पहनावा, लोकनृत्य, संगीत शैलियाँ और धार्मिक आस्थाएँ भिन्न होते हुए भी एक साझा सांस्कृतिक सूत्र से जुड़ी हुई हैं जो 'वसुधैव कुटुम्बकम्' और 'सर्वे भवन्तु सुखिनः' जैसे विचारों में अभिव्यक्त होता है। भारतीय समाज में विविधताओं के बावजूद राष्ट्रीय एकता की भावना स्वतंत्रता आंदोलन के दौरान और अधिक सशक्त रूप में उभरी जब विभिन्न वर्गों, भाषाओं और क्षेत्रों के लोगों ने औपनिवेशिक शासन के विरुद्ध एक साझा लक्ष्य के लिए संघर्ष किया, जिससे यह स्पष्ट हुआ कि सांस्कृतिक भिन्नताएँ विभाजन का नहीं बल्कि एकता का आधार बन सकती हैं। स्वतंत्र भारत में संविधान ने

इस सांस्कृतिक विविधता को सम्मान देते हुए सभी नागरिकों को समान अधिकार प्रदान किए और धर्मनिरपेक्षता, लोकतंत्र तथा सामाजिक न्याय जैसे मूल्यों के माध्यम से राष्ट्रीय एकता को सुदृढ़ किया। शिक्षा, साहित्य, सिनेमा और जनसंचार माध्यमों ने भी विभिन्न सांस्कृतिक पहचान को जोड़ने में महत्त्वपूर्ण भूमिका निभाई है जिससे आपसी समझ, सहिष्णुता और सहयोग की भावना विकसित हुई। आज के वैश्वीकरण के दौर में जब सांस्कृतिक समरूपता का दबाव बढ़ रहा है, तब भारतीय संस्कृति अपनी बहुलतावादी प्रकृति के कारण न केवल अपनी विशिष्ट पहचान बनाए हुए है बल्कि विविधता में एकता के आदर्श को व्यवहारिक रूप में प्रस्तुत करती है। इस प्रकार भारतीय संस्कृति, अपनी विविधता को संजोते हुए राष्ट्रीय एकता को मजबूत बनाती है और यह सिद्ध करती है कि भिन्नताओं के बावजूद साझा मूल्यों, ऐतिहासिक अनुभवों और संवैधानिक आदर्शों के माध्यम से एक सशक्त और समरस राष्ट्र का निर्माण संभव है।

भारतीय संस्कृति, विविधता और राष्ट्रीय एकता का विकास के संदर्भ में विश्लेषण किया जाए तो यह स्पष्ट होता है कि सांस्कृतिक बहुलता केवल सामाजिक पहचान का प्रतीक नहीं है, बल्कि यह समावेशी और सतत विकास की एक सशक्त आधारशिला भी है क्योंकि विकास तब ही सार्थक बनता है जब वह समाज के प्रत्येक वर्ग, क्षेत्र और समुदाय को साथ लेकर आगे बढ़े। भारत जैसे विविधतापूर्ण देश में आर्थिक, सामाजिक और मानव विकास की प्रक्रिया को सफल बनाने के लिए स्थानीय सांस्कृतिक मूल्यों, परंपरागत ज्ञान प्रणालियों और सामाजिक संरचनाओं को समझना और उन्हें विकास नीतियों में सम्मिलित करना अत्यंत आवश्यक है क्योंकि एक ही प्रकार की विकास नीति सभी क्षेत्रों पर समान रूप से लागू नहीं हो सकती। ग्रामीण आजीविका, कृषि, हस्तशिल्प, लोककला, आयुर्वेद, योग और पारंपरिक पर्यावरणीय ज्ञान जैसे क्षेत्र यह दर्शाते हैं कि भारतीय संस्कृति में निहित ज्ञान और कौशल विकास के वैकल्पिक तथा आत्मनिर्भर चित्र को प्रस्तुत करते हैं जो न केवल रोजगार सृजन को बढ़ावा देते हैं बल्कि सांस्कृतिक संरक्षण के साथ आर्थिक सशक्तिकरण भी सुनिश्चित करते हैं। विविध भाषाई और सांस्कृतिक समुदायों की सहभागिता से जब विकास योजनाएँ तैयार की जाती हैं, तब लोकतांत्रिक विकेंद्रीकरण, स्थानीय शासन

और जनभागीदारी को मजबूती मिलती है, जिससे राष्ट्रीय एकता को भी व्यवहारिक आधार प्राप्त होता है साथ ही सामाजिक समावेशन, लैंगिक समानता और हाशिए पर स्थित समुदायों के सशक्तिकरण जैसे विकासात्मक लक्ष्य भारतीय संविधान और सांस्कृतिक मूल्यों से गहराई से जुड़े हुए हैं, जो विकास को केवल भौतिक प्रगति तक सीमित न रखकर मानवीय गरिमा और सामाजिक न्याय से जोड़ते हैं। वर्तमान वैश्विक परिदृ श्य में जब विकास को प्रायः आर्थिक संकेतकों के माध्यम से आँका जा रहा है तब भारतीय दृष्टिकोण यह स्पष्ट करता है कि असमानता, सांस्कृतिक उपेक्षा और सामाजिक बहिष्करण विकास की प्रक्रिया को कमजोर कर सकते हैं, जबकि विविधता का सम्मान और राष्ट्रीय एकता का सुदृढ़ीकरण दीर्घकालिक स्थिरता को सुनिश्चित करता है। डिजिटल इंडिया, आत्मनिर्भर भारत और सतत विकास जैसे समकालीन प्रयास तभी प्रभावी हो सकते हैं जब वे विभिन्न सामाजिक–सांस्कृतिक संदर्भों के अनुरूप हों और नागरिकों में समान पहचान तथा सामूहिक उत्तरदायित्व की भावना को प्रोत्साहित करें। इस प्रकार भारतीय संस्कृति और विविधता, विकास को एक समावेशी, सहभागी और नैतिक दिशा प्रदान कर रहें है जहाँ राष्ट्रीय एकता केवल एक भावनात्मक अवधारणा नहीं है बल्कि सामाजिक–आर्थिक प्रगति की प्रेरक शक्ति बनकर उभर रही है।

भारतीय संस्कृति की समावेशी, बहुलतावादी और 'एकता में विविधता' की भावना जो विकसित भारत 2047 का आधार तथा वही मूलभूत शक्ति है जिसने भारत को हजारों वर्षों तक जीवित, प्रगतिशील और एकजुट बनाए रखा । वर्ष 2047 का भारत केवल आर्थिक रूप से शक्तिशाली राष्ट्र नहीं होगा बल्कि एक ऐसा सभ्यतागत राष्ट्र–राज्य होगा जिसकी प्रगति का केंद्र उसकी सांस्कृतिक जड़ें और सामाजिक समरसता होगी। भारतीय संस्कृति में "वसुधैव कुटुम्बकम्", "एकम् सद् विप्रा बहुधा वदन्ति" और "सर्वे भवन्तु सुखिनः" जैसे सिद्धांत सामाजिक न्याय, सामूहिक विकास और आध्यात्मिक समता की आधारशिला प्रदान करते हैं। 2047 तक भारत के सामाजिक ढांचे में यह देखा जाएगा कि बहुभाषिक, बहुधार्मिक और बहु–परंपरागत समाज अब केवल सह–अस्तित्व में नहीं, बल्कि समन्वित सह–उत्कर्ष में जी रहा होगा। नयी राष्ट्रीय शिक्षा नीति में भारतीय ज्ञान प्रणाली, मातृभाषा

आधारित शिक्षा और सांस्कृतिक जागरूकता पर जोर इसी दिशा का संकेत है। सांस्कृतिक विरासत के डिजिटलीकरण, राष्ट्रीय अभिलेखों के संरक्षण, स्थानीय कलाओं के पुनर्जीवन तथा जनजातीय संस्कृति के सशक्तिकरण से भारत अपनी सभ्यतागत निरंतरता को आधुनिकता के साथ जोड़ रहा है। सामाजिक सौहार्द और राष्ट्रीय एकता के लिए "एक भारत श्रेष्ठ भारत" कार्यक्रम, राष्ट्रीय एकता दिवस, सीमा क्षेत्रों का सामाजिक–आर्थिक एकीकरण, और आंतरिक संपर्क ये सभी 2047 तक भारत को अधिक मजबूत, आत्मविश्वासी और एकजुट बनाने में निर्णायक भूमिका निभाएँगे। वर्ष 2047 का भारत ऐसा होगा जहाँ सांस्कृतिक पहचान आधुनिकता के साथ संघर्ष न करके उसे ऊर्जा प्रदान करेगी, और विविधता एक बाधा नहीं बल्कि वैश्विक नेतृत्व की सबसे बड़ी ताकत होगी भारत विश्व को यह दिखाएगा कि आर्थिक विकास और सांस्कृतिक मूल्यों का संरक्षण दोनों एक साथ चल सकते हैं।

विकसित भारत 2047 का आर्थिक ढांचा एक ऐसी अर्थव्यवस्था का निर्माण करना है जो विश्व की शीर्ष तीन अर्थव्यवस्थाओं में स्थान प्राप्त करे और साथ ही सामाजिक न्याय, समान अवसर और सतत विकास को प्राथमिकता दे। पिछले वर्षों में भारत पाँचवीं सबसे बड़ी अर्थव्यवस्था के रूप में उभरा है तथा वैश्विक विकास दर में अग्रणी स्थान रखता है भारत का लक्ष्य इस आर्थिक मजबूती को एक उच्च–आय, कौशल–आधारित, तकनीक–प्रधान और निर्यात–संचालित मॉडल में परिवर्तित करना है। भारत की आर्थिक रणनीतियों में डिजिटल पब्लिक इंफ्रास्ट्रक्चर, मेक इन इंडिया. पीएम गति शक्ति, लॉजिस्टिक्स दक्षता) विश्वसनीय परिवहन पर निर्भर, भंडारण और भण्डारण पर निर्भर, व्यापक आपूर्ति श्रृंखला प्रबंध, हरित ऊर्जा, सेमीकंडक्टर निर्माण, आर्टिफिशियल इंटेलिजेंस मिशन और विनिर्माण उद्यम और सेवाएं प्रदान करने वाले उद्यम का आधुनिकीकरण प्रमुख स्तंभ है, इन पहलों से न केवल उत्पादकता बढ़ेगी बल्कि रोजगार और उद्यमिता के अवसर भी बढ़ेंगे। ग्रामीण अर्थव्यवस्था में कृषि ,फसल विविधीकरण, खाद्य प्रसंस्करण, किसान ड्रोन, तथा सहकारी क्षेत्र के सुदृ ढ़ीकरण से वर्ष 2047का विकसित भारत ग्रामीण–शहरी संतुलित विकास का मॉडल बनेगा। नारी–शक्ति, युवा जनसंख्या और डिजिटल समावेशन

भारत की अर्थव्यवस्था को जनसांख्यिकीय लाभांश का पूर्ण उपयोग करने में सक्षम बनाएंगे। यूपीआई, डिजिटल भुगतान, जनधन, आधार और डीबीटी जैसे मॉडल भारत को दुनिया की सबसे समावेशी डिजिटल अर्थव्यवस्था में बदल रहे हैं। इसका लक्ष्य केवल धनी राष्ट्र बनना नहीं, बल्कि ऐसा विकास मॉडल देना है जो विश्व के लिए प्रेरणास्रोत बन सके जहाँ विकास का लाभ अंतिम व्यक्ति तक पहुँचे और भारत "विकासशील" नहीं, बल्कि "विकास–प्रेरक" शक्ति के रूप में उभरे। विकसित भारत 2047 का मूल स्तंभ एक ऐसी शिक्षा प्रणाली का निर्माण है जो वैश्विक प्रतिस्पर्धा, रचनात्मकता, अनुसंधान, और मानवीय मूल्यों के अनुरूप हो राष्ट्रीय शिक्षा नीति भारत को एक ज्ञान–प्रधान अर्थव्यवस्था में रूपांतरित करने का व्यापक आधार प्रदान करती है। वर्ष 2047तक लक्ष्य यह है कि भारत केवल जनसंख्या में युवा राष्ट्र न रहे, बल्कि कौशल और नवाचार की विश्व राजधानी बने।

राष्ट्रीय शिक्षा नीति के अंतर्गत मातृभाषा–आधारित शिक्षा, समग्र पाठ्यक्रम, 5+3+3+ 4संरचना, कला एवं विज्ञान का एकीकरण, स्कूली शिक्षा का सार्वभौमीकरण और व्यावसायिक शिक्षा का विस्तार ये सभी सुधार शिक्षा को अधिक प्रभावी, व्यावहारिक और समावेशी बनाएंगे। लक्ष्य यह है कि 2047 तक विद्यार्थियों में आलोचनात्मक चिंतन, समस्या–समाधान, डिजिटल साक्षरता और सामाजिक संवेदनशीलता जैसे कौशल स्वाभाविक रूप से विकसित हों। उच्च शिक्षा के क्षेत्र में भारत ज्ञान–सृजन का वैश्विक केंद्र बनने की दिशा में अग्रसर है बहुविषयी विश्वविद्यालयों, शोध अनुदानों, राष्ट्रीय अनुसंधान प्रतिष्ठान, स्टार्टअप–इंक्यूबेशन और औद्योगिक एवं आकादमिक सहयोग से भारत 2047 तक शोध एवं विकास प्रधान अर्थव्यवस्था में परिवर्तित होगा। ग्रामीण और वंचित समुदायों के लिए डिजिटल शिक्षा, ऑनलाइन लर्निंग प्लेटफ़ॉर्म और शिक्षा के लोकतंत्रीकरण से प्रत्येक नागरिक को समान अवसर प्राप्त होंगे।

भारत का लक्ष्य केवल रोजगार देने योग्य शिक्षा नहीं, बल्कि मानव पूँजी का समग्र विकास है ऐसा नागरिक जो वैज्ञानिक दृष्टि रखता हो, परंतु सांस्कृतिक जड़ों से भी जुड़ा हो। विकसित भारत में शिक्षा विकास का

साधन ही नहीं बल्कि राष्ट्र–निर्माण का मार्गदर्शक तत्व बनेगी यह शिक्षा भारत को न केवल आर्थिक रूप से विकसित बल्कि बौद्धिक और नैतिक रूप से परिपक्व राष्ट्र बनाएगी। वर्ष 2047 का भारत डिजिटल इंडिया, डिजिटल अर्थव्यवस्था और डिजिटल नागरिक सशक्तिकरण का वैश्विक मॉडल होगा भारत ने पिछले दस वर्षों में डिजिटल पब्लिक इंफ्रास्ट्रक्चर के माध्यम से विश्व को दिखाया है कि तकनीक को समावेशी विकास के लिए कैसे उपयोग किया जा सकता है आधार, डिजिटल भुगतान और डिजिलॉकर जैसे मॉडल दुनिया के सबसे प्रभावी डिजिटल इकोसिस्टम के उदाहरण बन चुके हैं। भारत का लक्ष्य डिजिटल भुगतान में, एआइ समाधानों में, साइबर सुरक्षा में, रोबोटिक्स में और गवर्नेंस में तकनीक के उपयोग में विश्व नेतृत्व हासिल करना है। आर्टिफिशियल इंटेलिजेंस मिशन, सेमीकंडक्टर मिशन, भारत G6 विज़न, क्वांटम टेक्नोलॉजी, स्पेस टेक्नोलॉजी और क्लाउड इंडिया इंफ्रास्ट्रक्चर जैसे कार्यक्रम भारत के डिजिटल भविष्य की दिशा तय करेंगे। ग्रामीण विकास 2047 के भारत का सामाजिक–आर्थिक आधार है, जहाँ कृषि, बुनियादी ढाँचा, स्थानीय उद्योग, डिजिटल कनेक्टिविटी और सामाजिक सशक्तिकरण एक साथ मिलकर नए भारत का निर्माण करेंगे। विकसित भारत 2047 का लक्ष्य तभी पूरा होगा जब भारत के गाँव जो देश की आत्मा हैं सशक्त, समृद्ध और आधुनिक बनेंगे।

कृषि क्षेत्र में भारत 2047 तक कृषि 4.0 को अपनाएगा जैसे ड्रोन आधारित खेती, सेंसर–आधारित निगरानी, कृषि जैव–प्रौद्योगिकी, फसल विविधीकरण और स्मार्ट सिंचाई प्रणाली इससे उत्पादन बढ़ेगा, लागत घटेगी और किसानों को अधिक आय प्राप्त होगी। खाद्य प्रसंस्करण, कृषि निर्यात, किसान उत्पादक संगठन और सहकारी प्रणालियों के सुदृढ़ीकरण से ग्रामीण क्षेत्र रोजगार और उद्यमिता के प्रमुख केंद्र बनेंगे। प्रधानमंत्री ग्राम सड़क योजना, हर घर जल, ग्रामीण बिजलीकरण, डिजिटल सेवाएँ, और ग्रामीण उद्यमों का विस्तार 2047 तक ऐसा ग्रामीण ढाँचा विकसित करेगा जो शहरों से किसी भी मायने में पीछे नहीं रहेगा। श्रम–प्रधान उद्योग, स्थानीय कौशल, हस्तशिल्प, पारंपरिक कला, और सूक्ष्म लघु एवं मध्यम उद्योग के क्षेत्र ग्रामीण युवाओं के लिए नए अवसर पैदा करेंगे। सामाजिक

सशक्तिकरण विशेषकर महिलाओं, अनुसूचित जनजातियों और कमजोर वर्गों का ग्रामीण विकास का आधार है स्व–सहायता समूह, डिजिटल बैंकिंग, महिला उद्यमिता, और ग्रामीण कौशल विकास केंद्र 2047 में एक समावेशी ग्रामीण अर्थव्यवस्था का निर्माण करेंगे। ग्रामीण भारत केवल कृषि पर निर्भर न रहकर उत्पादन, सेवा, नवाचार और डिजिटल भागीदारी का केंद्र बनेगा यह परिवर्तन भारत को एक संतुलित, स्थायी और न्यायपूर्ण विकास मॉडल प्रदान करेगा जहाँ गाँव भारत की सबसे बड़ी शक्ति बनेंगे। वर्ष 2047 तक भारत सिर्फ आर्थिक शक्ति नहीं होगा बल्कि दुनिया का प्रमुख हरित राष्ट्र भी बनेगा जलवायु परिवर्तन, पर्यावरण संरक्षण और सतत विकास भारत की विकास रणनीति के मूल में हैं। भारत ने 2070 तक कार्बन उत्सर्जन नेट–जीरो का लक्ष्य घोषित करके विश्व को एक स्पष्ट संदेश दिया है कि उसका विकास मॉडल पर्यावरण–सम्मत होगा। नवीकरणीय ऊर्जा विशेषकर सौर, पवन और ग्रीन हाइड्रोजन 2047 तक भारत की ऊर्जा संरचना में मुख्य भूमिका निभाएंगे भारत पहले ही वैश्विक सौर गठबंधन और राष्ट्रीय हरित ऊर्जा मिशन के माध्यम से ऊर्जा परिवर्तन का नेतृत्व कर रहा है। वर्ष 2047तक देश अपनी अधिकांश ऊर्जा आवश्यकताओं को हरित स्रोतों से पूरा करेगा और जीवाश्म ईंधन पर निर्भरता कम करेगा।

सतत शहरीकरण, अपशिष्ट प्रबंधन, स्वच्छ जल, नदी संरक्षण, वायु गुणवत्ता सुधार और जैव विविधता संरक्षण 2047 के स्वच्छ भारत के प्रमुख लक्ष्य हैं। स्मार्ट सिटीज़ मिशन, नमामि गंगे, स्वच्छ भारत, मिशन लाइफ (-EFIL TNEMNORIVNE ROF ELYTSEFIL) जैसे कार्यक्रम नागरिकों को पर्यावरण के प्रति जिम्मेदार बनाने में महत्वपूर्ण भूमिका निभाएँगे। कृषि में प्राकृतिक खेती, जैविक खाद, जल संरक्षण और जलवायु–सहिष्णु फसलें ग्रामीण पर्यावरण की सुरक्षा में योगदान देंगी। सतत विकास का लक्ष्य केवल पर्यावरण का संरक्षण नहीं बल्कि अगली पीढ़ियों के लिए सुरक्षित और स्वस्थ भविष्य सुनिश्चित करना है विकसित भारत में आर्थिक विकास और पर्यावरण संरक्षण विरोधाभासी नहीं बल्कि एक–दूसरे के पूरक होंगे और भारत दुनिया को एक नया पर्यावरण–अनुकूल विकास मॉडल प्रस्तुत करेगा। भारत की सबसे बड़ी शक्ति उसकी सांस्कृतिक विविधता और सभ्यतागत निरंतरता है विश्व की सबसे प्राचीन जीवित सभ्यताओं में से

एक होने के नाते भारत हजारों वर्षों से अनेक भाषाओं, धर्मों, परंपराओं, कला रूपों, दर्शन, और जीवन मूल्यों का घर रहा है। विकसित भारत 2047 का लक्ष्य केवल आर्थिक या तकनीकी उन्नति नहीं, बल्कि एक ऐसे समाज का निर्माण भी है जो अपनी सांस्कृतिक आत्मा को सुरक्षित रखते हुए आधुनिकता को अपनाता है। भारत की सांस्कृतिक विविधता राष्ट्रीय एकता को कमजोर नहीं करती, बल्कि उसे अधिक मजबूत और समावेशी बनाती है। "वसुधैव कुटुंबकम्", "एकम् सत् विप्रा बहुधा वदन्ति" और "अनेकता में एकता" जैसे भारतीय विचार 2047 के भारत के सामाजिक ताने–बाने की नींव होंगे सभी भाषाओं, जातियों, समुदायों, जनजातियों और परंपराओं का सम्मान भारत को सामाजिक सौहार्द और सांस्कृतिक आत्मविश्वास प्रदान करता है। सांस्कृतिक विरासत का संरक्षण जैसे ऐतिहासिक स्मारकों का रखरखाव, पारंपरिक कला एवं शिल्प का पुनर्जीवन, शास्त्रीय संगीत–नृत्य का संवर्धन, जनजातीय परंपराओं का संरक्षण भारत को वैश्विक सांस्कृतिक मानचित्र पर विशेष स्थिति दिलाएगा डिजिटल अभिलेखन, वर्चुअल संग्रहालय और सांस्कृतिक पर्यटन 2047 तक बड़ी भूमिका निभाएंगे। युवा पीढ़ी में भारतीय संस्कृति की पहचान को मजबूत करने के लिए शिक्षा में भारतीय ज्ञान–परंपरा, योग, आयुर्वेद, साहित्य और स्थानीय भाषाओं पर अधिक बल दिया जाएगा। सांस्कृतिक कूटनीति जैसे अंतरराष्ट्रीय योग दिवस, भारतीय कला, सिनेमा, संगीत, खानपान भारत को विश्व के साथ जोड़ने का माध्यम बनेंगे। वर्ष 2047का भारत एक ऐसा राष्ट्र होगा जहाँ आधुनिकता और परंपरा सह–अस्तित्व में हों, और जहाँ विविधता किसी विभाजन का कारण नहीं बल्कि राष्ट्रीय एकता और सह–अस्तित्व की प्रेरक शक्ति हो यही सांस्कृतिक समृद्धि भारत को विश्वगुरु बनने की दिशा में अग्रसर करेगी।

विकसित भारत 2047 का लक्ष्य केवल आर्थिक प्रगति नहीं, बल्कि एक ऐसे सतत विकास मॉडल का निर्माण है जो सामाजिक न्याय, पर्यावरण संरक्षण और आर्थिक स्थिरता को समान महत्व देता है। भारत को आने वाले वर्षों में जनसंख्या वृद्धि, शहरीकरण, जलवायु परिवर्तन, संसाधनों के दबाव और वैश्विक प्रतिस्पर्धा जैसी चुनौतियों का सामना करना होगा। इसलिए विकास को बहुआयामी और टिकाऊ बनाना अत्यंत आवश्यक है। सामाजिक सततता शिक्षा, स्वास्थ्य, लैंगिक समानता, सामाजिक न्याय और

कमजोर वर्गों के उत्थान पर निर्भर करती है। गरीबी उन्मूलन, गुणवत्तापूर्ण शिक्षा, पोषण, आधुनिक स्वास्थ्य सेवाएँ और ग्रामीण विकास भारत के सामाजिक ताने–बाने को मजबूत करेंगे। भारत अपनी सांस्कृतिक विविधता, विरासत और सामाजिक समरसता को संरक्षित रखते हुए एक न्यायसंगत समाज का निर्माण करेगा, जहाँ हर नागरिक को समान अवसर मिलें। पर्यावरणीय सततता जल संरक्षण, स्वच्छ ऊर्जा, कचरा प्रबंधन, हरित परिवहन, जैव विविधता संरक्षण और जलवायु–अनुकूल कृषि के माध्यम से सुनिश्चित होगी। वर्ष 2047 तक भारत ग्रीन इकॉनमी का वैश्विक मॉडल बनेगा जहाँ विकास और प्रकृति एक–दूसरे के पूरक होंगे। इस प्रकार विकसित भारत 2047 का लक्ष्य एक ऐसी अर्थव्यवस्था प्रस्तुत करता है जो मजबूत, समावेशी, पर्यावरण–सम्मत, प्रौद्योगिकी–आधारित और भविष्य–केंद्रित हो यह भारत की आगामी पीढ़ियों के लिए सुरक्षित, समृद्ध और स्थायी भविष्य का मार्ग प्रशस्त करेगा।

सन्दर्भ ग्रंथ सूची

- Confederation of Indian Industry & Grant Thornton Bharat. (2025, November). Continuous improvement journey of Higher Education Institutions: Approaches and Practices Shaping the Future of Learning. PTI / Economic Times. Retrieved from https://economictimes.indiatimes.com/industry/services/education/india-needs-86-11-million-enrolments-by-2035-to-meet-nep-target-report/articleshow/125325569.cms Hindustan Times+2The Economic Times+2
- DD India. (2025, January 31). From 23.7% to 28.4%: India's rising higher education enrolment. Retrieved from https://ddindia.co.in/2025/01/from-23-7-to-28-4-indias-rising-higher-education-enrolment/ DD India
- Economic Times / Times of India. (2025, February 1). Economic Survey 2024-25: Higher education institutions grow by 13.8%, gross enrolment ratio rises to 28.4% from

23.7%. The Times of India. https://timesofindia.indiatimes.com/business/india-business/economic-survey-2024-25-higher-education-institutions-grow-by-13-8-gross-enrolment-ratio-rises-to-28-4-from-23-7/articleshow/117817185.cms The Times of India

- Ministry of New & Renewable Energy, Government of India / Press Information Bureau. (2025, February 1). Energy Security in India: Advancing Renewable Energy and Sustainability through Key Government Initiatives. Retrieved from https://static.pib.gov.in/WriteReadData/specificdocs/documents/2025/feb/doc202521493701.pdf Press Information Bureau
- India Brand Equity Foundation (IBEF). (2025). Renewable Energy in India. Retrieved from https://ibef.org/industry/renewable-energy India Brand Equity Foundation
- National Economic Forum. (2025). Economic Survey 2024-25 Analysis. Retrieved from https://nationaleconomicforum.org/wp-content/uploads/2025/02/Economic-Survey-2024-25-Analysis-1.pdf National Economic Forum
- Ahuja, R. (2014). Social problems in India (3rd ed.). Rawat Publications.
- Alias, S. (2018). Modernization in developing societies. Sage Publications.
- Bhat, A. (2017). Unemployment and youth in India. Routledge.
- Bryant, R. L., & Bailey, S. (2015). Environmental issues in the developing world. Routledge.
- Desai, A. R. (2019). Rural India and social change. Popular Prakashan.

- Jayaram, N. (2016). Education, society and development. Sage Publications.
- Kumar, A. (2017). Urbanization and social transformation. Rawat Publications.
- Kumar, K. (2012). Education and modernity. Routledge.

Chapter- 11

समावेशी विकसित भारत के निर्माण में स्त्री विमर्श : बौद्ध भिक्षुणी आम्रपाली के व्यक्तित्व का अध्ययन

डॉ० दिनेश कुमार

असिस्टेंट प्रोफेसर–हिन्दी
राजकीय स्नातकोत्तर महाविद्यालय, जलेसर, एटा।

स्त्री–विमर्श को जानने से पहले विमर्श शब्द को जानना आवश्यक है। विमर्श शब्द अंग्रेजी के Discourse शब्द का हिन्दी रूपान्तरण है, जिसका अर्थ है किसी स्थिति के सुधार या वर्ग आदि के अभ्युत्थान के लिए होने वाला वैचारिक मंथन जैसे स्त्री–विमर्श, दलित–विमर्श। स्त्री के सामाजिक, आर्थिक, राजनैतिक, सांस्कृतिक, धार्मिक अभ्युत्थान के लिए होने वाला वैचारिक मंथन स्त्री–विमर्श है। स्त्री–विमर्श में समानता, काम करने की स्वतंत्रता, असामाजिक तत्वों से सुरक्षा, अपने जीवन पर नियंत्रण, स्त्री–सशक्तीकरण, पितृसत्ता से मुक्ति, सामाजिक रूढ़ियों से मुक्ति, सांस्कृतिक रूढ़ियों से मुक्ति, धार्मिक रूढ़ियों से मुक्ति जैसे विषयों पर बल दिया गया है।

स्त्री–विमर्श का प्रारम्भ कब हुआ, इसके संबंध में विद्वान एकमत नहीं हैं। कुछ विद्वान स्त्री–विमर्श का प्रारम्भ मेरी वोल्सटनक्राफ्ट की पुस्तक 'A Vindication of the Rights of Woman' (स्त्री अधिकारों की औचित्य साधना) के प्रकाशन वर्ष 1792 से मानते है। कुछ विद्वान स्त्री–विमर्श का प्रारम्भ उन्नीसवीं शताब्दी से मानते हैं, जब पश्चिम में स्त्रियों को मताधिकार मिला और पाश्चात्य संस्कृति में स्त्रियों के योगदान पर चर्चा होने लगी थी। कुछ विद्वान स्त्री–विमर्श को बीसवीं शताब्दी की देन मानते हैं। बीसवीं शताब्दी में भी कुछ लोग इसका प्रारम्भ फ्रांसीसी लेखिका सिमोन द बोउवार की पुस्तक The Second Sex (1949) के

प्रकाशन वर्ष से मानते है। लेकिन अधिकांश विद्वान इस तरह के किसी वर्ष विशेष को स्त्री–विमर्श का प्रस्थान बिन्दु मानना उचित नहीं समझते, क्योंकि बीसवीं शताब्दी में ही इससे पहले भी स्त्री की अलग पहचान, उसके स्वतंत्र अस्तित्व और उसके अधिकारों की समस्याओं को उठाया जाने लगा था। 1949 ई० में प्रकाशित सिमोन द बोउवार की पुस्तक The Second Sex स्त्री–विमर्श के संदर्भ में मील का पत्थर साबित हुई है। इस पुस्तक ने यूरोप और अमरीका के स्त्री–विमर्श को ही नहीं, भारतीय स्त्री–विमर्श को भी प्रभावित किया है और इस तरह से हिन्दी में भी स्त्रीवाद को महत्व मिला।

हिन्दी में स्त्री–विमर्श ने बीसवीं शताब्दी के अन्त में जोर पकडा है। स्त्रीवादी मानते हैं कि स्त्री सामाजिक, सांस्कृतिक, राजनैतिक, धार्मिक, आर्थिक शोषण का शिकार है। सामाजिक संरचनाएं उसे शिक्षा और रोजगार के उचित अवसर प्रदान नहीं करतीं। उसका शाारीरिक स्तर पर शोषण किया जाता है। बच्चे पैदा करना और उन्हें पालना स्त्री का काम है। पुरुष की तुलना में शारीरिक रूप से दुर्बल होने के कारण उसे मारा पीटा जाता है। उसके साथ बलात्कार किया जाता है। सांस्कृतिक स्तर पर स्त्री शोषण का शिकार है। यौन शुद्धता या सतीत्व के मूल्य स्त्री से सम्बद्ध हैं। स्त्री को पतिव्रता होना चाहिए, पुरुष को पत्नीव्रती होने की जरूरत नहीं है। स्त्री–पुरुष की लम्बी उम्र के लिए करवाचौथ का व्रत रखती है। पुरुष को स्त्री की लम्बी उम्र के लिए करवाचौथ का व्रत रखने की जरूरत नहीं है। स्त्री इसी में खुश है। यह स्त्री का सांस्कृतिक शोषण है। मनोवैज्ञानिक स्तर पर भी स्त्री का शोषण किया जाता है। स्त्रियों के पास पुरुषों जैसे सबल तन, मन और मस्तिष्क नहीं। सुन्दरता कोमलता, समर्पण आदि उसके गुण हैं। शक्ति, कठोरता, शासन आदि पुरुष के गुण हैं, स्त्री के अवगुण। स्त्री–पुरुष का मौलिक अन्तर शताब्दियों से चली आ रही अवधारणा का ही यह सूत्रात्मक निष्कर्ष है कि पुरुष में स्त्री के गुण आ जाते हैं तो वह महात्मा बन जाता है, स्त्री में पुरुष के गुण आ जाते हैं तो वह कुलटा बन जाती है। सिमोन द बोउवार ने अपनी पुस्तक 'The Second Sex में इस अवधारणा का खण्डन किया है। उनकी स्थापना है कि बचपन से लेकर युवावस्था तक स्त्री को जिन स्थितियों में रखा जाता

है, जो शिक्षा–दीक्षा दी जाती है, उसके कारण ही स्त्री पुरुष से भिन्न बनती है। स्त्री और पुरुष के जिन भिन्न और परस्पर विरोधी गुणों की बात की जाती है, वे मौलिक या प्राकृतिक गुण नहीं है अपितु मानव सभ्यता की देन हैं।

जिस मानव सभ्यता ने स्त्री और पुरुष की गुणात्मक भिन्नता को जन्म दिया है, वह पितृसत्तात्मक मानव सभ्यता है। इस मानव सभ्यता में पिता शासक होता है। स्त्रीवादियों का कहना है कि पितृसत्ता घर, राज्य, धर्म संस्थानों, कानून, शिक्षा–संस्थानों अन्य सांस्कृतिक संस्थानों आदि में सर्वत्र सक्रिय है। यहाँ तक कि वह स्वयं स्त्रियों में भी सक्रिय है, क्योंकि पितृसत्तात्मक समाज में स्त्रियाँ भी उन मूल्यों को आत्मसात कर लेती हैं, जो उपर्युक्त सत्ता–संस्थानों के द्वारा उनके सामने परोसे जाते हैं। इन पितृसत्तात्मक संरचनाओं की बात मार्क्सवादियों और मनोविश्लेषणवादियों ने भी की है। लेकिन स्त्रीवादियों ने स्त्री पर पड़ने वाले इनके प्रभावों पर स्वयं को केन्द्रित किया है। उनका मानना है कि कोई भी दमनकारी संरचना जितना स्त्री को प्रभावित करती है, उतना पुरुष को नहीं। वे इन दमनकारी संरचनाओं का यथार्थ रूप सामने लाना चाहते हैं और इन्हें बदलना चाहते हैं। स्त्रीवादी साहित्य–सैद्धांतिकी का उपयोग भी इसके लिए करते हैं। उनके अनुसार पढ़ना–लिखना, चिंतन करना, आलोचना करना इन सबका लक्ष्य एक ही है, अर्थात् दमनकारी संरचनाओं के यथार्थ का उद्घाटन करना और उन्हें बदलना। इसलिए स्त्रीवादी स्वयं को उन सैद्धांतिकियों के साथ जोड़ते हैं, जिन्होंने मनुष्य और मनुष्य के बीच की अनेक प्रकार की विषमताओं के उद्घाटन और रेखांकन को अपना लक्ष्य बनाया है, जैसे मार्क्सवाद, मनोविश्लेषणवाद, रंगभेद संबंधी सैद्धांतिकी आदि। स्त्रीवादियों का मानना है कि स्त्री और पुरुष के बीच की विषमता की पक्षधर और स्त्री का शोषण और दमन करने वाली सामाजिक संरचनाओं को बदलने के लिए क्रांति की आवश्यकता है। हिन्दी में स्त्री–विमर्श की जो शुरूआत हुई है, वह पश्चिम से प्रभावित है। इसलिए पश्चिमी स्त्रीवादियों की स्थापनाओं की अनुगूंज हमें उसमें सुनायी देती है। पश्चिम में जो स्त्री–विमर्श चला उसने यह अनुभव किया कि साहित्यिक क्षेत्र में लेखिकाओं और उनकी रचनाओं की उपेक्षा की गयी है और साहित्यिक विमर्श में दृष्टि पुरुषवादी रही है। इसके प्रतिकार के लिए एक

ओर तो उन्होंने उपेक्षित लेखिकाओं का पुनरुद्धार और पुनर्मूल्यांकन किया और दूसरी ओर स्त्रीवादी साहित्यिक मूल्यों और कसौटियों के निर्माण का प्रयत्न किया। जिस तरह पश्चिम में स्त्री–विमर्शकों ने नये साहित्यिक मूल्यों को विकसित करने का प्रयत्न किया है, उस रूप में हिन्दी में नहीं। हिन्दी में इस दिशा में छुटपुट प्रयत्न तो हुए हैं, लेकिन अभी तक कोई बड़ा उल्लेखनीय काम नहीं हुआ है। हिन्दी में इस तरह की तमाम रचनाएं हैं जिनका स्त्रीवादी दृष्टि से विवेचन करके पुनर्मूल्यांकन किया जा सकता है।

स्त्रियों की समाज में स्थिति और उनकी समस्याओं पर बहुत समय से लिखा जाता रहा है। लेकिन आज स्त्री–विमर्श साहित्य के केन्द्र में है। पुरुष सत्तात्मक समाज में स्त्री अनेक वर्षों तक शक्तिहीन, निरीह बनी रही। उसे या तो देवी का दर्जा दिया गया या भोग्या बनाया गया। सदियों से हो रहे शोषण और दमन के प्रति स्त्री चेतना ने स्त्री–विमर्श को जन्म दिया। स्त्री ने अपने व्यक्तित्व और अस्मिता की पहचान के लिए जो संघर्ष किया उसने शीघ्र ही एक आन्दोलन का रूप ले लिया। जिससे स्त्री को निष्पक्ष न्याय मिल सके तथा समाज में व्याप्त लिंगभेद को समाप्त करने के लिए एक स्वस्थ दृष्टिकोण का विकास हो सके।

स्त्री–विमर्श को अनेक रूपों में देखना आवश्यक है। स्त्री–विमर्श के संदर्भ में समग्रता से विचार करने पर अनेक समस्याएं सामने आती हैं। जैसे बाल विवाह, विधवा विवाह, अनमेल विवाह, स्त्री शिक्षा, लड़कियों का पालन–पोषण, तलाक, सम्पत्ति में स्त्री का अधिकार, संतति निरोध, स्त्री संगठन, स्त्री की अवस्था, स्त्री के विकास की ऐतिहासिक प्रक्रिया, स्त्री–पुरुष के बीच मौजूद असमानता, पर्दा–प्रथा, वैध–अवैध वैवाहिक रिश्ते, परिवार संयुक्त और एकल, सती प्रथा, बलात्कार, दहेज , स्त्री स्वास्थ्य, स्त्री रोजगार, स्त्री आन्दोलन, संविधान में स्त्री की स्थिति इन सभी विषयों का स्त्री विमर्श में समावेश है।

स्त्री–विमर्श को साहित्यकारों ने अपने–अपने ढंग से परिभाषित किया है। मैत्रेयी पुष्पा के अनुसार "स्त्री विमर्श वह बातचीत है, तर्क–वितर्कों से भरी बहस और बहसों से निकलकर आने वाला वह निष्कर्ष है जो स्त्री के जीवन को पुरुष जीवन के साथ समानता के स्तर पर लाना

चाहता है।''[1] स्त्री विमर्श को लेकर निर्मला जैन लिखती हैं ''स्त्री–विमर्श की प्रेरणा इस बात से आती है कि भारत ही नहीं दुनिया के सभी समाजों में स्त्री और पुरुष के बीच भेदभाव होता है। कुछ गिने–चुने समुदायों को छोड़ दें तो स्त्री को प्रायः दूसरे दर्जे का नागरिक माना जाता रहा है। भारत में समस्या दोहरी है। एक ओर उसे देवी, पूज्य और माँ का दर्जा देकर एक छद्म की सृष्टि की जाती है। लेकिन ये सारी बातें केवल सैद्धान्तिक हैं। व्यवहार में जब भी निर्णायक क्षण आते हैं तभी यह पूज्य भाव काफूर हो जाता है। पुरुष अपना वर्चस्व बनाये रखने का कोई अवसर हाथ से नहीं जाने देता।''[2] राजी सेठ के अनुसार ''जीवन एक चीज है, साहित्य दूसरी चीज। समाज में लोग जब समस्याओं के प्रति सचेत होने लगते हैं तो उनकी परिभाषाएँ बनती हैं, विमर्श बनने लगते हैं। इसका एक लाभ यह होता है कि किसी विमर्श के हवाले से लोग एक–दूसरे से जुड़ जाते हैं और समस्याओं को सामूहिक चेष्टा और जागरूकता से देखने की प्रक्रिया शुरू हो जाती है। संगठित शक्ति बढ़ती है। दूसरे देशों की तरह भारत में स्त्री–विमर्श को एक ऐसे ही जागरूकता आभियान की तरह देखा जाना चाहिए।''[3]

आज के परिवेश ने स्त्रियों को यह सोचने के लिए विवश कर दिया है कि उन्हें भी उन सामाजिक सांस्कृतिक, आर्थिक और राजनैतिक मूल्यों की प्राप्ति हो जिन्हें पुरुषों ने परम्परा से अपने लिए सुरक्षित कर लिया है। आज भी स्त्री समाज विवशता की परधि से बाहर नहीं निकल सका है। स्त्री के अधिकारों को लेकर मनीषाजी ने लिखा है ''आज की शिक्षित, कामकाजी औरत भी मर्द की बराबरी पर नहीं खड़ी है। इसका सीधा–सा सामाजिक कारण है, उसे उसके हिस्से के अधिकारों से वंचित रखना। औरत को अधिकार देने के नाम पर कानून तो तमाम बनाए गए हैं परन्तु उन पर अमल यदि पचास प्रतिशत भी हो पाता तो आज स्थिति इतनी विषम न होती।''[4] स्त्रियों को समाज में स्थान दिलाने और पुरुष वर्चस्व से स्त्रियों को आजाद करने के लिए मृदुला गर्ग अपने लेख स्त्री विमर्श से दूर स्त्रीवाद में लिखती हैं कि ''स्त्रीवाद शुरू से हर जगह आन्दोलन की तरह उभरा। फिर आन्दोलन को बल और आधार देने के लिए विचारधाराओं ने जन्म लिया। अब चूंकि लिंग दो ही हैं इसलिए जो

आघात स्त्रियों ने स्त्री होने के अलावा वर्ग या जाति विशेष की सदस्या होने के नाते सहे हैं, उनका संबंध सत्ता और व्यवस्था से है। चूंकि सत्ता में पुरुष का वर्चस्व रहा है इसलिए यह सम्बन्ध भी पुरुष से जा जुड़ा है। स्त्रीवाद का मुख्य मुद्दा स्त्री को वे अधिकार दिलाना है जो पुरुष को प्राप्त हैं, पर स्त्री को नहीं।"[5] जूलिया क्रिस्तोबा, जर्मेन ग्रीयर, सिमोन द बोउवार और हिन्दी की प्रबुद्ध लेखिकाऐं स्त्री को सिर्फ लिंग के कारण महत्व न देने और इसी कारण उसका दमन करने का विरोध करती हैं। लिंग को आधार बनाकर मनीषा लिखती हैं "औरतों के पास क्योंकि लिंग नाम का हथियार नहीं, सिर्फ इसीलिए वह दोयम नहीं हो सकतीं। संस्कृति, परम्परा और मर्यादा के नाम पर औरतों के भावात्मक शोषण की जड़ें इस कदर गहरी हैं कि वे इन्हीं संकीर्णताओं और कायदे–कानूनों के बीच अपनी स्वतंत्रता के छोटे–मोटे जश्न मना लेती है। औरत के अभाव में परिवार नहीं बसता पर इस परिवार नाम की संस्था का मुखिया मर्द ही होता है चाहे वह उम्र में सबसे छोटा–ही क्यों न हो।"[6] अतीत के चलचित्र, स्मृति की रेखाएँ और श्रृंखला की कडियाँ नामक गद्य रचनाओं में महादेवी वर्मा ने स्वतंत्रता पूर्व की भारतीय स्त्री के बहुत से चित्र अंकित किए हैं। महादेवी वर्मा स्त्री के उस रूप की चर्चा करती हैं जो अपने अधिकारों के प्रति सजग हो रही है। उपेक्षित एवं उत्पीड़ित स्त्री की आन्तरिक वेदना का मार्मिक आख्यान भी वे प्रस्तुत करती हैं "अनेक बार नारी की बाह्‌य परिस्थितियों के परिवर्तन की ओर ध्यान न देकर मैं उसकी शक्तियों को जाग्रत करके परिस्थितियों में साम्य लाने वाली सफलता संम्भव कर सकती हूँ। समस्या का समाधान समस्या के ज्ञान पर निर्भर है और यह ज्ञान ज्ञाता की अपेक्षा रखता है।"[7]

श्रृंखला की कड़ियाँ में महादेवी वर्मा भारतीय समाज में स्त्रियों के लिए उचित स्थान की माँग करते हुए लिखती हैं "हमें न किसी पर जय चाहिए, न किसी से पराजय, न किसी पर प्रभुता चाहिए, न किसी का प्रभुत्व। केवल अपना वह स्थान, वह स्वत्व चाहिए जिनका पुरुषों के निकट कोई उपयोग नहीं है परन्तु जिनके बिना हम समाज का उपयोगी अंग बन नहीं सकेंगी। हमारी जाग्रति और साधन सम्पन्न बहनें इस दिशा में विशेष कार्य कर सकेंगी, इसमें सन्देह नहीं है।"[8] स्त्री–अधिकारों का ध्यान दिलाते हुए सिमोन द बोउवार लिखती हैं "एक ऐसी दुनियाँ, जिसमें स्त्री–पुरुष के

अधिकार समान हों अब हमारी सोच और चिन्तन का मुख्य विषय है। सोवियत संघ इसका प्रमाण है, जहाँ स्त्री और पुरुष को एक ही तरह का काम करना पड़ता है। यदि स्त्रियाँ अधिक शक्ति की माँग करने वाले कार्य नहीं कर सकतीं तो ऐसी स्थिति कई पुरूषों की भी होती है।''[9]

जर्मेन ग्रीयर ने अपनी पुस्तक द फीमेल यूनक के सार संक्षेप में स्त्रियों की स्थिति और उनके कर्तव्य को आधार बनाकर कहा है ''हम जानती हैं कि हम क्या हैं, लेकिन हम यह नहीं जानती कि हम क्या हो सकती हैं या हो सकती थीं। विज्ञान की मतान्धता यथास्थिति को नियम के अपरिहार्य परिणाम के रूप में अभिव्यक्त करती है, स्त्रियों को स्त्रैण सामान्यता की एकदम मूलभूत मान्यताओं के बारे में प्रश्न करना सीखना होगा ताकि विकास की वे संभावनाएँ जिन्हें अनुकूलन द्वारा लगातार बंद रखा गया है, फिर से खोली जा सकें।''[10]

वेदों से ही प्रेरणा लेकर पुराणों और स्मृतियों ने भी उत्तरोत्तर काल में पुरुष–प्रधान समाज के भोग व ऐश्वर्य के लिए नारी की गुलामी को और अधिक पुष्टता प्रदान की। स्मृति ग्रन्थों में सर्वप्रमुख मनुस्मृति में तो यहाँ तक लिखा गया ''बाल्ये पितुवसेतिष्ठेत प्राणि गृहस्थयौवने। पुत्राणां भर्त्तार प्रेतेन, भेजेस्त्रीमनाम स्वतंत्रताम्।'' अर्थात् बाल्यावस्था में नारी पिता के अधीन रहे, युवावस्था के प्रति और जब विधवा हो जाए तो पुत्रों के अधीन रहना चाहिए स्त्री कभी भी स्वतंत्र नहीं रहनी चाहिए। प्रो. के. टी. एस. सराओ लिखते हैं ''गौतमबुद्ध के जन्म के समय तक पुरुष–प्रधानता व पितृसत्तात्मकता, भारतीय समाज के मुख्य स्तम्भ बन चुके थे। जिसमें परिवार जैसे एक सामाजिक ढांचे के जरिये महिलाओं को नियन्त्रित रखा जाता था। लड़की का जन्म न केवल अनिच्छित, बल्कि दुर्भाग्यपूर्ण माना जाता था। बहुपत्नी प्रथा हरम व वेश्यावृत्ति जैसी महिलाओं को निम्नीकृत करने वाली सामाजिक कुरीतियाँ भारतीय समाज व आर्थिक जीवन का अभिन्न अंग बन चुकी थी।''[11] नारी विरोधी मानसिकता के ऐसे काल में भगवान् तथागत गौतम बुद्ध का जन्म हुआ। सर्वसुन्दरी महिलाओं को जनपद कल्याणी, नगरवधू या गणिका बनाकर बुद्ध–जन्म–काल का भारतीय समाज काम–भोग व विलासिता के जीवन में गोते लगा रहा था।

ऐसे ही काल में उस युग की विश्वसुन्दरी अम्बपाली का वैशाली नगर में जन्म हुआ।

वज्जिगणसंघ में अष्ट राजकुल सम्मिलित थे. उनमें लिच्छवियों की प्रतिष्ठा सर्वोच्च थी। लिच्छवियों की अधिकांश आबादी वैशाली में ही थी। ऐसे वैभवशाली लिच्छवियों की नगरी वैशाली में अम्बपाली का जन्म हुआ। अम्बपाली के वास्तविक माता–पिता का कहीं भी उल्लेख नहीं मिलता है क्योंकि वह वैशाली के एक आम्रवन में, उस उपवन के संरक्षक (माली) को सफेद कपड़े में लिपटी हुई, नवजात शिशु के रूप में एक आम के पेड़ के नीचे प्राप्त हुई थी। आम के उपवन में आम के पेड़ के पाद पर मिलने के कारण ही उसका नाम अम्बपाली (आम्रपाली) रखा गया। वर्तमान समय में बिहार राज्य के वैशाली जिले में स्थित बसाढ़ नामक गांव व उसके आस–पास के क्षेत्रों को प्राचीन वैशाली के रूप में चिन्हित किया गया है। बसाढ़ गांव से चार–पांच किलोमीटर के ही अन्तर पर मुजफ्फरपुर जिले का क्षेत्र आरम्भ हो जाता है। मुजफ्फरपुर जिले के कुछ गांव भी प्राचीन वैशाली के पुरातात्विक अवशेषों को संजोए हुए हैं। बासढ़ गांव से लगभग चार किलोमीटर की दूरी पर मुजफ्फरपुर जिले की सीमा में अम्बारा नामक एक गांव है। बहुत से पुरातात्विक व ऐतिहासिक विद्वान यह स्वीकार करते हैं कि यह अम्बारा शब्द उस प्राचीन आम्रवन का अपभ्रंश है। जहाँ पर अम्बपाली पैदा हुई थी।

इस लेख में ऐतिहासिक पृष्ठभूमि को लिखते समय यह सिद्ध हुआ कि बुद्ध–जन्म–पूर्व काल में वैदिक परम्परा ने नारी को लाचार, मजबूर व गुलाम बना दिया था। पुरुष–प्रधान भारतीय समाज ने काम भोग व विलासिता के लिए नारी–विरोधी व्यवस्था को स्थापित कर लिया था। ऐसे समय में युवा होने पर अम्बपाली के सौन्दर्य–आकर्षण ने सभी पुरुषों को मन्त्रमुग्ध कर दिया। सभी युवाओं में, चाहे वे श्रेष्ठि–पुत्र हों या राज–पुत्र हों, सभी में अम्बपाली को अपनी प्रेमिका, पत्नी या रखैल बनाने की होड़ लग गयी। अम्बपाली की सुन्दरता राज–कलह का कारण बन गयी, लोग एक–दूसरे का रक्त बहाने के लिए उन्मत हो गये। वज्जिगणसंघ की नारी विरोधी कानून व्यवस्था ने अम्बपाली को जनपद कल्याणी, नगरवधू या सार्वजनिक गणिका बनने के लिए बाध्य किया। इस प्रकार की घोषित गणिकाएं सार्वजनिक होती थी, उन्हें नृत्य गीत व वाद्य के द्वारा सम्पूर्ण

जनपद के पुरुषों का मनोरंजन करना पड़ता था। अम्बपाली कोई साधारण महिला नहीं थी, उसने पुरुषों का दंभ चूर करने के लिए, उनके मनोरंजन के बदले अथाह सम्पत्ति अर्जित की। गणिका जीवन जीते हुए, प्रेम–प्रसंग के सन्दर्भ में उसका नाम मात्र महान सम्राट बिम्बिसार के साथ ही जुडा, इससे अम्बपाली की महत्वाकांक्षा की पुष्टि होती है। पालि–साहित्य में उल्लेख प्राप्त होता है कि अम्बपाली व सम्राट बिम्बिसार से एक पुत्र भी पैदा हुआ जो बड़ा होकर भगवान बुद्ध के भिक्षु संघ में प्रव्रजित हुआ। जो कि विमलकोण्डञथेर के नाम से प्रसिद्ध हुआ। अम्बपाली के जीवन में सुख–समृद्धि, भोग–ऐश्वर्य, धन–सम्पत्ति इत्यादि की प्रचुरता रही। साधारण नारी के मन में पुरुष–प्रेम ही सर्वोत्तम सुख व आनन्द का प्रतिनिधित्व करता है। जिस प्रकार सिद्धार्थ गौतम के अलग–अलग ऋतुओं के महल में हजारों दास–दासियों के साथ रहने के बाद भी उनका मन सांसारिक बन्धनों से मुक्त रहा। उसी प्रकार अम्बपाली भी हजारों दास–दासियों के मध्य में रहने के बाद भी तमाम् सांसारिक वस्तुओं के आकर्षण से मुक्त रही। उसकी कामनाएं तृप्त नहीं हुई। उसकी प्यास तब तक नहीं बुझी, जब तक उसने धम्म–रस का पान नहीं किया। उसकी कामना तभी पूर्ण हुई. जब उसे बुद्ध वचनामृत का रसापान हुआ और उसने अपने सर्वस्व को धम्म पर न्योछावर कर दिया।

भगवान् बुद्ध अपने जीवन के अंतिम वर्ष में घूमते हुए वैशाली आए और अम्बपालिवन में रुके जब अम्बपाली ने सुना कि भगवान् वैशाली आये हैं और मेरे आम्रवन में विहार कर रहे हैं तब वह सुन्दर–सुन्दर यानों को जुड़वाकर एक सुन्दरयान पर चढ़ अपने दल–बल के साथ आम्रवन में जहाँ भगवान् थे, वहाँ गयी, जाकर अभिवादन कर एक ओर बैठ गयी। भगवान् ने धार्मिक कथा से उसे सम्प्रहर्षित समुत्तेजित किया। अन्त में अम्बपाली ने भगवान् से निवेदन कर कहा– "भन्ते! भगवान। भिक्षु–संघ के साथ मेरा कल का भोजन स्वीकार करें।"[12] भगवान बुद्ध की मौन सहमति पाकर अम्बपाली गणिका ने असीम गौरव का अनुभव किया और प्रसन्नचित्त मुद्रा में अपने महल को वापस हुई। वैशाली के लिच्छवियों ने भी भगवान् के आगमन की बात सुनी। जब वे सुसज्जित रथों पर अपने दल–बल के साथ भगवान् बुद्ध की ओर जा रहे थे तो अम्बपाली अपने दल–बल के साथ उधर से वापस आ रही थी। मार्ग में अम्बपाली ने तरुण–तरुण

लिच्छवियों के रथों से रथ, धुरों से धुरा, चक्कों से चक्का, जुए से जुआ टकरा दिया। तरुण लिच्छवियों ने अम्बपाली के इस गर्व का कारण पूछा तो अम्बपाली ने उन्हें जवाब दिया ''आर्य पुत्रों ! क्योंकि मैंने भिक्षु संघ के साथ कल के भोजन के लिए भगवान् को आमंत्रित किया है। लिच्छवियों ने अम्बपाली से कहा– ष्सौ हजार काषार्पण लेकर, यह भोजन हमें कराने दें। अम्बपाली ने इसका भी उत्तर दिया ''आर्य पुत्रों! यदि वैशाली जनपद भी दे दो, तब भी इस महान भोजन को मैं न दूंगी।''[13] दूसरे दिन भगवान् बुद्ध भिक्षुसंघ सहित अम्बपाली के महल पधारे और उसके उत्तम भोजन को ग्रहण किया। भोजनोपरान्त अम्बपाली ने भगवान् से निवेदन किया ''भन्ते! मैं इस आराम को बुद्ध–प्रमुख भिक्षु संघ को दान करती हूँ। इस प्रकार अम्बपाली भगवान् बुद्ध की श्रद्धा–सम्पन्न उपासिका बनी। भगवान् बुद्ध ने उसे अपनी उपासिका मान उसके इस दान व आतिथ्य को स्वीकार करके एक गणिका के जीवन को कृतार्थ किया। अम्बपाली का जीवन धन्य हो गया।

वैशाली के कूटागारशाला में ही भगवान् ने महाप्रजापति गौतमी को पांच सौ शाक्य महिलाओं के साथ, संघ में दीक्षित होने, प्रव्रज्या लेने व भिक्षुणी संघ के स्थापना की अनुमति दी थी ''महाप्रजापति गौतमी को स्वयं बुद्ध ने एवं उन शेष पांच सौ भिक्षुणियों को भगवान् के शिष्य नन्दक ने धम्म और विनय की दीक्षा दी थी।''[14] अम्बपाली और मगध सम्राट बिम्बिसार द्वारा उत्पन्न, उसका एक पुत्र विमलकोण्डञ था, जिसकी चर्चा पहले भी की जा चुकी है वह भगवान् के भिक्षु संघ में पहले ही प्रव्रजित होकर अर्हत्व की प्राप्ति कर चुका था। बुद्ध–उपासिका अम्बपाली ने अपने अर्हत् पुत्र विमलकोण्डञ्थेर से प्रव्रज्या ग्रहण की और अपना सर्वस्व धन–धान्य, प्रासाद व आराम, अपने जीवन भर की अर्जित सम्पूर्ण सम्पदा बुद्ध प्रमुख संघ को दान कर भिक्षुणी हो गयी। तथागत के धम्म में प्रतिष्ठित हो जिन–जिन ने ध्यान और भावना से यह जाना कि संसार परिवर्तनशील है, जीवन अनित्य है, सुख–दुःख क्षणिक हैं, जीवन व उससे सम्बन्धित सभी चीजों में आसक्ति दुःखों का मूल है। उन्होंने निर्वाण–सुख का साक्षात्कार किया। वृद्ध–थेरी अम्बपाली ने अपने अर्हत् पुत्र विमलकोण्डञ् थेर के उपदेश के प्रभाव में विदर्शन–भावना (विपश्यना) का अभ्यास पूर्ण किया। अपने ही जर्जरित शरीर को देखकर उसे भगवान् बुद्ध के प्रतीत्यसमुत्पाद

व अनित्यता के सिद्धान्त का बोध हुआ और उसने अपने देह की अनित्यता में बुद्ध वचनों को परिलक्षित होते हुए देखा। इस प्रकार उसे अर्हत–पद की प्राप्ति हुई।

अम्बपाली को अपने जीवन में अनित्यता के सिद्धान्त का जो अनुभव प्राप्त हुआ उसे उसने अपने उद्‌गारों में व्यक्त किया। थेरीगाथा नामक ग्रन्थ में अम्बपाली के उद्‌गारों को संग्रहित किया गया है जिसमें उसने सम्पूर्ण नारी–जगत को उपदेशित किया है कि "स्त्री–देह की सुन्दरता एक दिन क्षीण हो जायेगी, यह शरीर दुःखों का आलय बन जायेगा, यही बुद्ध वचन की सत्यता है।"[15] थेरीगाथा के बीसतिनिपातोवग्ग में अम्बपाली ने कहा है–"एदिसो अहु अयं समुस्सयो, जज्जरो बहुदुखानमालयो। सोपलेपपतितो जराघरो, सच्चवादिवचनं अनथा ति।"[16] अर्थात् "एक समय मेरा यह शरीर सुन्दर शोभायमान था, आज वही जर्जर और अनेक दुःखों का आलय बन गया है। यह मेरा शरीर आज ऐसे जीर्ण घर के समान है, जिसकी लीपन टूट–टूटकर नीचे गिर गयी है। बिना लेपादि के यह वृद्ध शरीर शीघ्र ही इस प्रकार गिर जायेगा, जैसे टूटी हुई लीपन वाला पुराना जीर्ण घर। सत्यवादी बुद्ध के वचन कभी मिथ्या नहीं होते। इस प्रकार अम्बपालीथेरी भगवान के धम्म में श्रद्धा–सम्पन्न होकर अन्य भिक्षुओं व भिक्षुणियों की भांति जीवनपर्यन्त, बुद्ध–वचनों की सार्थकता को बहुजन हिताय, बहुजन सुखाय प्रचारित करती रही।

तथागत भगवान् गौतम बुद्ध ने 2550 वर्ष पूर्व मौलिक रूप में जो उपदेश दिए, जो सिद्धान्त प्रतिपादित किए, उन सभी उपदेशों के परिणाम व निष्कर्ष मानव धरा में समाहित हो गये। बुद्ध–काल में उन सिद्धान्तों से मानव कल्याण तो हुआ ही तथापि आज भी बुद्ध के उपदेश विभिन्न विचार–सरणियों में नयी ऊर्जा को लिए हुए, मानव कल्याणार्थ संघर्ष कर रहे हैं। इस शरीर और जीवन की अनित्यता की बात आज भी प्रासंगिक है। स्त्री–देह की अनित्यता का वर्णन थेरीगाथा में अम्बपाली (आम्रपाली) और उस काल की तमाम् अन्य भिक्षुणियों ने भी किया जिसका प्रभाव वर्तमान समय में परिलक्षित हो रहा है। आधुनिक काल में भी फ्रेंच की प्रसिद्ध लेखिका सिमोन द बोवुआर अपनी सुप्रसिद्ध पुस्तक द सेकेंड सेक्स में लिखती हैं देह ही स्त्री की पहचान रह गयी है ... औरत पैदा नहीं होती

बनाई जाती है। सुप्रसिद्ध पत्रकार व लेखक राजेन्द्र यादव भी पुरुष–प्रधान समाज को कोसते हुए लिखते हैं पुरुष औरत को सिर्फ शरीर या उसके कुछ अंगों को ही उसकी सम्पूर्ण पहचान के रूप में देखने की जिद में रहता है, लेकिन जब औरत स्वयं को इस रूप में देखने या मानने लगती है तो बौखला उठता है..... स्त्री शरीर रहे, लेकिन अपने आपको सिर्फ उतना ही शरीर माने जितने की पुरुष को जरूरत है... उससे अधिक मानना उसकी उच्छृखलता और अमर्यादा है। देह, स्त्री की एक मात्र पहचान के रूप में उसका गुण भी है और गाली भी। जब तक वह पुरुष की इच्छा व वासना के नियंत्रण में हैं– वह सौन्दर्य है, उसके नियंत्रण से बाहर है तो भर्त्सनीय और दण्डनीय है। इसी नारी–देह के प्रति स्वयं नारी को और पुरुष को भी आसक्ति न रहे, देह की सत्यता का साक्षात्कार हो सके, संसार में सभी संस्कार अनित्य हैं–इसका भी बोध हो सके।

इस कारण से ही बुद्ध ने अनित्यता के सिद्धान्त को मूलतः प्रतीत्यसमुत्पाद के रूप में स्वयं अभ्यास किया और सम्पूर्ण मानव जगत के नर और नारी को विपश्यना के रूप में अभ्यास करना सिखाया। समाज में नर व नारी का उत्तरदायित्व समान होता है। अच्छी संस्कृति व सभ्यता के निर्माण में बुद्धकालीन महिलाएं भी अग्रणी रही हैं। अम्बपालीथेरी का एक घृणित–जीवन–पद्धति को त्यागकर सदाचार व ब्रह्मचर्यपूर्ण जीवन बिताना आधुनिक भारतीय समाज के लिए एक प्रेरणा स्त्रोत है, खासकर उन महिलाओं के लिए, जो कुसंस्कृति की शिकर होती आयी हैं। समाज में उच्च जीवन पद्धति के लिए आज भी अम्बपाली के उद्‌गारों को बार–बार दोहराए जाने की आवश्यकता है। अतः सारांश रूप में कहा जा सकता है कि अंबपाली का व्यक्तित्व समावेशी विकसित भारत के स्त्री विमर्श को एक नई दिशा प्रदान करने में सहायक हो सकता है।

सन्दर्भ–

- सम्पादक–ममता कालिया, उत्तर प्रदेश (पत्रिका), स्त्री विषेशांक मई 2003, पृ० 210,
- वही, पृ० 209

- वही, पृ० 212
- मनीषा, हम सभ्य औरतें, सामयिक प्रकाशन, नई दिल्ली, 2002, पृ० 14
- मृदुला गर्ग, लेख–स्त्री–विमर्श से दूर स्त्रीवाद, सहारा समय (साप्ताहिक) 24 मई 2003
- मनीषा, हम सभ्य औरतें, सामयिक प्रकाशन, नई दिल्ली, 2002, पृ० 6
- महादेवी वर्मा, श्रृंखला की कड़ियाँ, लोकभारती प्रकाशन, इलाहाबाद 2001, पृ० 10
- वही, पृ० 26
- सिमोन द बोउवार, द सेकेण्ड सेक्स, हिन्दी अनु० स्त्री उपेक्षिता, सरस्वती विहार, दिल्ली, 1991, पृ० 324
- जर्मेन ग्रीयर, द फीमेल यूनक, हिन्दी अनु०–बधिया स्त्री, राजकमल प्रकाशन, नई दिल्ली, 2001, पृष्ठ 16
- प्राचीन भारतीय बौद्ध धर्मः उद्भव, स्वरूप और पतन, प्रो. के. टी. एस. सराओ, हिन्दी माध्यम कार्यान्वयन निदेशालय, दिल्ली विश्वविद्यालय, दिल्ली– 06. 2004, पृ० 158
- दीघ निकाय (हिन्दी अनुवाद), अनु. भिक्षु राहुल सांकृत्यायन एवं भिक्षु जगदीश काश्यप, भारतीय बौद्ध शिक्षा परिषद्, लखनऊ, 1979 पृ० 128
- वही, पृ. 128
- विनय पिटक (हिन्दी अनुवाद), अनु, राहुल सांकृत्यायन, सारनाथ, 1935, पृष्ठ 519

- भगवान् बुद्ध और उनका धम्म (हिन्दी अनुवाद), डॉ. बी. आर अम्बेडकर, अनु भदन्त आनन्द कौशल्यायन, सिद्धार्थ प्रकाशन मुम्बई, 1991, पृ. 188
- थेरीगाथा. (हिन्दी अनुवाद), अनु. डॉ. विमलकीर्ति, सम्यक प्रकाशन, पश्चिमीपुरी, दिल्ली–63, 2003 पृष्ठ 214

Chapter- 12

भारत कल, आज और कल : विकसित भारत 2047 के विशेष सन्दर्भ में

मंतोष कुमार यादव

शोध छात्र

समाजशास्त्र विभाग

दी.द.उ.गोरखपुर विश्वविद्यालय

भारतवर्ष सिर्फ एक भौगोलिक इकाई ही नहीं एक जीवंत सभ्यता, एक अद्‌भुत सामाजिक संगम और विविधताओं के बीच एकता का प्रतीक है जिसने सहस्राब्दियों से सांस्कृतिक, सामाजिक और बौद्धिक विकास को आकार दिया है, भारत विविधताओं के बीच सामंजस्य और एकता का अद्वितीय उदाहरण है। भारत की ऐतिहासिक यात्रा सिर्फ घटनाओं और साम्राज्यों तक सीमित नहीं है यह विचार, दर्शन, विज्ञान, कला और सामाजिक संरचनाओं के निरंतर विकास का दर्पण भी है यहाँ का सामाजिक और सांस्कृतिक परिदृश्य समय की परीक्षा में सदैव जीवित रहा है जहाँ परिवर्तन और निरंतरता दोनों ने एक साथ योगदान दिया है। "भारतः कल, आज और कल" इस सतत प्रवाह का समाजशास्त्रीय विश्लेषण है जो अतीत की गौरवपूर्ण परंपराओं, वर्तमान की सामाजिक–आर्थिक चुनौतियों और भविष्य की संभावनाओं के बीच संतुलन को समझने का प्रयास है। प्रस्तुत अध्ययन न सिर्फ भारतीय सभ्यता की गहन समझ प्रदान करता है यह भी दर्शाता है कि किस प्रकार ऐतिहासिक दृष्टिकोण और आधुनिक प्रगतिशील विचार मिलकर एक समग्र और विकसित राष्ट्र की परिकल्पना को संभव बनाते हैं। भारत का अध्ययन केवल भौगोलिक या ऐतिहासिक दृष्टि से नहीं, बल्कि एक सतत विकसित सामाजिक–सांस्कृतिक प्रणाली के रूप में किया जाना चाहिए, भारत की

सभ्यता का इतिहास उस सतत प्रवाह का प्रतीक है जिसमें परिवर्तन और निरंतरता दोनों समान रूप से विद्यमान हैं, जहाँ अतीत के गौरव, वर्तमान की चुनौतियों और भविष्य की संभावनाओं के बीच से एक विकसित भारत की परिकल्पना उभर रही है।

"विकसित भारत 2047" की परिकल्पना भारत को उसके स्वतंत्रता के शताब्दी वर्ष तक एक ऐसे राष्ट्र के रूप में देखने का प्रयास है, जो न केवल आर्थिक दृष्टि से सशक्त हो, बल्कि सामाजिक न्याय, राजनीतिक पारदर्शिता, सांस्कृतिक समृद्धि, वैज्ञानिक नवाचार और मानवीय मूल्यों की दृष्टि से भी विश्व में अग्रणी बन सके। यह दृष्टि भारत की प्राचीन सभ्यताओं, ज्ञान–परंपराओं और नैतिक आदर्शों को आधुनिक विज्ञान, तकनीक और सुधारवादी दृष्टिकोण के साथ जोड़कर भविष्य के भारत का निर्माण करने पर केंद्रित है। इतिहास के संदर्भ में देखें तो उपनिवेशवाद से पहले भारत व्यापार, हस्तकला, कृषि, गणित, चिकित्सा और शिक्षा में अत्यंत उन्नत था, परंतु औपनिवेशिक शासन ने आर्थिक संरचनाओं को खोखला किया और सामाजिक–सांस्कृतिक ताने–बाने को गहराई से प्रभावित किया। स्वतंत्रता के समय देश के सामने गरीबी, बेरोजगारी, अशिक्षा, कमजोर उद्योगों, प्रशासनिक अव्यवस्था और आर्थिक ठहराव जैसी गंभीर चुनौतियाँ थीं। इसके बावजूद, भारत ने लोकतंत्र को मजबूती प्रदान की, योजना आधारित विकास शुरू किया, सार्वजनिक क्षेत्र और बुनियादी ढांचे को विस्तृत किया, और धीरे–धीरे आर्थिक स्थिरता की ओर कदम बढ़ाए। 1991 के आर्थिक सुधारों ने भारत को वैश्वीकरण के नए युग में प्रवेश कराया, जिससे तकनीकी विकास, उद्यमिता, निजी निवेश, विदेशी व्यापार, और डिजिटल नवाचार को अभूतपूर्व गति मिली। "विकसित भारत 2047" इसी बहुआयामी विकास यात्रा का उन्नत चरण है, जिसमें शिक्षा को भविष्य निर्माण का मूल स्तंभ माना गया है। राष्ट्रीय शिक्षा नीति 2020 इस दिशा में न सिर्फ गुणवत्तापूर्ण शिक्षा पर बल देती है, बल्कि शोध, बहुविषयक अध्ययन, कौशल विकास, डिजिटल दक्षता और भारतीय ज्ञान परंपरा के पुनर्जीवन पर भी ध्यान केंद्रित करती है। इसी प्रकार, सुशासन को विकास का आवश्यक आधार मानते हुए सरकार पारदर्शिता, दक्षता और जवाबदेही को मजबूत करने के लिए डिजिटल प्रशासन, प्रत्यक्ष लाभ अंतरण, ऑनलाइन सेवाएँ, आधार–आधारित पहचान प्रणाली और

नागरिक–केंद्रित योजनाओं का विस्तार कर रही है। तकनीकी क्षमता भी इस दृष्टि का केंद्रीय पहलू है, जहाँ भारत कृत्रिम बुद्धिमत्ता, अंतरिक्ष विज्ञान, क्वांटम तकनीक, जैव–प्रौद्योगिकी, सेमीकंडक्टर उत्पादन, साइबर सुरक्षा, नवीकरणीय ऊर्जा और डिजिटल पब्लिक इंफ्रास्ट्रक्चर के क्षेत्र में वैश्विक नेतृत्व की ओर अग्रसर है। पर्यावरणीय संतुलन की आवश्यकता को ध्यान में रखते हुए विकास मॉडल को हरित ऊर्जा, जल संरक्षण, प्रदूषण नियंत्रण, सतत कृषि, इको–फ्रेंडली परिवहन और जलवायु सहनशील शहरी नियोजन की दिशा में आगे बढ़ाया जा रहा है, साथ ही प्राचीन भारतीय पारिस्थितिक ज्ञान जैसे जल–संचयन, प्राकृतिक कृषि और सामुदायिक संसाधन प्रबंधन को भी महत्त्व दिया जा रहा है। इसके अतिरिक्त, यह दृष्टि समाज में एकता, समानता, न्याय और सांस्कृतिक पहचान की रक्षा को भी विकास का अभिन्न हिस्सा मानती है, ताकि भारत अपनी विविधता में एकता को बनाए रखते हुए लैंगिक समानता, सामाजिक सुरक्षा, कमजोर वर्गों के उत्थान और अधिक समावेशी समाज का निर्माण कर सके। बेरोजगारी, कौशल की कमी, ग्रामीण - शहरी अंतर, जलवायु संकट, सामाजिक असमानता और वैश्विक प्रतिस्पर्धा जैसी चुनौतियाँ अभी भी मौजूद हैं, परंतु इनसे निपटने के लिए दूरदर्शी नीतियाँ, नवाचार आधारित समाधान, राजनीतिक इच्छाशक्ति और नागरिकों की सक्रिय भागीदारी आवश्यक मानी गई है। अंततः "विकसित भारत 2047" एक ऐसी राष्ट्रीय परियोजना है, जो भारत की सांस्कृतिक जड़ों, वैज्ञानिक सोच, तकनीकी नवाचार, आर्थिक आत्मनिर्भरता और मानवीय संवेदनाओं को एक साथ जोड़कर एक ऐसे शक्तिशाली, समावेशी और प्रेरणादायी राष्ट्र की रचना करना चाहती है, जो 2047 तक न केवल विकसित हो, बल्कि विश्व को स्थिर, नैतिक और सतत विकास का मार्ग दिखाने में सक्षम हो सके।

प्राचीन भारत की सामाजिक, आर्थिक और राजनीतिक संरचना

प्राचीन भारत की सामाजिक संरचना वैदिक परंपराओं, समुदाय–आधारित जीवन, संयुक्त परिवार व्यवस्था और वर्ण–आश्रम प्रणाली पर आधारित थी। समाज में कर्तव्य, धर्म, सदाचार और सामूहिक उत्तरदायित्व को विशेष महत्त्व दिया जाता था। सामाजिक जीवन ग्राम–केन्द्रित था, जहाँ पंचायतें स्थानीय प्रशासन, न्याय और सामाजिक नियमों का संचालन करती थीं।

आर्थिक संरचना मुख्यतः कृषि प्रधान थी, किंतु व्यापार, हस्तकला, धातुकर्म, वस्त्र निर्माण, नौवहन और पशुपालन भी अत्यंत विकसित थे। सिंधु सभ्यता से लेकर मौर्य और गुप्त काल तक भारत सुव्यवस्थित शहरी नियोजन, मुद्रा–प्रणाली, व्यापार मार्गों और तकनीकी कौशल के लिए प्रसिद्ध रहा। मसाला -रेशम व्यापार और समुद्री व्यापार भारत की समृद्धि का आधार थे। राजनीतिक संरचना में गणतंत्र और राजतंत्र दोनों प्रकार की व्यवस्थाएँ विद्यमान थीं। सभा और समिति जैसे संस्थान लोकतांत्रिक परंपराओं के प्रारंभिक उदाहरण थे। मौर्य शासन में केन्द्रीयकृत प्रशासन, कर–व्यवस्था और दक्ष नौकरशाही विकसित हुई, जबकि गुप्त काल में विधि, शिक्षा, साहित्य और कला का उत्कर्ष देखा गया। शासन को नैतिकता और धर्मराज्य की अवधारणाओं से जोड़ा जाता था। समग्र रूप से प्राचीन भारत की सामाजिक - आर्थिक- राजनीतिक संरचना एक व्यवस्थित, संतुलित और स्थायी व्यवस्था थी, जिसने भारत की सभ्यता को दीर्घकालीन स्थिरता प्रदान की।

शिक्षा, विज्ञान और संस्कृति का उत्कर्ष

प्राचीन भारत शिक्षा, ज्ञान–विज्ञान और सांस्कृतिक उत्कर्ष का वैश्विक केंद्र माना जाता था। तक्षशिला, नालंदा, विक्रमशिला, वल्लभी और काशी जैसे विश्वविख्यात शिक्षा केंद्रों में दर्शन, गणित, खगोल विज्ञान, चिकित्सा, व्याकरण, राजनीति, कला और धर्मशास्त्र की उच्च शिक्षा प्रदान की जाती थी। गुरुकुल प्रणाली में शिक्षा का उद्देश्य केवल ज्ञान देना नहीं, बल्कि व्यक्तित्व निर्माण, नैतिक मूल्यों का संवर्धन और जीवनोपयोगी कौशल विकसित करना था। विज्ञान के क्षेत्र में आर्यभट्ट, ब्रह्मगुप्त, चरक, सुश्रुत और भास्कराचार्य जैसे विद्वानों ने गणित, बीजगणित, शल्य चिकित्सा, औषध विज्ञान और खगोल विज्ञान में अभूतपूर्व योगदान दिया। शून्य की खोज, दशमलव पद्धति, ग्रहों की गति के वैज्ञानिक सिद्धांत, धातुकर्म तकनीक और जल–प्रबंधन प्रणाली प्राचीन भारत की उन्नत वैज्ञानिक क्षमता को दर्शाते हैं। सांस्कृतिक रूप से भारत विविध भाषाओं, कलाओं, संगीत, नृत्य, स्थापत्य और साहित्य का केंद्र था। वेदों, उपनिषदों, गीता, अष्टाध्यायी, अर्थशास्त्र जैसी कृतियाँ ज्ञान–विरासत का आधार हैं। मंदिर

स्थापत्य, मूर्तिकला, लोककलाएँ और शिल्प परंपराएँ आज भी वैश्विक गौरव का विषय हैं। इस प्रकार शिक्षा, विज्ञान और संस्कृति का यह उत्कर्ष भारत को एक सभ्य, प्रगतिशील और ज्ञान–समृद्ध राष्ट्र बनाता है।

औपनिवेशिक काल में सामाजिक परिवर्तन और चुनौतियाँ

औपनिवेशिक काल ने भारतीय समाज की संरचना, अर्थव्यवस्था और सांस्कृतिक जीवन पर गहरा प्रभाव डाला। ब्रिटिश शासन ने पारंपरिक उद्योगों, कुटीर उत्पादन और ग्रामीण अर्थव्यवस्था को कमजोर किया, जिसके परिणामस्वरूप व्यापक गरीबी, बेरोजगारी और पलायन बढ़ा। भूमि–राजस्व प्रणालियों जैसे- ज़मींदारी, रैयतवाड़ी और महालवाड़ी ने किसानों पर भारी बोझ डाला और ग्रामीण समाज में असमानता बढ़ाई। सामाजिक दृष्टि से औपनिवेशिक शिक्षा ने आधुनिक चेतना, तार्किक विचार और वैज्ञानिक दृष्टिकोण को जन्म दिया, जिससे सुधारवादी आंदोलनों को गति मिली। राजा राममोहन राय, ज्योतिबा फुले, ईश्वरचंद्र विद्यासागर, महात्मा गांधी और डॉ. अंबेडकर जैसे नेताओं ने बाल विवाह, सती प्रथा, अस्पृश्यता, लैंगिक असमानता और जातिगत भेदभाव के खिलाफ आवाज उठाई। अंग्रेजों ने कानून, प्रशासन और परिवहन में परिवर्तन किए, परंतु इनका उद्देश्य शासन को मजबूत करना था, न कि भारतीय समाज का कल्याण। राजनीतिक जागरूकता बढ़ने से राष्ट्रवाद का उदय हुआ और स्वाधीनता आंदोलन व्यापक जन–सहभागिता के साथ आगे बढ़ा। साम्राज्यवाद ने एक ओर भारतीय समाज को विभाजित किया, वहीं दूसरी ओर एक साझा राष्ट्रीय पहचान को भी जन्म दिया औपनिवेशिक शासन सामाजिक परिवर्तन का कारण बना, परंतु चुनौतियाँ अत्यंत गंभीर और दूरगामी थीं।

समाजशास्त्र के अनुसार समाज में परिवर्तन विभिन्न आंतरिक और बाह्य कारकों के प्रभाव से होता है। परिवर्तन की प्रमुख प्रक्रियाओं में सांस्कृतिक प्रसार, आधुनिकीकरण, औद्योगीकरण, नगरीकरण, वैश्वीकरण, शिक्षा, संचार माध्यम, तकनीकी नवाचार और राजनीतिक आंदोलनों का महत्त्वपूर्ण योगदान होता है। सांस्कृतिक प्रसार से एक समाज दूसरे समाज की विचारधाराओं, तकनीकों, मान्यताओं और जीवनशैलियों को अपनाता है, जिससे नई सामाजिक संरचनाएँ विकसित होती हैं। आधुनिकीकरण व्यक्ति

में तार्किकता, वैज्ञानिक दृष्टिकोण, समानता और मानवाधिकार जागरूकता को बढ़ाता है। औद्योगीकरण और नगरीकरण से आर्थिक अवसर बढ़ते हैं, लेकिन साथ ही परिवार संरचना का परिवर्तन, प्रवासन, वर्ग निर्माण और सामाजिक गतिशीलता की नई स्थितियाँ उत्पन्न होती हैं। वैश्वीकरण ने सूचना, तकनीक, व्यापार और संस्कृति को वैश्विक पैमाने पर जोड़कर सामाजिक परिवर्तन की गति को तेज कर दिया है। शिक्षा सामाजिक परिवर्तन की केंद्र बिंदु है, क्योंकि यह व्यक्तित्व, दृष्टिकोण और व्यवहार को पुनर्गठित करती है। समाज में राजनीतिक आंदोलनों और सामाजिक सुधारों ने समानता, न्याय और स्वतंत्रता के मूल्यों को मजबूत किया है। इस प्रकार समाजशास्त्रीय दृष्टि से सामाजिक परिवर्तन एक सतत, बहु–आयामी और जटिल प्रक्रिया है, जो समाज को निरंतर नई दिशाओं में विकसित करती है।

स्वतंत्रता के बाद सामाजिक और आर्थिक नीतियों का प्रभाव

स्वतंत्रता के बाद भारत ने एक समावेशी और संतुलित विकास की दिशा में कई सामाजिक और आर्थिक नीतियाँ लागू कीं। भूमि सुधार, सार्वजनिक क्षेत्र का विकास, नियोजित औद्योगिक प्रोत्साहन, और पंचायती राज जैसी स्थानीय शासन व्यवस्थाएँ ग्रामीण और पिछड़े क्षेत्रों में विकास के लिए महत्वपूर्ण रही। पंचायती राज ने ग्राम स्तर पर प्रशासन और निर्णय लेने की प्रक्रिया में जनता की भागीदारी सुनिश्चित की। योजना आयोग और बाद में नीति आयोग के माध्यम से केंद्र और राज्य स्तर पर योजनाबद्ध विकास को गति मिली। सामाजिक दृष्टि से संविधान ने समानता, अल्पसंख्यक अधिकार, अनुसूचित जाति- जनजाति के लिए आरक्षण और महिला सशक्तिकरण के लिए कानून बनाए, जिससे समाजिक न्याय और अवसरों की समानता सुनिश्चित हो सकी। आर्थिक दृष्टि से 1950– 1990 के दशक में उद्योग और कृषि में विकास के लिए सार्वजनिक निवेश और औद्योगिक नीतियों को महत्व दिया गया, जबकि 1991के आर्थिक उदारीकरण ने निजी क्षेत्र और वैश्विक व्यापार को प्रोत्साहन दिया। इन नीतियों ने गरीबी कम करने, शिक्षा और स्वास्थ्य सेवाओं तक पहुँच बढ़ाने,

और सामाजिक गतिशीलता को सशक्त बनाने में योगदान दिया, असमानता और क्षेत्रीय अंतर अभी भी चुनौतियाँ हैं।

वर्तमान सामाजिक संरचना: परिवार, जाति, वर्ग और लिंग की स्थिति

वर्तमान भारतीय समाज में परिवार, जाति, वर्ग और लिंग के कारक समाज की संरचना को प्रभावित करते हैं। परिवार पारंपरिक संयुक्त परिवार से धीरे–धीरे छोटे, एकल परिवारों की ओर बढ़ रहा है, विशेषकर शहरी क्षेत्रों में। इसका प्रभाव सामाजिक समर्थन, मूल्य प्रणाली और संसाधनों के वितरण पर देखा जा सकता है। जाति संरचना सामाजिक पहचान, विवाह, और अवसरों के वितरण में अभी भी प्रभावशाली है, हालांकि संविधान और सामाजिक आंदोलनों ने जातिगत भेदभाव को कम करने के प्रयास किए हैं। वर्ग संरचना आर्थिक स्थिति, शिक्षा, पेशा और संपत्ति के आधार पर विकसित होती है। भारत में मध्यम वर्ग का विस्तार और उच्च वर्ग की वैश्विक संपर्क क्षमता बढ़ी है। लैंगिक दृष्टि से महिलाएं शिक्षा और रोजगार में अधिक सक्रिय हो रही हैं, लेकिन लैंगिक असमानता, घरेलू जिम्मेदारियाँ, और समान वेतन की कमी जैसी चुनौतियाँ अभी भी विद्यमान हैं। शिक्षा, मीडिया, डिजिटल प्लेटफ़ॉर्म और कानूनी सुधार समाज की समग्र गतिशीलता को प्रभावित कर रहे हैं। आधुनिक भारत में ये सभी कारक परस्पर जुड़े हुए हैं और सामाजिक परिवर्तन, समानता और अवसरों की व्यापकता में निर्णायक भूमिका निभाते हैं।

तकनीकी और डिजिटल उन्नति

भारत ने पिछले दो दशकों में तकनीकी और डिजिटल क्षेत्र में अभूतपूर्व विकास किया है। डिजिटल इंडिया अभियान, आधार प्रणाली, यूपीआई और ई–गवर्नेंस जैसी पहलों ने सरकारी सेवाओं और वित्तीय लेन–देन को अधिक पारदर्शी और सुलभ बनाया है। सूचना प्रौद्योगिकी उद्योग ने न केवल रोजगार के अवसर बढ़ाए, बल्कि वैश्विक अर्थव्यवस्था में भारत की प्रतिस्पर्धात्मक स्थिति को भी सुदृढ़ किया। स्टार्ट–अप इकोसिस्टम, ई–कॉमर्स, स्मार्ट सिटीज, क्लाउड सेवाएँ, आर्टिफिशियल इंटेलिजेंस, और डेटा एनालिटिक्स के क्षेत्र में भारत तेजी से अग्रणी बन रहा है। तकनीकी नवाचार ने शिक्षा, स्वास्थ्य, कृषि, और प्रशासनिक प्रक्रिया को भी डिजिटल रूप दिया है। ग्रामीण क्षेत्रों में मोबाइल और इंटरनेट पहुँच ने डिजिटल

साक्षरता बढ़ाई है इसके साथ ही साइबर सुरक्षा, डिजिटल भेदभाव और डेटा गोपनीयता जैसी चुनौतियाँ भी सामने आई हैं। समग्र रूप से, तकनीकी और डिजिटल विकास ने भारत की आर्थिक उत्पादकता, प्रशासनिक दक्षता, नवाचार क्षमता और वैश्विक प्रतिस्पर्धा को सुदृढ़ किया है, जिससे देश आधुनिक, स्मार्ट और समावेशी राष्ट्र बनने की दिशा में आगे बढ़ रहा है।

समकालीन चुनौतियाँ: बेरोजगारी, असमानता, भ्रष्टाचार, पर्यावरणीय संकट

आज भारत अनेक समकालीन सामाजिक और आर्थिक चुनौतियों का सामना कर रहा है। बेरोजगारी- विशेषकर युवा और उच्च शिक्षा प्राप्त वर्ग में चिंता का विषय है जो सामाजिक असंतोष, अपराध दर और आर्थिक विषमता को बढ़ाता है। आर्थिक असमानता ग्रामीण और शहरी क्षेत्रों, जाति और वर्ग के बीच अवसरों में अंतर पैदा करती है, जिससे समाज में असंतुलन और सामाजिक संघर्ष की संभावना बढ़ती है। भ्रष्टाचार सरकारी और निजी संस्थाओं में पारदर्शिता और विश्वसनीयता को प्रभावित करता है, और विकास योजनाओं के प्रभाव को कमजोर करता है। पर्यावरणीय संकट भी गहन है, जिसमें जलवायु परिवर्तन, वायु और जल प्रदूषण, जंगलों और जैव विविधता का नुकसान शामिल है। औद्योगिकीकरण, नगरीकरण, अत्यधिक ऊर्जा खपत और रासायनिक कृषि ने प्राकृतिक संसाधनों पर दबाव बढ़ाया है और इसका समाधान नीति सुधार, रोजगार सृजन, पारदर्शिता, सतत विकास, तकनीकी नवाचार और नागरिक जागरूकता के माध्यम से ही संभव है। इसके अलावा, सामाजिक और वैश्विक सहयोग की भूमिका भी महत्वपूर्ण है, क्योंकि वैश्विक पर्यावरणीय संकट और आर्थिक असमानताएँ अकेले किसी राष्ट्र द्वारा हल नहीं की जा सकतीं। इस प्रकार, भारत की विकास यात्रा इन चुनौतियों से निपटने के लिए समन्वित रणनीति, राजनीतिक इच्छाशक्ति और नागरिक सहभागिता पर निर्भर करती है।

भारत में सतत विकास की अवधारणा

भारत में सतत विकास का सिद्धांत प्राकृतिक संसाधनों की सुरक्षा, आर्थिक वृद्धि, सामाजिक न्याय और पर्यावरणीय संतुलन को एक साथ जोड़ने पर आधारित है। सतत विकास का उद्देश्य वर्तमान पीढ़ी की आवश्यकताओं को पूरा करना है, बिना भविष्य की पीढ़ियों की जरूरतों और संसाधनों पर खतरा डाले। भारत ने इसके लिए नवीकरणीय ऊर्जा, जल प्रबंधन, हरित परिवहन, कचरा प्रबंधन और जैव विविधता संरक्षण जैसी योजनाओं को अपनाया है। शिक्षा, स्वास्थ्य, महिला सशक्तिकरण और ग्रामीण विकास भी सतत विकास के महत्वपूर्ण आयाम हैं। डिजिटल तकनीक और नवाचार संसाधनों के कुशल उपयोग में सहायक हैं। सतत विकास की वैश्विक अवधारणा की शुरुआत 1987में संयुक्त राष्ट्र की ब्रंटलैंड आयोग की रिपोर्ट ष्आवर कॉमन फ्यूचरष से हुई, जिसमें सतत विकास की परिभाषा दी गई थी। वर्ष 2000में सहस्त्राब्दी विकास लक्ष्य लागू किए गए, जिनके आठ लक्ष्य दुनिया के सामाजिक और आर्थिक विकास के मानदंड बने। वर्ष 2015 में इसे और व्यापक रूप देकर सतत विकास लक्ष्य घोषित किए गए, जिनमें 17लक्ष्यों के तहत गरीबी उन्मूलन, शिक्षा, स्वास्थ्य, लैंगिक समानता, जल और स्वच्छता, ऊर्जा, जलवायु कार्रवाई और वैश्विक साझेदारी शामिल हैं। भारत ने इन लक्ष्यों को अपने राष्ट्रीय विकास कार्यक्रमों और नीति आयोग के माध्यम से लागू किया है। सतत विकास का यह दृष्टिकोण सामाजिक समावेशन, आर्थिक अवसरों की समानता और पर्यावरण संरक्षण को जोड़कर भारत के लिए दीर्घकालिक और संतुलित विकास मार्ग प्रस्तुत करता है। यदि यह रणनीति सही ढंग से लागू की जाए, तो भारत आर्थिक, सामाजिक और पर्यावरणीय स्थिरता में अग्रणी बन सकता है।

विकसित भारत 2047 का लक्ष्य

विकसित भारत 2047 का **लक्ष्य** स्वतंत्रता के सौवें वर्ष तक भारत को एक संपूर्ण विकसित राष्ट्र बनाने का लक्ष्य रखता है। यह **लक्ष्य** केवल आर्थिक वृद्धि तक सीमित नहीं है, बल्कि मानव संसाधन, सामाजिक समानता, न्याय, पर्यावरणीय संतुलन और सांस्कृतिक मूल्यों के विकास को भी समाहित करती है। इस **लक्ष्य** के अनुसार भारत को वैश्विक मंच पर एक

प्रभावशाली, नवाचार–सक्षम और तकनीकी रूप से अग्रणी राष्ट्र के रूप में स्थापित किया जाना है। इसके लिए शिक्षा, स्वास्थ्य, रोजगार, डिजिटल नवाचार और सतत विकास पर विशेष ध्यान दिया गया है। विकसित भारत का विज़न सामाजिक समावेशन और समान अवसर पर भी केंद्रित है। इसमें ग्रामीण और शहरी क्षेत्रों के बीच संतुलन, कमजोर वर्गों का सशक्तिकरण, महिला और युवाओं की भागीदारी, और लैंगिक समानता पर जोर दिया गया है। डिजिटल और तकनीकी क्षेत्रों में निवेश, स्टार्ट–अप इकोसिस्टम, स्मार्ट सिटीज़, कृत्रिम बुद्धिमत्ता और विज्ञान–आधारित नवाचार इसे सशक्त बनाने के प्रमुख साधन हैं। इसके साथ ही पारंपरिक ज्ञान प्रणाली, जैसे आयुर्वेद, योग, कृषि परंपराएँ और स्थानीय हस्तकला, भी इस विज़न में शामिल हैं, जिससे विकास सांस्कृतिक और सामाजिक मूल्यों के साथ संतुलित हो। विकसित भारत 2047में पर्यावरणीय स्थिरता भी एक अनिवार्य तत्व है जलवायु परिवर्तन, प्रदूषण, संसाधन क्षरण और जैव विविधता ह्रास जैसी चुनौतियों का समाधान नवीकरणीय ऊर्जा, स्वच्छ परिवहन, सतत कृषि और जल संरक्षण के माध्यम से किया जाएगा। इस दृष्टि में नवाचार और तकनीकी प्रगति के साथ–साथ नैतिक और सामाजिक मूल्यों की भी अहम भूमिका है। इसके अतिरिक्त यह **लक्ष्य** वैश्विक नेतृत्व की दिशा में भारत को एक ऐसा राष्ट्र बनने की योजना है जो न केवल अपनी जनता के लिए समृद्धि और न्याय सुनिश्चित करे, बल्कि वैश्विक स्तर पर सतत विकास, नवाचार और सांस्कृतिक आदान–प्रदान में योगदान दे। इसके लिए सरकारी नीतियाँ, निजी क्षेत्र, शैक्षिक संस्थाएँ और नागरिक समाज मिलकर कार्य करेंगे। यदि यह **लक्ष्य** सफलतापूर्वक लागू होता है, तो भारत 2047तक एक समृद्ध, समानतापूर्ण, तकनीकी रूप से सक्षम और विश्व स्तर पर जिम्मेदार राष्ट्र के रूप में उभर सकता है।

शिक्षा, रोजगार और सामाजिक न्याय की संभावनाएँ

शिक्षा, रोजगार और सामाजिक न्याय भारत के समग्र विकास के प्रमुख स्तंभ हैं। शिक्षा के माध्यम से मानव पूंजी का विकास होता है और यह नवाचार, कौशल और सामाजिक चेतना को बढ़ावा देती है। राष्ट्रीय शिक्षा नीति *2020*बहुविषयक और कौशल–केंद्रित शिक्षा पर जोर देती है, जिससे रोजगार की संभावनाएँ और सामाजिक समावेशन बढ़ता है। रोजगार सृजन केवल आर्थिक वृद्धि नहीं सुनिश्चित करता, बल्कि सामाजिक स्थिरता और समान अवसर प्रदान करता है। इसमें डिजिटल और तकनीकी क्षेत्रों में नए अवसर विशेष रूप से युवाओं के लिए महत्वपूर्ण हैं। सामाजिक न्याय के अंतर्गत अनुसूचित जाति, जनजाति, महिला और अन्य कमजोर वर्गों के लिए समान अवसर, आरक्षण और सशक्तिकरण शामिल है। शिक्षा और रोजगार के माध्यम से समाज में लैंगिक समानता, सामाजिक समावेशन और अवसरों की समानता सुनिश्चित की जा सकती है। यह तीनों क्षेत्र आपस में जुड़े हुए हैं और समग्र विकास की नींव रखते हैं। यदि सही नीतियाँ और कार्यक्रम लागू किए जाएँ, तो भारत न केवल आर्थिक रूप से सशक्त बन सकता है, बल्कि सामाजिक न्याय और समान अवसर के आदर्श को भी पूर्ण रूप से प्राप्त कर सकता है।

तकनीकी नवाचार और सामाजिक परिवर्तन

तकनीकी नवाचार समाज में बदलाव और विकास के प्रमुख साधन बन गए हैं भारत में डिजिटल इंडिया, आर्टिफिशियल इंटेलिजेंस, क्लाउड तकनीक, डेटा एनालिटिक्स, स्टार्ट–अप इकोसिस्टम और स्मार्ट सिटीज जैसे पहल ने प्रशासन, शिक्षा, स्वास्थ्य और व्यवसाय में क्रांति ला दी है। तकनीकी नवाचार ने पारंपरिक प्रक्रियाओं को सरल, त्वरित और अधिक प्रभावशाली बनाया है। शिक्षा और स्वास्थ्य सेवाओं तक पहुँच डिजिटल प्लेटफ़ॉर्म के माध्यम से बढ़ी है, और रोजगार के नए अवसर उत्पन्न हुए हैं। तकनीकी विकास ने सामाजिक गतिशीलता को भी प्रभावित किया है, जैसे ग्रामीण क्षेत्रों में डिजिटल साक्षरता, ऑनलाइन व्यापार और स्टार्ट–अप संस्कृति के माध्यम से स्थानीय अर्थव्यवस्था को सुदृढ़ करना। इसके साथ ही, तकनीकी नवाचार सामाजिक समानता, महिला सशक्तिकरण और कमजोर

वर्गों के लिए अवसर पैदा करने में भी सहायक है। डिजिटल विभाजन, साइबर सुरक्षा और डेटा गोपनीयता जैसी चुनौतियाँ भी उभर रही हैं समग्र रूप से, तकनीकी नवाचार न केवल आर्थिक और प्रशासनिक क्षेत्र में बल्कि सामाजिक परिवर्तन और मानव विकास में भी निर्णायक भूमिका निभा रहा है।

युवाओं और महिलाओं की भूमिका

युवाओं और महिलाओं का विकास और समाज में भागीदारी भारत के भविष्य को निर्धारित करने वाले कारक हैं युवा वर्ग देश की नवाचार क्षमता, उद्यमिता और सामाजिक ऊर्जा का स्रोत है सही शिक्षा, कौशल प्रशिक्षण और रोजगार अवसर उन्हें सशक्त बनाते हैं और आर्थिक वृद्धि में योगदान करते हैं। महिला सशक्तिकरण समाजिक समानता, लैंगिक न्याय और परिवारिक और समुदायिक विकास के लिए आवश्यक है शिक्षा, रोजगार, नेतृत्व और नीति निर्माण में महिलाओं की भागीदारी समाज की समग्र प्रगति को सुनिश्चित करती है। युवाओं और महिलाओं की सक्रिय सहभागिता सामाजिक बदलाव, नवाचार और लोकतांत्रिक प्रक्रियाओं को भी सुदृढ़ करती है। सरकारी योजनाओं, आरक्षण और कौशल विकास कार्यक्रमों के माध्यम से यह समूह अधिक सशक्त और स्वतंत्र बन रहा है। युवा और महिला नेतृत्व केवल आर्थिक विकास तक सीमित नहीं है, बल्कि वे सामाजिक न्याय, पर्यावरणीय जागरूकता और सांस्कृतिक संरक्षण में भी महत्वपूर्ण भूमिका निभा रहे हैं। यदि युवाओं और महिलाओं को सही दिशा और अवसर दिए जाएँ, तो भारत **2047** तक एक सशक्त, समानतापूर्ण और समृद्ध राष्ट्र के रूप में विकसित हो सकता है।

चरण	मुख्य विशेषताएँ	सामाजिक परिवर्तन	आर्थिक स्थिति / सुधार	तकनीकी व प्रशासनिक परिवर्तन	विकसित भारत 2047 से संबंध
प्राचीन भारत	उच्च शिक्षा (तक्षशिला, नालंदा), उन्नत कृषि, गणित, चिकित्सा, वास्तुकला का विकास	वर्ण-व्यवस्था, संयुक्त परिवार व्यवस्था, स्थानीय स्वशासन	कृषि-प्रधान अर्थव्यवस्था, व्यापारिक नेटवर्क	धातुकर्म, जल-प्रबंधन, आयुर्वेद, ज्योतिष	भारत की ज्ञान परंपरा 2047 के "Knowledge Economy" का आधार
मध्यकालीन भारत	सांस्कृतिक समन्वय, कला, स्थापत्य, संगीत का विकास	नई सामाजिक मिश्रित संस्कृति, सूफी-भक्ति आंदोलन	कृषि और कुटीर उद्योग केंद्र में	सिंचाई प्रणालियाँ, स्थापत्य तकनीक	सांस्कृतिक विविधता 2047 की "Inclusive Society" को मजबूत करती है
औपनिवेशिक काल	संघर्ष, दमन, संसाधनों का दोहन	सामाजिक सुधार आंदोलन का उदय	पारंपरिक उद्योगों का पतन, गरीबी	पश्चिमी शिक्षा, रेलवे, पोस्ट, प्रशासनिक ढाँचा	आधुनिक शासन व्यवस्था का आधार

					जो 2047 में पारदर्शिता व सुशासन की नींव बनता है
स्वतंत्र भारत (1947–1990)	राष्ट्र निर्माण, संविधान, लोकतंत्र की स्थापना	समानता, आरक्षण, पंचायती राज की शुरुआत	योजना-आधारित अर्थव्यवस्था, सार्वजनिक क्षेत्र का विस्तार	वैज्ञानिक संस्थानों की स्थापना, हरित क्रांति	सामाजिक न्याय व बुनियादी ढाँचा जिन पर 2047 की विकास योजना निर्भर
उदारीकरण युग (1991–2014)	वैश्वीकरण, निजीकरण, उदारीकरण	नया मध्यम वर्ग, शहरीकरण	विदेशी निवेश, IT सेक्टर, तेज आर्थिक वृद्धि	कंप्यूटराइजेशन, डिजिटल बैंकिंग	"Digital India" की जड़ें जिनसे 2047 की तकनीकी शक्ति उत्पन्न
न्यू इंडिया युग (2014–वर्तमान)	सबका साथ–सबका विकास, सबका विश्वास	महिलाओं, युवाओं व ग्रामीणों की भागीदारी	स्टार्टअप, इंफ्रास्ट्रक्चर, मेक इन इंडिया	UPI, Aadhaar, AI, 5G, स्मार्ट सिटीज़	2047 के लिए मजबूत आर्थिक-तकनीकी नींव
वर्तमान चुनौति	बेरोजगारी, सामाजिक	जाति-लिंग	कौशल की कमी,	साइबर सुरक्षा, डेटा	2047 लक्ष्य इन

याँ	असमानता, ग्रामीण-शहरी अंतर	आधारित असमानता	संसाधनों का असमान वितरण	संरक्षण	चुनौतियों को दूर करने पर केंद्रित
सतत विकास	स्वच्छता, शिक्षा, स्वास्थ्य, ऊर्जा	लैंगिक समानता, समावेशन	पर्यावरण संरक्षण आधारित अर्थव्यवस्था	नवीकरणीय ऊर्जा, ग्रीन टेक	2047 का आधार: पर्यावरण + अर्थव्यवस्था + समाज तीनों का संतुलन
तकनीकी क्रांति	AI, Robotics, Blockchain, Biotechnology	डिजिटल सहभागिता	Gig economy, Digital Jobs	UPI, DigiLocker, Smart Governance	2047 में "Tech-Powered Nation" बनने की दिशा
विक्सित भारत 2047 का लक्ष्य	आत्मनिर्भर, समावेशी, आधुनिक भारत	सामाजिक न्याय, समान अवसर	विश्व की शीर्ष 3 अर्थव्यवस्थाओं में स्थान	AI-Based Governance, Green Energy	2047: विकसित, न्यायपूर्ण, स्थायी और वैश्विक नेतृत्व वाला भारत

भारत की विकास यात्रा का निष्कर्ष

भारत की विकास यात्रा सदियों से विविध सामाजिक, आर्थिक और राजनीतिक प्रक्रियाओं का परिणाम रही है। उपनिवेशीय युग में शोषण और संसाधनों की लूट ने समाज की आर्थिक और सामाजिक संरचना को प्रभावित किया। स्वतंत्रता के बाद भारत ने समावेशी विकास, शिक्षा और औद्योगिकरण पर ध्यान दिया। ग्रामीण क्षेत्रों में पंचायत व्यवस्था और सामाजिक योजनाओं ने समाजिक न्याय और नागरिक सहभागिता को बढ़ावा दिया। **1991** के आर्थिक उदारीकरण ने वैश्विक अर्थव्यवस्था से जुड़कर तकनीकी नवाचार और निजी क्षेत्र की भागीदारी को बढ़ाया। शिक्षा और स्वास्थ्य क्षेत्रों में सुधार ने मानव पूंजी का निर्माण किया, जबकि डिजिटल तकनीक ने प्रशासन और सेवाओं में क्रांति लाई। विकास की यह यात्रा केवल आर्थिक प्रगति तक सीमित नहीं है, बल्कि सामाजिक समावेशन, लैंगिक समानता, सांस्कृतिक संरक्षण और पर्यावरणीय स्थिरता का संतुलन सुनिश्चित करती है। यह निष्कर्ष स्पष्ट करता है कि भारत का विकास समग्र और सतत दृष्टिकोण पर आधारित है, जिसमें सामाजिक संरचना, नीति निर्माण और नागरिक सहभागिता का महत्वपूर्ण योगदान है।

आने वाले कल के लिए तैयारियाँ

आने वाले कल के लिए भारत को एक समग्र और सतत विकास रणनीति अपनानी होगी इसके लिए शिक्षा और कौशल विकास को प्राथमिकता दी जानी चाहिए, ताकि युवा रोजगार, नवाचार और सामाजिक प्रगति में सक्रिय भूमिका निभा सकें। डिजिटल तकनीक, स्टार्ट–अप इकोसिस्टम और स्मार्ट सिटीज़ जैसी पहलों से प्रशासनिक दक्षता और आर्थिक अवसर बढ़ेंगे। सामाजिक संरचनाओं में समान अवसर, महिला और कमजोर वर्गों की भागीदारी, सामाजिक न्याय और लैंगिक समावेशन सुनिश्चित करना आवश्यक है। पर्यावरणीय स्थिरता, जलवायु अनुकूल बुनियादी ढांचा और नवीकरणीय ऊर्जा के उपाय भी भविष्य की तैयारी का हिस्सा हैं। इसके साथ ही नागरिकों, शैक्षिक संस्थाओं और सरकारी नीतियों के बीच सहयोग और जिम्मेदारी भी अनिवार्य है। वैश्विक साझेदारी, तकनीकी और सांस्कृ

तिक सहयोग भारत को अंतरराष्ट्रीय स्तर पर प्रतिस्पर्धी और जिम्मेदार राष्ट्र बनाएंगे। आने वाले कल की तैयारी यह सुनिश्चित करती है कि भारत न केवल आर्थिक रूप से सशक्त हो, बल्कि सामाजिक न्याय, मानव विकास और पर्यावरणीय स्थिरता के साथ एक संतुलित और समावेशी राष्ट्र बने।

विकसित भारत 2047 का समाजशास्त्रीय दृष्टिकोण से विवेचन

विकसित भारत 2047का समाजशास्त्रीय विश्लेषण यह स्पष्ट करता है कि देश का विकास केवल आर्थिक वृद्धि या तकनीकी नवाचार तक सीमित नहीं हो सकता। यह दृष्टिकोण समाज में समान अवसर, सामाजिक न्याय, सांस्कृतिक समावेशन और मानव विकास पर केंद्रित है। सामाजिक संरचना और परिवर्तन के अध्ययन के आधार पर यह स्पष्ट होता है कि शिक्षा, स्वास्थ्य, रोजगार, महिला और युवा सशक्तिकरण, और सामाजिक संस्थाएँ विकास की रीढ़ हैं। सामाजिक गतिशीलता और सामाजिक समावेशन सुनिश्चित करने के लिए नीति निर्माण, योजनाओं का प्रभावी कार्यान्वयन और नागरिकों की सक्रिय भागीदारी आवश्यक है। वैश्वीकरण और डिजिटल तकनीक के माध्यम से भारत वैश्विक स्तर पर प्रतिस्पर्धा में अग्रणी बन सकता है, लेकिन इसके साथ सामाजिक असमानताओं और सांस्कृतिक मूल्यों का संतुलन बनाए रखना भी आवश्यक है। समाजशास्त्रीय दृष्टिकोण यह बताता है कि विकसित भारत 2047केवल भौतिक संसाधनों और आर्थिक प्रगति से नहीं, बल्कि सामाजिक न्याय, मानव गरिमा और पर्यावरणीय स्थिरता के संतुलन से ही स्थायी रूप से सशक्त बन सकता है।

सन्दर्भ ग्रंथ सूची

- Altekar, A. S. (1965). *Education in Ancient India.* Nand Kishore & Bros.
- Basu, K. (2015). *India's economic transition: The impact of reforms.* Oxford University Press.

- Basham, A. L. (2001). *The Wonder That Was India* (3rd ed.). Rupa Publications.
- Bhagat, R. B., & Mohanty, S. (2010). *Youth unemployment in India: Challenges and strategies.* Economic and Political Weekly, 45(11), 36–44.
- Chandra, B. (2016). *India's Struggle for Independence* (2nd ed.). Penguin Books.
- Chattopadhyaya, D. (1991). *Science and Society in Ancient India.* Research India Publications.
- Chakraborty, P. (2010). *Planning and development in post-independence India.* Sage Publications.
- Choudhury, P. (2020). *Digital India: Opportunities and challenges.* Journal of Technology and Society, 12(3), 45–60.
- Desai, A. R. (1948). *Social Background of Indian Nationalism.* Popular Prakashan.
- Garla, S., & Tiwari, S. (2025). *Vision of Viksit Bharat @2047: A Bird's Eye View.* BIM GKP Journal. Retrieved from PDF of the journal.
- Gulati, A. U. P. (2025). *Leave No One Behind: AI Powered Inclusive Development for Viksit Bharat 2047.* Ushus: Journal of Business Management. DOI: 10.12725/ujbm.68.2
- Kamboj, G., Mili, D., Bala, M., & Sharma, T. (Eds.). (2025). *Viksit Bharat @2047: Innovation, Inclusion and Sustainable Development.* Bhumi Publishing. DOI: 10.5281/zenodo.17056182
- Karthikeyan, T. (2025). *Envisioning the Future of MSMEs in India: A Study of Opportunities and Challenges in Vision VIKSIT BHARAT @2047.* International Journal of Scientific Innovation (IJSCI), 2(8), 338–354. DOI: 10.70849/IJSCI
- Kolekar, P. N. (2025). *Viksit Bharat 2047: Pathways to a Developed, Inclusive and Sustainable India.* ಅಕ್ಷರಸೂರ್ಯ (Aksharasurya), 9(02), 06–11.

- Kumar, A., & Singh, R. (2019). *E-Governance and Digital Transformation in India.* Springer.
- Kumar, P. (2025). *Atmanirbhar Krishi for Viksit Bharat 2047: Roadmap for Self Reliance.* Agricultural Engineering Today, 49(2). DOI: 10.52151/aet2025492.1843
- Kumar, S., Pandita, P., & Singh, K. (2025). *Reimagining Indian Education for Viksit Bharat @2047: Addressing the Challenges of Shadow Education and Inequity.* RESEARCH REVIEW: International Journal of Multidisciplinary, 10(6), 72–81. DOI: 10.31305/rrijm.2025.v10.n6.009
- Kosambi, D. D. (1990). *An Introduction to the Study of Indian History* (3rd ed.). Popular Prakashan.
- Mehta, P. (2025). *VIKSIT BHARAT @ 2047: A Vision for Prosperity and Progress.* Archives. DOI: 10.25215/9389476593.04
- Metcalf, T., & Metcalf, B. (2012). *A Concise History of Modern India* (2nd ed.). Cambridge University Press.
- Ministry of Environment, Forest and Climate Change [MoEFCC]. (2018). *National Report on Sustainable Development in India.* Government of India.
- Ministry of Human Resource Development [MHRD]. (2020). *National Education Policy 2020.* Government of India.
- Rao, M. S. A. (2013). *Social Movements and Gender in India.* Orient Blackswan.
- Sharma, R. (2025). *Vision Viksit Bharat 2047: A Development Economics Perspective.* VEETHIKA: An International Interdisciplinary Research Journal, 10(04). DOI: 10.48001/veethika.1004007
- Sharma, R. S. (2005). *India's Ancient Past* (2nd ed.). Oxford University Press.
- Singh, J., & Gauba, S. (2025). *Key Challenges for Viksit Bharat@2047 Vision: Voice of Youth.* International Journal of Innovation and Multidisciplinary Research (IJIAMR), 4(1).

- Srinivas, M. N. (1966). *Social Change in Modern India.* University of California Press.
- Transparency International. (2021). *Corruption Perceptions Index 2021.* Transparency International.
- Uberoi, P. (2006). *Family, Kinship and Marriage in India.* Oxford University Press.
- United Nations Development Programme [UNDP]. (2020). *Sustainable Development Goals: India Progress Report.* UNDP.
- Veethika Journal. (2024). *Vision Viksit Bharat 2047: Integrated Framework of Traditional Knowledge and Development Economics.* VEETHIKA, 10(4). DOI:10.48001/veethika.1004007
- World Bank. (2019). *India: Digital Economy Report.* World Bank Publications.

Chapter- 13
विकसित भारत 2047 की रणनीतिः
वस्तु एवं सेवा कर

सौम्या रंजन

एम0ए0, एम0फिल0

पीएच0डी0 शोध छात्रा, अर्थशास्त्र, वीर बहादुर सिंह पूर्वांचल विश्वविद्यालय, जौनपुर (उ0प्र0)

वस्तु एवं सेवा कर (Goods and Services Tax : GST) को विकसित भारत 2047 की एक महत्वपूर्ण रणनीति समझी जा रही है। एक ऐतिहासिक कर बदलाव के रूप में वस्तु एवं सेवा कर (जीएसटी) को 1 जुलाई 2017 से लागू किया गया।

एक राष्ट्र, एक कर, एक बाजार

जीएसटी एक व्यापक अप्रत्यक्ष कर है जिसमें केन्द्र सरकार एवं राज्य सरकार उदगृहित एवं एकत्र किये जाने वाले कई अप्रत्यक्ष करों को सम्मिलित किया गया है। वस्तु एवं सेवा कर से 17 केन्द्रीय एवं राज्य कर तथा 22 प्रकार के उप कर एक ही कर में शामिल हो गए हैं।

- केन्द्र सरकार द्वारा उदगृहित एवं एकत्र किये जाने वाले निम्नलिखित करों को जीएसटी में सम्मिलित किया गया है–
    - ❖ केन्द्रीय उत्पाद शुल्क
    - ❖ उत्पाद शुल्क (औषधिक एवं प्रसाधन उत्पाद)
    - ❖ अतिरिक्त उत्पाद शुल्क (विशेष महत्व की वस्तुएँ)

- ❖ अतिरिक्त उत्पाद शुल्क (टेक्सटाइल एवं टेक्सटाइल उत्पाद)
- ❖ अतिरिक्त सीमा शुल्क (सामान्यतया इसे Countervailing Duty–सीवीडी के नाम से जाना जाता है)
- ❖ अतिरिक्त विशेष सीमा शुल्क (एसएडी)
- ❖ सेवा कर
- ❖ केन्द्रीय अधिभार एवं उप कर, जहाँ तक ये वस्तुओं और सेवाओं की आपूर्ति से सम्बन्धित है।

- राज्य सरकार द्वारा उद्गृहित एवं एकत्र किये जाने वाले निम्नलिखित करों को जीएसटी में सम्मिलित किया गया है–
  - ❖ राज्य वैट
  - ❖ केन्द्रीय बिक्री कर
  - ❖ विलासिता कर
  - ❖ क्रय कर (Purchase Tax)
  - ❖ प्रवेश कर (Entry Tax)
  - ❖ मनोरंजन कर (उनको छोड़कर जो स्थानीय निकायों द्वारा लगाए जाते हैं)
  - ❖ विज्ञापनों पर कर
  - ❖ लॉटरी, सट्टेबाजी एवं जुए पर कर
  - ❖ राज्य अधिभार एवं उपकर, जहाँ तक ये वस्तुओं एवं सेवाओं की आपूर्ति से सम्बन्धित है।

इस प्रकार जीएसटी में केन्द्र सरकार एवं राज्य सरकार को उपर्युक्त अप्रत्यक्ष करों को सम्मिलित करके एक एकीकृत कर (वस्तु एवं सेवा कर) का निर्माण किया गया है। स्वतन्त्रता के पश्चात् किया गया

सबसे बड़ा कर बदलाव जीएसटी 'एक देश, एक कर, एक बाजार' के लक्ष्य को पूरा करने के लिए संकल्पित है।

जीएसटी के पूर्व एवं जीएसटी के बाद की कर व्यवस्था

जीएसटी की पूर्ववर्ती व्यवस्था में जब कोई ग्राहक अपने व्यक्तिगत उपभोग के लिये किसी विशेष वस्तु/सेवा की खरीद करता था, तो उससे पहले उस वस्तु/सेवा को उत्पादन और आपूर्ति श्रृंखला के अनेक चरणों से होकर गुजरना पड़ता था, जिससे विभिन्न चरणों पर उस पर एक या अधिक अप्रत्यक्ष कर लगाए जाते थे। इनमें से कुछ कर केन्द्र सरकार और कुछ सम्बन्धित राज्य सरकारों द्वारा लगाए जाते थे। उदाहरण के लिए– भारत में निर्मित एक फ्रिज पर कारखाने से निकलने से पहले उत्पाद शुल्क लगाया जाता था, अगर उसमें आयातित पुर्जों या उपकरणों का प्रयोग किया जाता था तो इन वस्तुओं पर सीमा शुल्क लगाया जाता था, फिर निर्माता से थोक व्यापारी तक पहुँचने के सफर में उस पर बिक्री कर लगाया जाता था। फिर थोक व्यापारी से खुदरा व्यापारी तक पहुँचने पर उस फ्रिज पर वैट लगता था। राज्यों के बीच वस्तुओं की आवाजाही की स्थिति में यह व्यवस्था और जटिल हो जाती थी, क्योंकि तब उन वस्तुओं पर केन्द्रीय बिक्री कर लगता था, साथ ही हर राज्य में कर की दर भी अलग–अलग थी।

जीएसटी को वस्तुओं के विनिर्माण या वस्तुओं की बिक्री या सेवाओं के प्रावधान पर जो कर की पूर्ववत् अवधारणा थी, के एवज में वस्तुओं और सेवाओं की आपूर्ति पर लगाया गया है।

जीएसटी उत्पत्ति आधारित करारोपण के पूर्ववर्ती सिद्धान्त के बदले गन्तव्य आधारित उपभोग करारोपण के सिद्धान्त पर आधारित है अर्थात् यह एक गन्तव्य आधारित उपभोग कर है। जहाँ वस्तु एवं सेवा का उपभोग होगा, उसी राज्य अथवा संघ राज्य क्षेत्र को यह कर उपार्जित होगा। उदाहरणस्वरूप– यदि तमिलनाडु के एक उत्पादक ने तमिलनाडु से ही कच्चा माल खरीदा और वहीं पर वस्तु का उत्पादन करता है, लेकिन वस्तु का विक्रय एवं उपभोग दिल्ली में होता है तो दिल्ली को कर लाभ प्राप्त होगा, क्योंकि वस्तु का उपभोग दिल्ली में हुआ है। जीएसटी एक दोहरा कर है, जिसमें केन्द्र और राज्य दोनों एक साथ समान कर आधार पर कर

का उद्ग्रहण एवं संग्रहण करेंगे। वस्तुओं अथवा सेवाओं के राज्यान्तर्गत प्रदायों पर केन्द्र सरकार द्वारा वसूला जाने वाला जीएसटी केन्द्रीय जीएसटी (सीजीएसटी) और राज्यों के द्वारा (इनमें वे संघ राज्य क्षेत्र भी आते हैं, जिनका अपना विधानमण्डल है) लगाए जाने वाले जीएसटी को राज्य जीएसटी (एसजीएसटी) कहा जाएगा। बिना विधानमण्डल वाले संघ राज्यों द्वारा लगाए जाने वाले जीएसटी का संघ राज्य जीएसटी (यूटीजीएसटी) कहा जाएगा।

समेकित जीएसटी (आईजीएसटी) को वस्तुओं और सेवाओं की अन्तर्राज्यीय आपूर्ति पर लगाया जाएगा। इसे केन्द्र द्वारा वसूला जाएगा, ताकि 'क्रेडिट चेन' में कोई व्यवधान न आए। इस प्रकार,

- ❖ वस्तुओं के आयात को अन्तर्राज्यीय आपूर्ति माना जाएगा और इस पर लागू सीमा शुल्क के अलावा समेकित जीएसटी (आईजीएसटी) लगेगा।
- ❖ सेवाओं के आयात को अन्तर्राज्यीय आपूर्ति माना जाएगा और इन पर आईजीएसटी लगेगा।
- ❖ सीजीएसटी, एसजीएसटी, यूटीजीएसटी एवं आईजीएसटी को उस दर से लगाया जाएगा, जिस पर जीएसटी परिषद् सहमत हो।

जीएसटी की आवश्यकता के पीछे कारण

जीएसटी के प्रमुख कारण निम्नवत् है–

1. वस्तुओं एवं सेवाओं पर अलग–अलग कर की दरें

भारत में वस्तुओं एवं सेवाओं के कर अलग–अलग थे। ऐसे में वस्तुओं एवं सेवाओं के कर को एक ही कर व्यवस्था के अन्तर्गत लाना अनिवार्य था। ऐसी व्यवस्था में बहुत सारे करदाता अपने उत्पाद को कभी वस्तु मानते तो कभी सेवा एवं जिस पर भी कर की दर निम्न होगी उसी के अन्तर्गत अपने उत्पाद को रखते थे, जैसे– सॉफ्टवेयर। जीएसटी के द्वारा सभी वस्तुओं एवं सेवाओं पर कर की दर एक समान कर दी गई है।

2. सेनवैट एवं वैट की कर पर कर (Cascading) की समस्या

केन्द्र सरकार द्वारा वस्तुओं के उत्पादन पर लिया जाने वाला कर 'केन्द्रीय मूल्य वर्द्धित कर' (CENVAT) एवं राज्यों द्वारा वस्तुओं के विक्रय पर लिया जाने वाला कर 'मूल्य वर्द्धित कर' (VAT) के कारण 'कर पर कर' (Cascading) की समस्या विद्यमान थी, जिसका समाधान किया जाना आवश्यक था। जीएसटी के द्वारा इस समस्या का समाधान हो गया है।

3. अलग–अलग राज्यों में मूल्य वर्द्धित कर (वैट) की दरों में भिन्नता

भारत में अलग–अलग राज्यों में मूल्य वर्द्धित कर (VAT) की दर अलग–अलग चल रही थी, क्योंकि राज्यों में प्रतिस्पर्धा के परिणामस्वरूप एक राज्य अपने कर राजस्व को बढ़ाने के लिए मूल्य वर्द्धित कर (VAT) की दर को कम रखता है, ताकि वहाँ व्यापार अधिक तीव्र गति से बढ़ सके। इसके साथ ही 'एक राष्ट्र' की संकल्पना को साकार करने हेतु सम्पूर्ण देश में कर की एक समान दर अर्थात् एक ही कर प्रणाली आवश्यक थी। जीएसटी के माध्यम से पूरे देश में एक समान कर व्यवस्था लागू हो सकी।

4. प्रवेश कर एवं चुंगी कर की समस्या

एक वस्तु को किसी एक राज्य से दूसरे राज्य में भेजने पर उसके मार्ग में आने वाले प्रत्येक राज्य की सीमा पर प्रवेश कर एवं प्रत्येक नगरपालिका की सीमा पर चुंगी देनी पड़ती थी, जिससे उस वस्तु की लागत में वृद्धि हो जाती थी। इस वजह से एक ही कर की संकल्पना की आवश्यकता महसूस की गई, जिससे राज्यों के बीच वस्तुओं एवं सेवाओं का आवागमन आसान हो सके।

5. कर अनुपालन में आसानी

जीएसटी से 17 केन्द्रीय और राज्य कर तथा 22 प्रकार के उपकर केवल एक कर में शामिल हो गये हैं। इसके फलस्वरूप विविध करों की जटिलता समाप्त हो गयी है एवं अप्रत्यक्ष करों में महत्वपूर्ण सरलीकरण को प्राप्त किया जा सका है। विभिन्न राज्यों के मूल्य वर्द्धित कर (वैट) में 97

प्रकार के रिटर्न्स होते थे, जिन्हें भरने के लिए 28 ब्यौरों (Declarations) और 317 अनुबन्धों (Annexures) का आश्रय लेना पड़ता था। इसी तरह केन्द्रीय उत्पादन शुल्क के लिये 13 रिटर्न फॉर्म्स भरने के साथ एक ब्यौरा भी देना होता था। यहाँ तक कि चालान भी 12 तरह के होते थे। अब इन सभी की जगह पूरे देश में समान रूप से केवल एक चालान के साथ 12 फॉर्म भरने होते हैं। जीएसटी से कर का भुगतान करना और रिटर्न्स भरना सरल हो गया है। इससे कर अनुपालन आसान हो गया है।

6. केन्द्र सरकार और राज्य सरकारों के करों को जोड़ना

भारत में केन्द्र और राज्यों के अलग–अलग करों के कारण, भारत में करों की बहुलता की समस्या पाई जाती थी। इसलिए केन्द्र एवं राज्यों के करों को जोड़ना आवश्यक था, ताकि नागरिक आसानीपूर्वक करों का भुगतान कर सके। जीएसटी के द्वारा 'एक राष्ट्र–एक कर एक बाजार' की संकल्पना के उद्देश्य को प्राप्त किया जा रहा है।

जीएसटी प्रणाली की श्रेष्ठता

किसी वस्तु को उत्पादन से लेकर उपभोग तक कई चरणों से होकर गुजरना पड़ता है। भारत की कर व्यवस्था में 'कर पर कर' (Cascading) की समस्या मिलती थी। जैसे किसी वस्तु के निर्माण के लिये कच्चा माल खरीदने पर वैट (VAT) का भुगतान करना पड़ता था। उस कच्चे माल से निर्मित वस्तु को बेचने पर सेनबैट (CENVAT) का भुगतान करना पड़ता था। इसके बाद जब उत्पादक वस्तु को थोक विक्रेता को बेचते थे तब फिर से वैट (VAT) एवं थोक विक्रेता के द्वारा खुदरा विक्रेता को बेचने पर वैट (VAT) और फिर उपभोक्ता के क्रय करने पर भी फिर से वैट (VAT) का भुगतान किये जाने के कारण 'कर पर कर' (Cascading) की समस्या बनी हुई थी।

जीएसटी एक बहुचरणीय कर है। जीएसटी वस्तु के निर्माण से लेकर उपभोग तक हर चरण पर लगेगा। यह बहुस्तरीय संग्रहण विधि का अनुसरण करता है। इसमें प्रदाय (सप्लाई) के हर स्तर पर कर का भुगतान होता है और पिछले स्तर पर चुकाए गए कर का क्रेडिट प्रदाय के अगले

स्तर पर सैट ऑफ के लिए उपलब्ध होता है। प्रत्येक चरण पर जीएसटी लगने के परिणामस्वरूप 'कर पर कर' (Cascading) की समस्या का समाधान हो जाता है। प्रत्येक स्तर की आउटपुट कर देयताओं (Output Tax Liabilities) में से पीछे का इनपुट टैक्स क्रेडिट (Input Tax Credit) निकलता जाता है।

जीएसटी एक प्रकार से मूल्य वर्द्धित कर (VAT) है। मूल्य वर्द्धित कर किसी वस्तु के उत्पादन से लेकर उसके उपभोग तक प्रत्येक चरण पर किये जाने वाले मूल्य वर्द्धन (Value Addition) पर लगने वाला कर है।

इस प्रकार, जीएसटी में प्रत्येक चरण में कर भुगतान किया जाता है एवं किसी चरण में जितना कर भुगतान किया जाता है, उसमें से उससे पहले वाले चरण में किये गए कर भुगतान को घटा दिया जाता है। इस तरह, स्वतन्त्रता के पश्चात् किया गया सबसे बड़ा कर बदलाव जीएसटी 'एक देश, एक कर, एक बाजार' के लक्ष्य को पूरा करने के लिए संकल्पित है।

जीएसटी की श्रेणियाँ

भारत में जीएसटी की चार श्रेणियाँ (Categories) हैं–

CGST = Central Goods and Services Tax

SGST = State Goods and Services Tax

IGST = Integrated Goods and Services Tax

UTGST = Union Territory Goods and Services Tax

भारत एक संघीय 'राज्य' है, जहाँ केन्द्र और राज्यों को उपयुक्त कानून के माध्यम से करारोपण और करों को एकत्र करने की शक्तियाँ प्रदान की गई हैं। यह कर केन्द्र और राज्यों के द्वारा एक साथ सामान्य कर आधार पर आरोपित दोहरा कर है। कर का प्रशासन केन्द्र और राज्य सरकारों द्वारा किया गया है। एक राज्य के भीतर होने वाले लेन–देन पर केन्द्र सरकार द्वारा लगाये गये कर को केन्द्रीय जीएसटी (सीजीएसटी)

कहा जाता है एवं सीजीएसटी केन्द्र सरकार के खाते में जमा किया जाता है। राज्यों द्वारा लगाए करों को राज्य जीएसटी (एसजीएसटी) कहा गया है और एसजीएसटी सम्बन्धित राज्य सरकार के खाते में जमा किया जाता है। इसी प्रकार केन्द्र द्वारा प्रत्येक अन्तर–राज्य वस्तुओं और सेवाओं की आपूर्ति पर एकीकृत जीएसटी (आईजीएसटी) लगाने और प्रशासित करने को व्यवस्था है।

जीएसटी के अन्तर्गत निम्नलिखित तरीके से क्रेडिट का उपयोग करने की अनुमति है–

- ❖ सीजीएसटी और आईजीएसटी के भुगतान के लिए सीजीएसटी के इनपुट टैक्स क्रेडिट की अनुमति है।
- ❖ एसजीएसटी और आईजीएसटी के भुगतान के लिए एसजीएसटी के इनपुट टैक्स क्रेडिट की अनुमति है।
- ❖ यूटीजीएसटी और आईजीएसटी के भुगतान के लिए यूटीजीएसटी के इनपुट टैक्स क्रेडिट की अनुमति है।
- ❖ आईजीएसटी, सीजीएसटी और एसजीएसटी/यूटीजीएसटी के भुगतान के लिए आईजीएसटी के इनपुट टैक्स क्रेडिट की अनुमति है।
- ❖ एसजीएसटी/यूटीजीएसटी के भुगतान के लिए सोजीएसटी के इनपुट टैक्स क्रेडिट का उपयोग नहीं किया जाता और न ही सीजीएसटी के भुगतान के लिए एसजीएसटी/यूटीजीएसटी के इनपुट टैक्स क्रेडिट का उपयोग किया जाता है।

वस्तु एवं सेवा कर (जीएसटी) की विभिन्न दरें

जीएसटी से सम्बन्धित सभी महत्वपूर्ण मुद्दों (दर सहित) पर निर्णय लेने का पूरा अधिकार जीएसटी परिषद् (जीएसटी काउंसिल) को दिया गया है। जीएसटी के तहत प्रत्येक वस्तु या सेवा पर चार दरों में से कोई एक दर/स्लैब लागू होगा– 5 प्रतिशत, 12 प्रतिशत, 18 प्रतिशत, 28 प्रतिशत। इसके अलावा कुछ वस्तुओं को जीएसटी से छूट प्राप्त होगी जिसका अर्थ है कि इस स्थिति में यह स्लैब 0 प्रतिशत का होगा।

जीएसटी व्यवस्था के तहत किसी भी वस्तु या सेवा पर केवल एक ही कर की दर लागू होगी, जो देश के सभी राज्यों में एक समान होगी।

जीएसटी के तहत कृषि एवं सामान्य खाद्य उत्पादों, जैसे– छिलका उतरे हुए अनाज, अंडे, दालों, फल, सब्जियों, दूध इत्यादि को कर से छूट दी गई है। अन्य रोजमर्रा की आवश्यक वस्तुओं को 5 प्रतिशत की जीएसटी दर के अन्तर्गत रखा गया है। गौरतलब है कि जीएसटी परिषद् द्वारा विभिन्न वस्तुओं एवं उत्पादों पर जीएसटी की दरों में परिवर्तन किया जा सकता है।

जीएसटी दरें				
आईजीएसटी (प्रतिशत में)			**वर्गीकृत मदों की संख्या**	**जीएसटी के बाहर मुख्य वस्तुएँ**
सीजीएसटी (प्रतिशत में)	**एसजीएसटी (प्रतिशत में)**	**कुल (प्रतिशत में)**		
0 1.5 2.5	0 1.5 2.5	0 3 5	183 (15.07%) स्वर्ण एवं आभूषण 308 (25.37%)	• एल्कोहॉल • पेट्रोलियम और ऊर्जा • बिजली • भूमि और स्थावर सम्पदा
6 9 14	6 9 14	12 18 28	178 (14.66%) 517 (42.59%) 28 (2.31%)	• शिक्षा • स्वास्थ्य देखभाल

नोट– 1. आईजीएसटी केन्द्र और राज्य जीएसटी का योग है।

2. बिना तराशे हीरों पर जीएसटी की दर 0.25 प्रतिशत तथा तराशे एवं पॉलिश किये हीरों पर जीएसटी की दर 1.5 प्रतिशत है।

जीएसटी के दायरे से बाहर की वस्तुएँ

101वें संविधान संशोधन अधिनियम, 2016 के तहत अनुच्छेद 366 (12A) में जीएसटी की परिभाषा के माध्यम से मानव उपभोग के लिये

ऐल्कोहॉल को जीएसटी से बाहर रखा गया है। अस्थायी रूप से पाँच पेट्रोलियम उत्पाद अर्थात् पेट्रोलियम क्रूड, मोटर स्पिरिट (पेट्रोल), हाई स्पीड डीजल, प्राकृतिक गैस और विमानन टरबाइन ईंधन को जीएसटी से बाहर रखा गया है। इसके अलावा विद्युत को जीएसटी से बाहर रखा गया है। सभी पाँच विशिष्ट पेट्रोलियम उत्पादों (पेट्रोलियम क्रूड, पेट्रोल, डीजल, नेचुरल गैस, एटीएफ) पर उस तारीख से जीएसटी लगाया जाएगा जिस तारीख से लगाने के लिये जीएसटी परिषद् सिफारिश करेगी। इस प्रकार,

तम्बाकू और तम्बाकू उत्पादों पर भी जीएसटी लगाया जाएगा। इसके अतिरिक्त केन्द्र इस पर केन्द्रीय उत्पाद शुल्क लगाता रहेगा।

जीएसटी से छूट प्राप्त वस्तुओं एवं सेवाओं की सूची केन्द्र और सभी राज्यों के लिए समान होगी। जीएसटी एक व्यापक अप्रत्यक्ष कर है। यह कर पूरे भारत में एक समान रूप से लागू होता है।

जीएसटी 2.0

भारत में अप्रत्यक्ष कर सुधार (जीएसटी 2.0) को 22 सितम्बर 2025 को सम्पूर्ण देश में लागू किया गया। अब सिर्फ दो स्लैब– पाँच (5), तथा अठारह (18) प्रतिशत की दर से जीएसटी लागू रहेगा। इससे 12 और 28 प्रतिशत की दर खत्म हो गई है। 12 प्रतिशत के स्लैब में सम्मिलित 99 प्रतिशत वस्तुएँ 5 प्रतिशत के कर स्लैब में आ चुकी है। इसी तरह, 28 प्रतिशत के स्लैब में सम्मिलित अधिकांश वस्तुओं और सेवाओं पर अब 18 प्रतिशत कर लगेगा।

जीएसटी 2.0 की देरे निम्नवत् हैं–

ऐसे घटी जीएसटी की दरें

रोजमर्रा का जरूरी सामान सस्ता

वस्तुएँ	पहले	अब
तेल, शैम्पू, टूथपेस्ट, साबुन, ब्रश, शेविंग क्रीम	12%	5%
मक्खन, घी, पनीर व डेयरी स्प्रेड्स	12%	5%
नमकीन, भुजिया, मिक्सचर (पैक्ड)	12%	5%
फीडिंग बोतल, नैपकिन, क्लिनिकल, डायपर	12%	5%
सिलाई मशीन, पुर्जे और बर्तन	12%	5%

स्वास्थ्य, जीवन बीमा पर शून्य कर

वस्तुएँ	पहले	अब
स्वास्थ्य और जीवन बीमा	18%	शून्य
थर्मामीटर	18%	5%
मेडिकल ग्रेड ऑक्सीजन	12%	5%
ग्लूकोमीटर और टेस्ट स्ट्रिप	12%	5%
नजर के चश्मे	12%	5%

शिक्षा क्षेत्र में राहत

वस्तुएँ	पहले	अब
नक्शे, चार्ट, ग्लोब, पेंसिल	12%	शून्य
शार्पनर, क्रेयॉन्स, कॉपी	12%	शून्य
श्रबर	5%	शून्य

इलेक्ट्रॉनिक उपकरण

वस्तुएँ	पहले	अब
एसी	28%	18%
टेलीविजन (32 इंच से अधिक)	28%	18%

40 प्रतिशत का विशेष स्लैब

40 प्रतिशत के विशेष स्लैब में लग्जरी वस्तुएँ, महँगी कारें, कोल्ड ड्रिंक, सोडा वाले अन्य पेय और अन्य हानिकारक वस्तुएँ होंगी।

टिप्पणी

- 309 वस्तुओं पर 5 प्रतिशत जीएसटी लागू है।
- शेष सभी वस्तुएँ (40 प्रतिशत की स्लैब में आने वाली वस्तुओं को छोड़कर), 18 प्रतिशत की जीएसटी स्लैब के अंतर्गत हैं।
- 40 प्रतिशत का जीएसटी स्लैब मादक व हानिकर वस्तुओं पर लागू रहेगा।

जीएसटी के लाभ

जीएसटी पूरे देश के लिए एक लाभदायक व्यवस्था है। इससे अर्थव्यवस्था के सभी हितधारकों, केन्द्र सरकार, राज्य सरकारों, उद्यमियों, व्यापारियों एवं उपभोक्ताओं को लाभ होगा। जीएसटी से अर्थव्यवस्था को प्रोत्साहन मिलेगा और भारतीय वस्तुएँ एवं सेवाएँ वैश्विक स्तर पर प्रतिस्पर्धी बनेंगी। जीएसटी का लक्ष्य कर की दरों और प्रक्रियाओं में समरूपता लाकर और आर्थिक बाधाओं को हटाकर भारत की एक साझा राष्ट्रीय बाजार बनाना है, जिससे राष्ट्रीय स्तर पर एक एकीकृत अर्थव्यवस्था का मार्ग प्रशस्त हो सके।

जीएसटी से लाभ के विभिन्न बिन्दु निम्नलिखित हैं–

1. अर्थव्यवस्था को लाभ

- जीएसटी भारत के लिए एक एकीकृत सामान्य राष्ट्रीय बाजार बनाने में मदद करेगा, जिससे भारत में विदेशी निवेश को और 'मेक इन इंडिया' अभियान एवं 'व्यापार करने में आसानी' को बढ़ावा मिलेगा जिससे भारत को विनिर्माण केन्द्र बनाया जा सकेगा।
- जीएसटी के द्वारा 'कर पर कर' (Cascading) की समस्या को रोका जा सकेगा, क्योंकि इनपुट टैक्सस क्रेडिट सभी प्रकार की

वस्तुओं और सेवाओं पर तथा इनकी आपूर्ति के हर स्तर पर उपलब्ध होगी, जिससे वस्तुओं और सेवाओं की कीमतें कम हो जाएँगी। हमारे उत्पाद अन्तर्राष्ट्रीय बाजारों में प्रतिस्पर्धा कर सकेंगे तथा इस प्रकार निर्यात को बढ़ावा मिलेगा।

- जीएसटी के लागू होने से पूरे देश में केन्द्र एवं राज्यों के कर कानूनों, प्रक्रियाओं और कर की दरों में एकरूपता आएगी जिससे एक साझा राष्ट्रीय बाजार विकसित होगा तथा व्यापार करने में निश्चितता का माहौल बढ़ेगा।
- राज्य जीएसटी और समेकित जीएसटी की एक समान दरों से कर अपवंचन में कमी आएगी, क्योंकि इससे पड़ोसी राज्य अपनी मर्जी से कर की दर लागू नहीं कर सकेंगे एवं प्रत्येक राज्य में एक समान दर ही लागू होगी।
- इससे देश में समग्र निवेश के परिवेश में सुधार आएगा, जिससे राज्यों के आर्थिक विकास में मदद मिलेगी।
- जीएसटी के द्वारा उत्पादन क्रियाकलापों एवं निर्यात को बढ़ावा मिलेगा जिससे रोजगार के नए–नए अवसरों का सृजन होगा और अंततः गरीबी उन्मूलन में मदद मिलेगी, क्योंकि इससे बेहतर वित्तीय संसाधन विकसित किये जा सकेंगे और पर्याप्त आर्थिक विकास हो सकेगा।
- प्रधानमंत्री के अनुसार जीएसटी 2.0 (भारत में अप्रत्यक्ष कर में नव सुधार, जो कि 22 सितम्बर 2025 से सम्पूर्ण देश में लागू हो चुका है, से भारतीय अर्थव्यवस्था "आत्मनिर्भर भारत" की दिशा में महत्वपूर्ण कदम उठा चुका है।
- जीएसटी 2.0 सुधारों से गरीब, मध्यमवर्ग, युवा, किसान, महिलाएं, व्यापारी और दुकानदार (फर्मों)– सभी वर्गों को लाभ मिलेगा।

2. व्यापार एवं उद्योगों को लाभ

- जीएसटी के लागू होने से कर व्यवस्था आसान होगी। इससे भारत में व्यापार करना आसान हो जाएगा।
- करों की बहुलता में कमी आएगी, जो कि इस समय अप्रत्यक्ष कर व्यवस्था में विद्यमान है। इससे कर प्रणाली में सरलता एवं एकरूपता आएगी।
- विभिन्न प्रक्रियाएँ, जैसे– पंजीकरण, रिटर्न, रिफण्ड, कर भुगतान इत्यादि सरल और स्वचालित हो सकेंगी, जिससे कर प्रणाली में सुनिश्चितता आएगी।
- छोटे पैमाने के आपूर्तिकर्ताओं को बड़े सेगमेंट के समझौतों के अन्तर्गत मिले लाभ के परिणामस्वरूप उत्पाद की लागत को कम करने में मदद मिलेगी।
- जीएसटी 2.0 की दरों में सुधार भारत के विकास की नयी कहानी लिखेंगे जिससे व्यापार एवं उद्योगों को भी भरपूर लाभ होगा।
- प्रधानमंत्री जी के अनुसार जीएसटी 2.0 सुधारों से स्टार्टअप, मेक इन इण्डिया आदि स्वदेशी अभियानों को लाभ पहुँचेगा जिससे घरेलू, सूक्ष्म, लघु एवं मध्यम उद्योगों (MSMEs) का विकास होगा तथा व्यापार में इन उद्योगों की भागीदारी बढ़ेगी।

3. उपभोक्ताओं को लाभ

- उपभोक्ताओं, खुदरा विक्रेताओं और सेवा प्रदाताओं के बीच इनपुट टैक्स क्रेडिट के निर्बाध प्रवाह के कारण वस्तुओं की अन्तिम कीमतें कम हो सकेंगी।
- इससे कम्पनियों पर औसत कर भार कम होगा, जिससे वस्तुओं एवं सेवाओं की कीमतों में कमी आने की उम्मीद है और कीमतों में कमी होने के परिणामस्वरूप वस्तुओं एवं सेवाओं के उपभोग में बढ़ोत्तरी होगी।

- जीएसटी 2.0 से जीएसटी बचत उत्सव शुरू हो चुका है। प्रधानमंत्री के अनुसार इन कर सुधारों' से उपभोक्ताओं की क्रयशक्ति बढ़ेगी और अर्थव्यवस्था के उपभोग– बाजार में उल्लास का वातावरण बनेगा।

- देश की अर्थव्यवस्था– उपभोक्ताओं को अधिक मजबूती मिलेगी। जीएसटी 2.0 की दरों से प्रत्येक व्यक्ति की उन्नति होगी।

4. केन्द्र एवं राज्य सरकार को लाभ

- जीएसटी के कारण कराधार बढ़ने और कर अनुपालन में सुधार होने से सरकारी राजस्व में वृद्धि होने का अनुमान है। सकल घरेलू उत्पाद में 1.5 से 2 प्रतिशत तक वृद्धि होने का अनुमान लगाया गया है।

- जीएसटी लागू होने से कर अनुपालन लागत में कमी आएगी, क्योंकि अब तरह–तरह के करों को बनाए रखने के लिए ढेर सारे रिकॉर्ड्स की जरूरत नहीं पड़ेगी, इससे रिकॉर्ड्स को बनाए रखने के लिए संसाधनों एवं श्रम शक्ति में ज्यादा निवेश नहीं करना पड़ेगा।

- जीएसटी मुख्यतः प्रौद्योगिकी संचालित है। इससे मानवीय हस्तक्षेप बहुत हद तक कम हो जाएगा, जिससे निर्णय निर्माण की प्रक्रिया तीव्र हो सकेगी।

- केन्द्र और राज्य स्तर पर अभी तक लगने वाले सभी अप्रत्यक्ष करों के मुकाबले जीएसटी को प्रशासित करना सरल और आसान है।

- जीएसटी से सम्बन्धित सम्पूर्ण क्रियाएँ जीएसटी नेटवर्क (जीएसटीएन) के सामान्य पोर्टल पर हो सकेगी, जिससे कर प्रशासन सरल एवं सुगम हो सकेगा।

- मजबूत आईटी तन्त्र होने के कारण जीएसटी कर अनुपालन में बेहतर साबित होगा। इससे इनपुट टैक्स क्रेडिट का ऑनलाइन

सत्यापन हो सकेगा और इस प्रकार कर प्रक्रिया और अधिक पारदर्शी तथा उत्तरदायी होगी।

सारांश यह है कि जीएसटी वैट (VAT) आधारित एक प्रगतिशील कर प्रणाली (a progressive tax system) है। इस प्रणाली ने पूर्ववर्ती कर–संरचना की जटिलता को दूर किया है और भारतीय अप्रत्यक्ष कराधान को एक नई दिशा दी है। इस तरह, जीएसटी 'एक देश, एक कर, एक बाजार' को संकल्पित है।

जीएसटी नेटवर्क

1 जुलाई, 2017 को भारत ने अब तक के अपने सर्वाधिक क्रान्तिकारी कर सुधार के रूप में जीएसटी की शुरूआत कर दी है। इससे पूरे देश के बाजार का एकीकरण होगा और अर्थव्यवस्था को मजबूती भी मिलेगी।

जीएसटी नेटवर्क या जीएसटीएन की कल्पना जीएसटी के आईटी अवसंरचना के रूप में की गई। यह संगठन नई प्रणाली के लिए आईटी ढाँचे की समुचित व्यवस्था करेगा और करदाताओं को विविध प्रणालियों से एकल प्रणाली में लाने में सहायक होगा। भारत सरकार और राज्य सरकारों ने एक साथ मिलकर एक विशेष उद्देश्य की प्राप्ति के लिए गैर–सरकारी और गैर–लाभकारी संगठन के रूप में जीएसटी नेटवर्क को विकसित किया है, जिसमें केन्द्र 24.5 प्रतिशत और सभी राज्य 24.5 प्रतिशत की हिस्सेदारी रखते हैं। शेष बची हुई 51 प्रतिशत हिस्सेदारी गैर–सरकारी वित्तीय संस्थानों की है। जीएसटीएन केन्द्रीय और राज्य सरकारों, करदाताओं और अन्य हितधारकों को जीएसटी के कार्यान्वयन के लिए आईटी बुनियादी सुविधाएँ साझा करेगा।

सूच्य है कि, जीएसटी परिषद् ने 4 मई, 2018 को आयोजित 27वीं बैठक में संकल्प लिया था कि जीएसटीएन में सरकारी हिस्सेदारी को 51 प्रतिशत से बढ़ाकर 100 प्रतिशत कर दिया गया है।

जीएसटी नेटवर्क (जीएसटीएन) में रजिस्टर होने वाले प्रत्येक व्यक्ति या कम्पनी को प्रत्येक माह निश्चित तिथियों को GSTR–1, GSTR–2 एवं GSTR–3 भरना है जिसमें पिछले पूरे महीने का हिसाब

होगा कि पिछले महीने में कितना इनपुट अर्थात् कच्चा माल आया एवं कितना आउटपुट अर्थात् निर्मित माल तैयार किया गया। इसमें यह देखा जाएगा कि कितना उत्पादन किया गया एवं कितना टैक्स बनता है। इसके साथ ही एक चालान फॉर्म प्राप्त किया जाएगा, जिसमें टैक्स से सम्बन्धित सभी आवश्यक सूचनाएँ होंगी। करदाता बैंक में जाकर अपने कर का भुगतान कर सकता है या फिर ऑनलाइन भुगतान कर सकता है। इस प्रकार प्रत्येक महीने में 3 चालान विवरण तथा एक वर्ष में 36 चालान विवरण भरने होंगे। इसके साथ ही एक चालान GSTR–9 को वार्षिक आधार पर भरा जाएगा। GSTR से सम्बन्धित तारीखों एवं समय–सीमा में आवश्यकतानुसार परिवर्तन किया जा सकता है।

अन्त में हम कह सकते हैं कि 101वें संविधान संशोधन अधिनियम, 2016 के द्वारा अनुच्छेद 366 में एक नया खण्ड (12A) जोड़ा गया, जिसके अनुसार 'वस्तु एवं सेवा कर' का अर्थ है– मानव उपभोग के लिए मादक पेय पदार्थों की आपूर्ति पर लगने वाले कर को छोड़कर वस्तुओं या सेवाओं या दोनों की आपूर्ति पर लगने वाला कर। जीएसटी एक आधुनिक कर व्यवस्था है जो पहले से अधिक सरल एवं पारदर्शी और भ्रष्टाचार को रोकने में मददगार है। जीएसटी से सरकार, उद्योग और उपभोक्ता सभी हितधारक लाभान्वित हो रहे हैं। भारत में जीएसटी के लागू होने से उपभोक्ताओं को दोहरे कराधान (कर पर कर– Cascading) से मुक्ति मिली है जिससे होने वाले लाभों के कारण वस्तुओं एवं सेवाओं की कीमतों में कमी की अपेक्षा की जा रही है।

इस तरह, जीएसटी एक अप्रत्यक्ष (परोक्ष) कर है जो पूरे देश में वस्तुओं एवं सेवाओं की आपूर्ति करने में विनिर्माण से उपभोक्ता तक' एकल कर (सिंगल टैक्स) होता है।

संदर्भ ग्रंथ सूची

- गुप्ता, शिवनारायण (2014–15) : लोक वित्त एवं अन्तर्राष्ट्रीय व्यापार, अग्रवाल पब्लिकेशन्स, आगरा, अ0 18
- भारत सरकार (अगस्त 2017) : 'योजना' (अंग्रेजी), पब्लिकेशंस डिवीजन, नयी दिल्ली
- भारत सरकार (जनवरी 2018) : इकॉनोमिक सर्वे : 2017–18, आक्सफोर्ड यूनिवर्सिटी प्रेस, नयी दिल्ली, अ0 2
- गुप्ता, शिवनारायण (2022) : मुद्रा, बैंकिंग एवं लोक वित्त, अग्रवाल पब्लिकेशंस, आगरा, अ0 34
- साहू एवं अन्य (2024) : विकिसित भारत, 2047 न्यू सेंचुरी पब्लिकेशंस, नयी दिल्ली, अ0 4
- दत्त एवं सुन्दरम् (2024) : 'इण्डियन इकॉनॉमी', एस0 चन्द, नयी दिल्ली, अ0 19
- भारत सरकार (दिसम्बर 2025) : योजना, चैम्पियंस : 2025, पब्लिकेशंस डिवीजन, नयी दिल्ली

Chapter- 14

विकसित भारत 2047 बनाने में सामाजिक न्याय एवं समावेशी विकास की भूमिका का समाजशास्त्रीय अध्ययन

डॉ. अनुपम सिंह (प्रभारी प्राचार्य)
असिस्टेंट प्रोफेसर–समाजशास्त्र
लोकमाता अहिल्याबाई होल्कर
राजकीय महिला महाविद्यालय भरापुरा, अलीगंज, एटा
anupamsingh384@gmail.com, Mob:8532082425

शोध सारः-

भारत सरकार ने वर्ष 2047 तक 'विकसित भारत' की परिकल्पना प्रस्तुत की है जिसमें आर्थिक समृद्धि, सामाजिक न्याय और समावेशी विकास को केंद्रीय स्तंभ माना गया है। प्रस्तुत शोध पत्र 'विकसित भारत 2047' के स्वप्न को साकार करने में सामाजिक न्याय एवं समावेशी विकास की भूमिका का समाजशास्त्रीय दृष्टिकोण से विश्लेषण करता है। शोध में वर्णनात्मक पद्धति का प्रयोग किया गया है तथा द्वितीयक स्रोतों – सरकारी प्रतिवेदनों, नीति-दस्तावेजों, शोध-पत्रिकाओं एवं पुस्तकों – पर आधारित साक्ष्य एकत्र किए गए हैं।

शोध यह स्थापित करता है कि जाति-आधारित विषमता, लैंगिक असमानता, आदिवासी अधिकारों की उपेक्षा, अल्पसंख्यकों का सामाजिक-आर्थिक पिछड़ापन और दिव्यांगजनों के प्रति भेदभाव जैसी चुनौतियाँ विकसित भारत की राह में गहरे अवरोध उत्पन्न करती हैं। समावेशी विकास की रणनीतियों – शिक्षा का सार्वभौमिकरण, स्वास्थ्य सेवाओं की पहुँच,

ग्रामीण-शहरी असंतुलन का निराकरण और सामाजिक सुरक्षा जालों का विस्तार — को लागू किए बिना विकसित भारत का लक्ष्य अधूरा रहेगा।

शोध का केंद्रीय निष्कर्ष यह है कि सामाजिक न्याय और समावेशी विकास एक-दूसरे के पूरक हैं; जहाँ सामाजिक न्याय समाज के अंतिम व्यक्ति को समान अवसर प्रदान करता है, वहीं समावेशी विकास उस अवसर को वास्तविक भागीदारी में रूपांतरित करता है। राष्ट्रीय शिक्षा नीति 2020, आयुष्मान भारत, जन धन योजना और MGNREGA जैसी नीतियाँ इस दिशा में ठोस प्रयास हैं, परंतु इनके प्रभावी क्रियान्वयन और वंचित वर्गों तक पहुँच सुनिश्चित करना अभी भी एक बड़ी चुनौती है।

मुख्य शब्द: विकसित भारत, सामाजिक न्याय, समावेशी विकास, समाजशास्त्र, लैंगिक समानता, हाशियाकरण, SDG, नीति-विश्लेषण।

1.प्रस्तावना:- 15 अगस्त 2022 को भारत की स्वतंत्रता की 75वीं वर्षगाँठ पर माननीय प्रधानमंत्री ने 'विकसित भारत 2047' का संकल्प राष्ट्र के समक्ष रखा। इस संकल्प में भारत को वर्ष 2047 तक एक विकसित राष्ट्र के रूप में स्थापित करने का लक्ष्य निहित है। इस दृष्टि में आर्थिक विकास, आधुनिक अवसंरचना, तकनीकी नवाचार और सुशासन के साथ-साथ सामाजिक न्याय और समावेशी विकास को भी अनिवार्य घटक माना गया है। परंतु प्रश्न यह है — क्या भारत की विद्यमान सामाजिक संरचना इस स्वप्न को साकार करने के लिए पर्याप्त रूप से समतामूलक है?

भारत विश्व की सबसे बड़ी लोकतांत्रिक व्यवस्थाओं में से एक है, परंतु यह विविधताओं का भी एक जटिल समुच्चय है। यहाँ जाति, वर्ग, धर्म, भाषा, लिंग और क्षेत्र के आधार पर गहरी विषमताएं विद्यमान हैं। संयुक्त राष्ट्र विकास कार्यक्रम (UNDP) की मानव विकास रिपोर्ट 2022 के अनुसार भारत का मानव विकास सूचकांक (HDI) 0.633 है जो इसे 191 देशों में 132वें स्थान पर रखता है। यह आँकड़ा बताता है कि आर्थिक विकास की दर भले ही उत्साहवर्धक हो, परंतु वह विकास समाज के सभी वर्गों तक समान रूप से नहीं पहुँचा है।

समाजशास्त्रीय दृष्टिकोण से 'विकास' की अवधारणा केवल जी.डी.पी. वृद्धि से नहीं मापी जा सकती। अमर्त्य सेन की 'विकास-स्वतंत्रता' की अवधारणा (1999) और महबूब उल हक का मानव विकास सिद्धांत (1990) स्पष्ट करते हैं कि वास्तविक विकास वह है जिसमें प्रत्येक नागरिक — चाहे वह किसी भी जाति, वर्ग, लिंग या क्षेत्र का हो — को अपनी क्षमताओं का पूर्ण विकास करने का अवसर मिले। इसी दृष्टिकोण को 'समावेशी विकास' की संज्ञा दी जाती है।

सामाजिक न्याय और समावेशी विकास के बीच एक गहरा सहसंबंध है। जब तक दलितों, आदिवासियों, महिलाओं, अल्पसंख्यकों और दिव्यांगजनों को शिक्षा, स्वास्थ्य, रोजगार और राजनीतिक प्रतिनिधित्व में समान अवसर नहीं मिलते, तब तक विकसित भारत की परिकल्पना एक अधूरा स्वप्न ही बनी रहेगी। प्रस्तुत शोध पत्र इन्हीं जटिल अंतःसंबंधों का विवेचन करते हुए एक समाजशास्त्रीय विश्लेषण प्रस्तुत करता है।

2.संबंधित साहित्य का पुनरावलोकन:- सामाजिक न्याय और समावेशी विकास के विषय पर भारतीय और अंतर्राष्ट्रीय दोनों परंपराओं में विपुल साहित्य उपलब्ध है।

अमर्त्य सेन (1999) ने 'डेवलपमेंट एज़ फ्रीडम' में तर्क दिया कि वास्तविक विकास व्यक्ति की स्वतंत्रता और क्षमताओं के विस्तार में निहित है। उनके अनुसार गरीबी, उत्पीड़न, सामाजिक बाधाएं और राजनीतिक अधिकारहीनता विकास की प्रमुख बाधाएं हैं। भारतीय संदर्भ में यह दृष्टि विशेष रूप से प्रासंगिक है जहाँ जातिगत और लैंगिक भेदभाव व्यक्ति की मूलभूत क्षमताओं को बाधित करते हैं।

रावल्स (1971) ने अपनी कृति 'ए थ्योरी ऑफ जस्टिस' में न्याय के दो सिद्धांत प्रस्तुत किए। प्रथम यह कि प्रत्येक व्यक्ति को मूलभूत स्वतंत्रताओं का समान अधिकार हो, और द्वितीय यह कि सामाजिक-आर्थिक विषमताएं तभी

स्वीकार्य हैं जब वे सबसे वंचित वर्गों के लाभ में हों। भारतीय संविधान का अनुच्छेद 14 से 18 और अनुच्छेद 46 इसी भावना को प्रतिबिंबित करते हैं।

भीमराव रामजी अम्बेडकर (1936) ने 'एनिहिलेशन ऑफ कास्ट' में जाति-व्यवस्था को भारतीय समाज में समानता की सबसे बड़ी बाधा बताया। उनके अनुसार जब तक जाति का उन्मूलन नहीं होगा, तब तक भारत में सच्चा लोकतंत्र और सामाजिक न्याय संभव नहीं है। योजना आयोग (2013) की रिपोर्ट 'समावेशी विकास: योजना एवं कार्यान्वयन' भी इस बात की पुष्टि करती है कि SC, ST और OBC वर्गों में विकास के फल समान रूप से नहीं पहुँचे हैं।

नीति आयोग (2023) की 'विकसित भारत @ 2047: विजन एवं रणनीति' रिपोर्ट में समावेशी विकास को पाँच स्तंभों पर आधारित बताया गया है — नागरिकों की समृद्धि, आर्थिक शक्ति, बुनियादी अवसंरचना, हरित ऊर्जा और सुशासन। परंतु इस रिपोर्ट में सामाजिक न्याय के आयाम को अपेक्षाकृत कम महत्त्व दिया गया है जो एक गंभीर सीमा है।

पिल्लई और त्रिपाठी (2018) ने अपने शोध 'इंक्लूजन एंड इक्विटी इन इंडियन डेवलपमेंट' में पाया कि भारत में आर्थिक वृद्धि और सामाजिक समानता के बीच की खाई पिछले दो दशकों में और गहरी हुई है। ऑक्सफैम (2023) की रिपोर्ट के अनुसार भारत में शीर्ष 1% की संपत्ति कुल राष्ट्रीय संपत्ति के 40% से अधिक है।

हिंदी विद्वानों में चंद्रशेखर (2015) की 'भारत में सामाजिक न्याय और राज्य', मिश्र (2019) की 'समावेशी विकास की राजनीति' और वर्मा (2021) की 'दलित-आदिवासी विकास: चुनौतियाँ और संभावनाएं' जैसी कृतियों ने इस विषय पर भारतीय दृष्टिकोण को सशक्त रूप से प्रस्तुत किया है। इन सभी अध्ययनों के आलोक में यह स्पष्ट होता है कि सामाजिक न्याय को विकास नीति के केंद्र में रखे बिना विकसित भारत की परिकल्पना अधूरी रहेगी।

3.शोध का उद्देश्य और महत्त्वः-

शोध का उद्देश्य :-

(1) विकसित भारत 2047 की परिकल्पना में सामाजिक न्याय एवं समावेशी विकास की भूमिका का समाजशास्त्रीय विश्लेषण करना।

(2) वर्तमान भारतीय समाज में सामाजिक न्याय की प्राप्ति के मार्ग में विद्यमान प्रमुख चुनौतियों की पहचान करना।

(3) समावेशी विकास के लिए प्रभावी नीतिगत रणनीतियों का मूल्यांकन करना।

(4) सामाजिक न्याय और समावेशी विकास के परस्पर सहसंबंध को स्थापित करना।

शोध का महत्त्व :-

यह शोध नीति-निर्माताओं को यह समझने में सहायक है कि सामाजिक असमानता न केवल नैतिक दृष्टि से अस्वीकार्य है, बल्कि यह आर्थिक विकास की गति को भी अवरुद्ध करती है। जब समाज के एक बड़े वर्ग को विकास की मुख्यधारा से बाहर रखा जाता है, तो मानव पूँजी का विशाल भंडार अनुपयोगी रह जाता है। यह शोध सिद्ध करता है कि समतामूलक विकास और राष्ट्रीय उत्पादकता परस्पर-पोषक हैं। इसके अतिरिक्त, यह शोध SDG लक्ष्यों, विशेषकर SDG-10 (असमानता में कमी) और SDG-16 (शांति, न्याय और सशक्त संस्थाएं), के साथ भारत की प्रगति का मूल्यांकन करने में भी उपयोगी है।

4.सामाजिक न्याय के लिए चुनौतियाँ एवं रणनीतियाँ :-

जाति-आधारित भेदभाव और असमानता :-

भारतीय समाज में जाति-व्यवस्था एक ऐसी संरचनात्मक बाधा है जो आज भी शिक्षा, रोजगार और सामाजिक गतिशीलता को बाधित करती है। राष्ट्रीय परिवार स्वास्थ्य सर्वेक्षण (NFHS-5, 2021) के अनुसार अनुसूचित जाति और जनजाति के परिवारों में गरीबी दर, शिशु मृत्यु दर और कुपोषण क्रमशः उच्च वर्णीय परिवारों की तुलना में काफी अधिक है। संविधान के अनुच्छेद 17 ने अस्पृश्यता को अपराध घोषित किया है और SC/ST अत्याचार निवारण अधिनियम 1989 जैसे कानून बनाए गए हैं, परंतु इनका क्रियान्वयन अभी भी अपर्याप्त है।

रणनीति: आरक्षण नीति को और अधिक प्रभावी बनाने के साथ-साथ शिक्षा और कौशल-विकास में विशेष निवेश आवश्यक है। 'क्रीमी लेयर' की अवधारणा को पुनर्परिभाषित कर वास्तविक वंचितों को लाभ सुनिश्चित किया जाना चाहिए।

लैंगिक असमानता :-

विश्व आर्थिक मंच के वैश्विक लैंगिक अंतराल सूचकांक 2023 में भारत 127वें स्थान पर है। महिला श्रम-शक्ति भागीदारी दर (FLFPR) मात्र 24% है जबकि चीन में यह 60% से अधिक है। ग्रामीण क्षेत्रों में महिलाओं की शिक्षा, स्वास्थ्य और आर्थिक निर्णय-शक्ति आज भी पुरुषों की तुलना में न्यून है। बेटी बचाओ-बेटी पढ़ाओ, मातृत्व वंदना योजना और उज्ज्वला योजना जैसे कार्यक्रमों ने कुछ सुधार किया है, परंतु संरचनात्मक परिवर्तन की गति धीमी है।

रणनीति: महिलाओं की कानूनी साक्षरता, पंचायत स्तर पर वास्तविक प्रतिनिधित्व और कार्यस्थल पर सुरक्षा सुनिश्चित करना आवश्यक है। लैंगिक संवेदनशील बजटिंग (Gender Responsive Budgeting) को अनिवार्य बनाया जाना चाहिए।

आदिवासी अधिकार और वन-निर्भर समुदाय :-

देश की जनजातीय जनसंख्या लगभग 10.45 करोड़ है। वन अधिकार अधिनियम 2006 के बावजूद आदिवासियों का विस्थापन जारी है। बड़े बाँधों, खनन परियोजनाओं और वन-संरक्षण नीतियों के नाम पर आदिवासियों को उनकी पारंपरिक भूमि और जीविका से वंचित किया जा रहा है। जनजातीय क्षेत्रों में साक्षरता दर, स्वास्थ्य सूचकांक और मानव विकास सूचकांक राष्ट्रीय औसत से काफी नीचे है।

रणनीति: ग्राम सभाओं को वास्तविक निर्णय-शक्ति देना, वन अधिकार अधिनियम का समुचित क्रियान्वयन और आदिवासी भाषाओं में शिक्षा सुनिश्चित करना प्राथमिकता होनी चाहिए।

शहरी-ग्रामीण विषमता और प्रवासी श्रमिक :-

भारत में शहरी और ग्रामीण विकास के बीच की खाई चिंताजनक है। शहरी प्रति व्यक्ति आय ग्रामीण की तुलना में तीन गुनी है। COVID-19 महामारी ने प्रवासी श्रमिकों की दुर्दशा को उजागर किया। आनुमानित 40-50 करोड़ अनौपचारिक श्रमिकों के पास न सामाजिक सुरक्षा है, न रोजगार की गारंटी।

रणनीति: MGNREGA जैसी योजनाओं का विस्तार, 'वन नेशन वन राशन कार्ड' का प्रभावी क्रियान्वयन और प्रवासी श्रमिकों के पंजीकरण की अनिवार्यता इस दिशा में महत्त्वपूर्ण कदम हैं। श्रम संहिताओं को श्रमिक-हितैषी बनाना और न्यूनतम मजदूरी की गारंटी सुनिश्चित की जानी चाहिए।

डिजिटल असमानता :-

विकसित भारत की परिकल्पना में डिजिटल तकनीक एक महत्त्वपूर्ण भूमिका निभाती है, परंतु डिजिटल विभाजन (Digital Divide) एक नई

असमानता को जन्म दे रहा है। TRAI की रिपोर्ट 2023 के अनुसार ग्रामीण क्षेत्रों में इंटरनेट पहुँच 40% से कम है। महिलाओं, वृद्धों और वंचित वर्गों में डिजिटल साक्षरता का अभाव उन्हें सरकारी योजनाओं और डिजिटल अर्थव्यवस्था से बाहर रखता है।

रणनीति: पंचायत स्तर तक ब्रॉडबैंड कनेक्टिविटी, डिजिटल साक्षरता अभियान और सरकारी सेवाओं को ऑफलाइन मोड में भी उपलब्ध कराना डिजिटल समावेश के लिए अनिवार्य है।

5.विकसित भारत में समावेशी विकास की भूमिका का मूल्यांकन :-

समावेशी विकास वह विकास है जो आर्थिक वृद्धि के लाभों को समाज के सभी वर्गों — विशेषकर वंचित, हाशिये पर धकेले गए और पिछड़े समूहों — तक न्यायसंगत रूप से पहुँचाता है। विकसित भारत 2047 की परिकल्पना में समावेशी विकास की भूमिका निम्नलिखित आयामों में दिखती है:

मानव पूँजी का विकास: शिक्षा और स्वास्थ्य में निवेश समावेशी विकास का आधार है। राष्ट्रीय शिक्षा नीति 2020 ने प्रारंभिक बाल्यावस्था शिक्षा, व्यावसायिक प्रशिक्षण और उच्च शिक्षा की पहुँच को सार्वभौमिक बनाने का लक्ष्य रखा है। आयुष्मान भारत के अंतर्गत 50 करोड़ से अधिक लाभार्थियों को स्वास्थ्य बीमा प्रदान किया गया है। ये प्रयास दीर्घकालिक मानव पूँजी निर्माण में सहायक हैं।

वित्तीय समावेशन: प्रधानमंत्री जन धन योजना के माध्यम से 50 करोड़ से अधिक बैंक खाते खोले गए हैं। DBT (प्रत्यक्ष लाभ हस्तांतरण) के माध्यम से सब्सिडी सीधे लाभार्थियों तक पहुँचाई जा रही है। मुद्रा योजना और स्टार्टअप इंडिया ने लघु उद्यमियों को वित्तीय सहायता प्रदान की है।

बुनियादी सेवाओं की पहुँच: स्वच्छ भारत मिशन, हर घर जल और उज्ज्वला योजना ने क्रमशः स्वच्छता, जल और ऊर्जा की पहुँच में उल्लेखनीय सुधार किया है। PMGSY के माध्यम से ग्रामीण सड़क संपर्क में व्यापक वृद्धि हुई है जिससे ग्रामीण अर्थव्यवस्था सुदृढ़ हुई है।

हालाँकि इन सभी उपलब्धियों के बावजूद कुछ महत्त्वपूर्ण प्रश्न अनुत्तरित हैं। क्या इन योजनाओं के लाभ वास्तव में अंतिम व्यक्ति तक पहुँच रहे हैं? क्या कार्यान्वयन में पारदर्शिता है? ऑक्सफैम (2023) और वर्ल्ड इनइक्वालिटी लैब (2022) की रिपोर्टें यह दर्शाती हैं कि आर्थिक असमानता वास्तव में बढ़ी है। विकसित भारत के लिए आवश्यक है कि विकास की गति के साथ-साथ वितरण की न्यायिता भी सुनिश्चित की जाए।

6.सामाजिक न्याय और समावेशी विकास का सहसंबंध

सामाजिक न्याय और समावेशी विकास का संबंध द्विदिशीय (bidirectional) और पारस्परिक-पोषक (mutually reinforcing) है। यह संबंध निम्नलिखित स्तरों पर स्पष्ट होता है:

प्रथम, सामाजिक न्याय समावेशी विकास की पूर्व-शर्त है। जब तक जाति, लिंग और वर्ग-आधारित भेदभाव समाप्त नहीं होता, तब तक समाज के वंचित वर्ग विकास की प्रक्रिया में पूरी क्षमता से भाग नहीं ले सकते। भेदभाव का अर्थ है मानव पूँजी की बर्बादी — जब एक दलित छात्र शैक्षणिक भेदभाव के कारण आगे नहीं बढ़ पाता, या एक महिला सामाजिक प्रतिबंधों के कारण आर्थिक गतिविधि से दूर रहती है, तो राष्ट्र की उत्पादकता प्रत्यक्ष रूप से प्रभावित होती है।

द्वितीय, समावेशी विकास सामाजिक न्याय को व्यावहारिक धरातल पर साकार करता है। अधिकार और समानता की घोषणाएं तब तक अर्थहीन हैं जब तक उन्हें आर्थिक क्षमता और भौतिक संसाधनों का समर्थन नहीं मिलता। MGNREGA ने ग्रामीण दलितों और महिलाओं को आर्थिक स्वतंत्रता प्रदान कर सामाजिक न्याय को व्यावहारिक बनाया है।

तृतीय, दोनों मिलकर 'सामाजिक पूँजी' का निर्माण करते हैं। जब समाज न्यायपूर्ण होता है और विकास समावेशी होता है, तो नागरिकों में संस्थाओं के

प्रति विश्वास बढ़ता है, सामाजिक सामंजस्य बढ़ता है और लोकतंत्र सुदृढ़ होता है। यह 'सामाजिक पूँजी' विकसित भारत के लिए सबसे महत्त्वपूर्ण संसाधन है।

7.निष्कर्ष :-

प्रस्तुत शोध के समग्र विश्लेषण से यह निष्कर्ष उभरता है कि 'विकसित भारत 2047' का स्वप्न तभी साकार हो सकता है जब सामाजिक न्याय और समावेशी विकास को केवल नारे नहीं, बल्कि क्रियाशील नीति का आधार बनाया जाए। भारत की जनसांख्यिकीय विविधता, जो प्रायः चुनौती के रूप में देखी जाती है, वास्तव में एक असीमित संभावना है — बशर्ते कि समाज के प्रत्येक वर्ग को अपनी क्षमताओं के विकास का अवसर मिले।

विकसित भारत का अर्थ केवल $5 ट्रिलियन की अर्थव्यवस्था नहीं है; इसका अर्थ है एक ऐसा समाज जिसमें दलित किसान की बेटी IIT में पढ़ सके, आदिवासी युवक अपनी भाषा में तकनीक का उपयोग कर सके, दिव्यांग नागरिक सार्वजनिक जीवन में बिना भेदभाव के भाग ले सके और महिला उद्यमी बिना किसी बाधा के अपना व्यवसाय चला सके। यही भारत के संविधान का सपना है और यही विकसित भारत का वास्तविक लक्ष्य होना चाहिए।

शोध यह भी संकेत करता है कि सरकार, नागरिक समाज, शैक्षणिक संस्थाओं और निजी क्षेत्र को मिलकर एक ऐसा पारिस्थितिकी तंत्र विकसित करना होगा जिसमें सामाजिक न्याय की संस्थागत गारंटी हो और समावेशी विकास की नीतियाँ जमीनी स्तर पर प्रभावी रूप से लागू हों। 2047 की समय-सीमा चुनौतीपूर्ण है, परंतु असंभव नहीं — यदि हम समता, स्वतंत्रता और बंधुत्व के संवैधानिक मूल्यों के प्रति सच्चे अर्थों में प्रतिबद्ध हों।

संदर्भ ग्रन्थ सूची :-

- अम्बेडकर, भीमराव रामजी। (1936)। जाति का विनाश (हिंदी अनुवाद: ललई सिंह यादव, 1968)। बहुजन प्रकाशन।
- अम्बेडकर, भीमराव रामजी। (1948)। अछूत कौन थे और वे अछूत कैसे बने? (हिंदी अनुवाद, 2010)। सम्यक प्रकाशन।
- चंद्रशेखर, के.एन.। (2015)। भारत में सामाजिक न्याय और राज्य: एक समाजशास्त्रीय विश्लेषण। राजकमल प्रकाशन।
- तिवारी, रमेश। (2017)। भारतीय समाज में असमानता: कारण और समाधान। किताब घर प्रकाशन।
- नीति आयोग। (2023)। विकसित भारत @ 2047: विजन एवं रणनीति दस्तावेज। भारत सरकार।
- पिल्लई, सुनीता और त्रिपाठी, अनुराग। (2018)। भारत में समावेश और समता। ऑरियंट ब्लैकस्वान।
- प्रसाद, कमलेश। (2016)। दलित विकास और सामाजिक न्याय। अनामिका पब्लिशर्स।
- भारत सरकार। (2020)। राष्ट्रीय शिक्षा नीति 2020। शिक्षा मंत्रालय।
- भारत सरकार। (2011)। सामाजिक-आर्थिक और जाति जनगणना 2011: मुख्य रिपोर्ट। ग्रामीण विकास मंत्रालय।
- मिश्र, उदय भानु। (2019)। समावेशी विकास की राजनीति: भारतीय परिप्रेक्ष्य। सारांश प्रकाशन।
- मुखर्जी, अरुण। (2014)। भारत में गरीबी और असमानता। ओरियंट ब्लैकस्वान।

- योजना आयोग। (2013)। बारहवीं पंचवर्षीय योजना (2012-17): समावेशी एवं धारणीय विकास (खंड 3)। भारत सरकार।
- शर्मा, रेखा। (2018)। भारत में महिला सशक्तिकरण और लैंगिक न्याय। मनोज पब्लिकेशंस।
- सिंह, अवतार। (2021)। अनुसूचित जाति और जनजाति कल्याण नीतियाँ: एक आलोचनात्मक समीक्षा। ग्रंथशिल्पी।
- सेन, अमर्त्य। (1999)। विकास एक स्वतंत्रता है (हिंदी अनुवाद: अनिल रंजन भौमिक, 2003)। राजकमल प्रकाशन।
- सेन, अमर्त्य। (2009)। न्याय का विचार (हिंदी अनुवाद, 2015)। राजकमल प्रकाशन।
- संयुक्त राष्ट्र विकास कार्यक्रम। (2022)। मानव विकास रिपोर्ट 2022: अनिश्चितता के समय में। UNDP।
- त्रिपाठी, आलोक। (2022)। डिजिटल भारत और सामाजिक समावेश: अवसर एवं चुनौतियाँ। इन्फोसिस फाउंडेशन पब्लिकेशंस।
- वर्मा, सुरेश। (2021)। दलित-आदिवासी विकास: चुनौतियाँ और संभावनाएं। विकास प्रकाशन।
- विश्व बैंक। (2023)। भारत का आर्थिक परिदृश्य: समावेशी विकास की ओर। वर्ल्ड बैंक रिपोर्ट।
- वर्ल्ड इकोनॉमिक फोरम। (2023)। वैश्विक लैंगिक अंतराल रिपोर्ट 2023। WEF प्रकाशन।

CHAPTER- 15

ग्रामीण कृषक परिवारों का सशक्तिकरणः विकसित भारत 2047 के विशेष संदर्भ में।

डॉ॰ कौशलेंद्र विक्रम सिंह
असिस्टेंट प्रोफेसर – समाजशास्त्र
राजकीय महाविद्यालय हरदत्तनगर गिरंट जमुनहा श्रावस्ती

सारांश

विकसित भारत के लक्ष्य की प्राप्ति में ग्रामीण समाज की भूमिका को नजरंदाज नहीं किया जा सकता है। ग्रामीण समाज में मुख्य रूप से कृषक परिवारों की भूमिका अत्यंत महत्वपूर्ण है। भारत की अधिकांश आबादी आज भी प्रत्यक्ष या अप्रत्यक्ष रूप से कृषि एवं ग्रामीण अर्थव्यवस्था पर निर्भर है। वर्तमान अध्ययन में ग्रामीण कृषक परिवारों के सशक्तिकरण के सामाजिक, आर्थिक एवं सांस्कृतिक आयामों का गहन विश्लेषण किया गया है। अध्ययन का उद्देश्य यह पता लगाना है कि कृषक परिवारों के सर्वांगीण विकास के माध्यम से विकसित भारत की संकल्पना को किस प्रकार मूर्त रूप दिया जा सकता है। शोध पत्र में ग्रामीण कृषक परिवारों के समक्ष विद्यमान चुनौतियों, सरकारी प्रयासों तथा भविष्य की संभावनाओं का समाजशास्त्रीय विश्लेषण प्रस्तुत किया गया है।

मुख्य शब्दः ग्रामीण समाज, कृषक परिवार, सशक्तिकरण, सामाजिक परिवर्तन, विकसित भारत, ग्रामीण विकास।

प्रस्तावनाः

भारत की सामाजिक संरचना में ग्रामीण समाज का विशेष महत्व रहा है। भारत को गाँवों का देश कहा जाता है। आज भी एक बड़ी आबादी गांवों निवास करती है तथा अपनी आजीविका के लिए कृषि एवं उससे संबंधित क्षेत्रों पर निर्भर है। ग्रामीण कृषक परिवार केवल आर्थिक इकाई नहीं हैं, बल्कि वे सामाजिक, सांस्कृतिक एवं सामुदायिक आधारित जीवन पद्धति का अप्रतिम उदाहरण हैं।

2047 तक भारत को विकसित राष्ट्र बनाने का लक्ष्य केवल आर्थिक सशक्तिकरण करना ही नहीं है, बल्कि सामाजिक न्याय, समान अवसर, समावेशी विकास तथा मानव संसाधन का सशक्तिकरण भी है। इस लक्ष्य की प्राप्ति में ग्रामीण कृषक परिवारों की भूमिका प्रमुख है।

वैश्वीकरण, उदारीकरण, निजीकरण आधुनिकीकरण, नगरीकरण, तकनीकी विकास तथा संचार क्रांति ने ग्रामीण जीवन की पारंपरिक संरचना को बहुत अधिक प्रभावित किया है। ग्रामीण जीवन का कोई भी क्षेत्र इसके प्रभाव से अछूता नहीं है। एक ओर कृषि में नवीन तकनीकों, डिजिटल सेवाओं एवं सरकारी योजनाओं के माध्यम से अवसरों का विस्तार हुआ है, वहीं दूसरी ओर भूमि का बटवारा, बेरोजगारी, पलायन, सामाजिक असमानता, जलवायु परिवर्तन तथा बाजार की अनिश्चितता जैसी चुनौतियाँ भी सामने आई हैं।

ग्रामीण कृषक परिवारों के संदर्भ में सशक्तिकरण का तात्पर्य आर्थिक सुरक्षा, शिक्षा, स्वास्थ्य, समान अवसर की उपलब्धता, लैंगिक समानता, तकनीकी पहुँच, राजनीतिक भागीदारी तथा सामाजिक प्रतिष्ठा में वृद्धि से है।

प्रस्तुत शोध–पत्र में विकसित भारत के विशेष संदर्भ में ग्रामीण कृषक परिवारों के सशक्तिकरण का समाजशास्त्रीय विश्लेषण किया गया है। इसमें ग्रामीण सामाजिक संरचना, सशक्तिकरण की अवधारणा, सरकारी नीतियों एवं योजनाओं, सामाजिक परिवर्तन की प्रक्रियाओं तथा ग्रामीण विकास की चुनौतियों एवं संभावनाओं का अध्ययन किया गया है। यह शोध

इस तथ्य को रेखांकित करता है कि विकसित भारत की संकल्पना तभी साकार हो सकती है, जब ग्रामीण कृषक परिवार राष्ट्र की जीडीपी में सब्सिडी पाने वाले समुदाय से बाहर निकलकर सकल आय बढ़ाने और सामाजिक, आर्थिक एवं सांस्कृतिक दृष्टि से सशक्त होकर राष्ट्रीय विकास की मुख्यधारा में सक्रिय भागीदारी सुनिश्चित करें।

अध्ययन के उद्देश्य–

1-ग्रामीण कृषक परिवारों की वर्तमान सामाजिक एवं आर्थिक स्थिति का अध्ययन करना।

2-कृषक परिवारों के सशक्तिकरण की समाजशास्त्रीय अवधारणा का विश्लेषण करना।

3- विकसित भारत के संदर्भ में कृषक परिवारों की भूमिका का मूल्यांकन करना।

4- कृषक परिवारों के समक्ष विद्यमान प्रमुख चुनौतियों का अध्ययन करना।

5- ग्रामीण कृषक परिवारों के सशक्तिकरण हेतु सुझाव प्रस्तुत करना।

शोध पद्धति–

यह शोध–पत्र मुख्यतः द्वितीयक तथ्यों पर आधारित है। अध्ययन हेतु पुस्तकों, शोध–पत्रों, सरकारी रिपोर्टों, नीति आयोग, कृषि मंत्रालय, जनगणना रिपोर्टों तथा विभिन्न राष्ट्रीय एवं अंतरराष्ट्रीय संस्थाओं के प्रकाशित आँकड़ों का उपयोग किया गया है। अध्ययन की प्रकृति वर्णनात्मक एवं विश्लेषणात्मक है।

ग्रामीण कृषक परिवारः

परिवार एक सामाजिक संस्था है, जिसमें व्यक्ति सामाजिक व्यवहार, नैतिक मूल्यों, संस्कृति तथा सामाजिक जीवन के नियमों, मानको को सीखता है। ग्रामीण समाज में परिवार के सदस्य कृषि कार्यों में प्रत्यक्ष या अप्रत्यक्ष रूप से भाग लेते हैं तथा उत्पादन एवं संसाधनों के प्रबंधन में सहयोग प्रदान करते हैं। इस प्रकार कृषक परिवार की आर्थिक इकाई होने के साथ–साथ सामाजिक संगठन का भी आधार है। एमिल दुर्खीम के

अनुसार समाज का एकीकरण सामाजिक एकता और सामूहिक चेतना पर आधारित होती है। ग्रामीण कृषक परिवारों में पारस्परिक सहयोग, सामूहिक श्रम, परंपरागत विश्वास तथा सामुदायिक संबंध सामाजिक एकता को मजबूत करते हैं। खेती–बाड़ी से जुड़े कार्यों, धार्मिक अनुष्ठानों एवं सामुदायिक आयोजनों में परिवारों की सक्रिय भागीदारी ग्रामीण समाज में सामाजिक सामंजस्य को बनाए रखती है।

श्यामाचरण दुबे ने भारतीय ग्रामों को सामाजिक संबंधों एवं सांस्कृतिक परंपराओं का जीवंत केंद्र माना है। उनके अनुसार ग्रामीण परिवार सामाजिक संगठन की मूल इकाई है, जिसके माध्यम से सामाजिक मूल्य एक पीढ़ी से दूसरी पीढ़ी तक हस्तांतरित होते हैं। इसी तरह ए. आर. देसाई ने ग्रामीण समाज के अध्ययन में आर्थिक संरचना एवं वर्ग संबंधों को महत्वपूर्ण माना है। उनके अनुसार भूमि स्वामित्व, संसाधनों की उपलब्धता तथा उत्पादन संबंध ग्रामीण समाज की सामाजिक संरचना को प्रभावित करते हैं।

वर्तमान समय में ग्रामीण कृषक परिवार सामाजिक परिवर्तन की तीव्र प्रक्रिया से गुजर रहे हैं। आधुनिकीकरण, वैश्वीकरण, शिक्षा के प्रसार, सूचना प्रौद्योगिकी के विकास तथा नगरीकरण ने ग्रामीण जीवन में व्यापक परिवर्तन उत्पन्न किए हैं। पारंपरिक संयुक्त परिवारों का स्थान धीरे–धीरे एकल परिवार ले रहे हैं। कृषि कार्यों में आधुनिक तकनीकों का उपयोग बढ़ा है तथा युवाओं का गैर–कृषि व्यवसायों की ओर झुकाव भी दिखाई देता है। इन परिवर्तनों ने ग्रामीण सामाजिक संबंधों, पारिवारिक संरचना एवं आर्थिक गतिविधियों को प्रभावित किया है। ग्रामीण परिवार उत्पादन, उपभोग, समाजीकरण तथा सामाजिक नियंत्रण की प्रमुख इकाई है। यद्यपि ग्रामीण समाज को पहले की तरह उत्पादन और उपभोग की इकाईं मानकर अध्ययन करना उचित नहीं है। हरित क्रांति के बाद कृषक पैटर्न में व्यापक बदलाव आया है। राबर्ट रेडफील्ड की अवधारणा ग्राम – नगर सांतत्य अब अधिक व्यावहारिक है। ग्रामीण समाज नगरो से अब अछूते नहीं हैं। वे भी उन पर अब निर्भर हैं। फ्लिपकार्ट और एमेजॉन के डिलीवरी ब्वॉय गाँब में अब आसानी से देखे जा सकते हैं। यद्यपि ग्रामीण समाज में अभी भी निर्धनता की समस्या है। सांस्कृतिक रूप से आज भी ग्रामीण

समाज परंपरागत समाज के रूप में अपनी पहचान बनाए हुए है। ग्रामीण परिवार कृषि उत्पादन के साथ–साथ सामाजिक मूल्यों, परंपराओं एवं सांस्कृतिक विरासत के संरक्षण में भी महत्वपूर्ण भूमिका निभाते हैं। कृषक परिवार आर्थिक इकाई होने के साथ–साथ सामाजिक संबंधों एवं सामुदायिक जीवन का आधार भी हैं।

ग्रामीण समाज का सशक्तिकरण:

सशक्तिकरण का अर्थ केवल आर्थिक उन्नति नहीं है, बल्कि निर्णय लेने, संसाधनों तक पहुँच प्राप्त करने तथा सामाजिक अवसर की समान पहुँच और गरिमापूर्ण जीवन से भी है। ग्रामीण कृषक परिवारों का सशक्तिकरण विकसित भारत बनाने की दृष्टि से अहम है। केवल आय वृद्धि से ही नहीं, बल्कि आर्थिक, सामाजिक, राजनीतिक एवं तकनीकी क्षमताओं के समग्र विकास की आवश्यकता है। कृषक परिवार के बहुआयामी सशक्तिकरण के बिना समावेशी विकास का लक्ष्य पूरा नहीं हो सकता।

आर्थिक सशक्तिकरण कृषक परिवारों की आत्मनिर्भरता का मूल आधार है। कृषि आय में वृद्धि, उत्पादकता में सुधार, संस्थागत ऋण तक पहुँच तथा कृषि आधारित उद्यमिता का विकास विकसित गाँव के लिए अपरिहार्य शर्ते हैं। सरकारी आँकड़ों के अनुसार वित्तीय समावेशन, किसान क्रेडिट कार्ड, किसान उत्पादक संगठन तथा कृषि विविधीकरण जैसी पहलों ने किसानों की आर्थिक सुरक्षा को मजबूत किया है। ई मंडी, फसल बीमा और उसका त्वरित भुगतान, खेत से ही खड़ी फसलों की बिक्री तथा उचित प्रतिस्पर्धी दर पर भुगतान की दिशा में कार्य किए बिना कृषकों की आय बढ़ाना कठिन है।

शिक्षा, स्वास्थ्य, सामाजिक समानता एवं लैंगिक न्याय भी आर्थिक सशक्तिकरण की तरह ही महत्वपूर्ण है। ग्रामीण समाज में शिक्षा एवं जागरूकता, सामाजिक परिवर्तन को बढ़ावा देती है। स्वास्थ्य सुविधाओं तक पहुँच स्वस्थ ग्रामीण समाज की समाज के लिए आवश्यक है। महिला शिक्षा एवं महिला सहभागिता में वृद्धि से कृषक परिवारों की सामाजिक एवं आर्थिक स्थिति मजबूत होती है। इससे परिवार पर निर्भरता

अनुपात घटता है। सामाजिक समानता एवं लैंगिक न्याय समावेशी विकास की अनिवार्य शर्त हैं।

राजनीतिक सशक्तिकरण के अंतर्गत पंचायतों में सक्रिय सहभागिता, स्थानीय नेतृत्व का विकास तथा निर्णय प्रक्रिया में सक्रिय भागीदारी शामिल है। पंचायती राज संस्थाओं ने ग्रामीण समुदायों को विकास योजनाओं के निर्माण एवं क्रियान्वयन में भागीदारी का अवसर प्रदान किया है, जिससे लोकतांत्रिक विकेंद्रीकरण को बल मिला है। जनजागरुकता के बाद भी ग्राम सभा की बैठकें कागजी पूर्ति के लिए होती है। बिना जवाबदेही के पंचायती राज व्यवस्था बनाने का उद्देश्य सफल नहीं हो सकता है।

तकनीकी सशक्तिकरण वर्तमान समय की आवश्यकता है। डिजिटल साक्षरता, आधुनिक कृषि तकनीकों का उपयोग, ई–नाम जैसे डिजिटल विपणन मंच तथा सूचना एवं संचार प्रौद्योगिकी किसानों को बाजार, मौसम तथा कृषि संबंधी सूचनाओं तक त्वरित पहुँच प्रदान कर रहे हैं। इस प्रकार ग्रामीण कृषक परिवारों का बहुआयामी सशक्तिकरण विकसित भारत की दिशा में एक निर्णायक कदम सिद्ध हो सकता है।

ग्रामीण कृषक परिवारों के समक्ष प्रमुख चुनौतियाँ–

बढ़ती जनसंख्या के कारण कृषि जोत का औसत आकार लगातार घट रहा है, जिससे कृषि उत्पादकता प्रभावित हो रही है। अनियमित वर्षा, सूखा एवं बाढ़ जैसी समस्याएँ कृषि उत्पादन को प्रभावित करती हैं। तकनीकी विकास के बावजूद कृषि जोखिम को कम करने में वांछित सफलता नहीं मिली है। ग्रामीण भारत में बेरोजगारी की समस्या के कारण ग्रामीण युवाओं का शहरों की ओर पलायन, ग्रामीण सामाजिक संरचना को प्रभावित कर रहा है। स्थानीय स्तर पर रोजगार सृजन और आधारभूत संरचना की दिशा में अभी और काम किए जाने की आवश्यकता है। ग्रामीण क्षेत्रों में गुणवत्तापूर्ण शिक्षा एवं स्वास्थ्य सुविधाओं का अभाव अभी भी विद्यमान है।

विकसित भारत 2047 और ग्रामीण कृषक परिवार–

विकसित भारत 2047 की अवधारणा समावेशी विकास पर आधारित है। इस दृष्टिकोण में ग्रामीण समृद्धि, कृषि आधुनिकीकरण, डिजिटल सशक्तिकरण तथा सामाजिक न्याय को विशेष महत्व दिया गया है। कृषक परिवारों की आर्थिक सुरक्षा, सामाजिक उन्नयन एवं तकनीकी सशक्तिकरण विकसित भारत के लक्ष्य की आधारशिला हैं।

सुझाव–

- कृषि को अधिक लाभकारी बनाने हेतु बाजार सुधार किए जाएँ।
- ग्रामीण क्षेत्रों में डिजिटल अवसंरचना का विस्तार किया जाए।
- कृषक परिवारों के लिए गुणवत्तापूर्ण शिक्षा एवं स्वास्थ्य सुविधाएँ उपलब्ध कराई जाएँ।
- महिला/ वंचित तबकों के कृषकों के सशक्तिकरण पर विशेष ध्यान दिया जाए।
- स्वयं सहायता समूहों को अधिक प्रोत्साहन दिया जाए।
- जलवायु अनुकूल कृषि तकनीकों का प्रसार किया जाए।
- ग्रामीण युवाओं के कौशल विकास एवं उद्यमिता को बढ़ावा दिया जाए।

निष्कर्ष–

ग्रामीण कृषक परिवारों का सशक्तिकरण विकसित भारत की नींव है। विकसित गाँव के बिना विकसित राष्ट्र का सपना साकार नहीं हो सकता। जब तक ग्रामीण कृषक परिवार आर्थिक रूप से आत्मनिर्भर, सामाजिक रूप से सशक्त तथा तकनीकी रूप से सक्षम नहीं होंगे, तब तक विकसित भारत का लक्ष्य प्राप्त नहीं किया जा सकता। अतः यह जरूरी है कि विकास की नीतियों के केंद्र में कृषक परिवारों को रखा जाए। ग्रामीण समाज की नीतियों को बनाते समय ग्रासरूट स्तर से सलाह ली जाए। ग्रामीणों को नीति निर्धारण में सहभागी बनाया जाए। ग्रामीण समाज के समग्र विकास के माध्यम से ही भारत एक समृद्ध, समावेशी एवं विकसित

राष्ट्र के रूप में विश्व पटल पर अपनी विशिष्ट पहचान स्थापित कर सकेगा।

अतः स्पष्ट है कि ग्रामीण कृषक परिवारों का सशक्तिकरण एक बहुआयामी प्रक्रिया है, जिसमें आर्थिक, सामाजिक, राजनीतिक, शैक्षिक, तकनीकी तथा सांस्कृतिक सभी आयाम सम्मिलित हैं। समाजशास्त्रीय दृष्टि से यह प्रक्रिया केवल व्यक्तियों के विकास तक सीमित नहीं है, बल्कि संपूर्ण ग्रामीण समाज के परिवर्तन एवं प्रगति से जुड़ी हुई है। विकसित भारत के लक्ष्य की प्राप्ति तभी संभव है जब ग्रामीण कृषक परिवारों को विकास प्रक्रिया के केंद्र में रखकर उनके समग्र सशक्तिकरण हेतु प्रभावी नीतियाँ एवं कार्यक्रम संचालित किए जाएँ।

संदर्भ सूची–

- Desai, A. R. (2016). Rural Sociology in India (5th Ed.). Mumbai: Popular Prakashan.
- Dube, S. C. (2018). Indian Village. New Delhi: Routledge India.
- Durkheim, Émile. (2001). The Division of Labour in Society. London: Macmillan.
- Doshi, S. L. & Jain, P. C. (2020). Rural Sociology. Jaipur: Rawat Publications.
- Jodhka, Surinder S. (2012). Village Society. New Delhi: Orient Blackswan.
- Marx, Karl & Engels, Friedrich. (1970). The German Ideology. New York: International Publishers
- Oommen, T. K. (2010). Rural Transformation in India. New Delhi: Oxford University Press.
- Parsons, Talcott. (1951). The Social System. New York: Free Press.

- Sharma, K. L. (2017). Indian Social Structure and Change. Jaipur: Rawat Publications.
- Srinivas, M. N. (2009). Social Change in Modern India. New Delhi: Orient Blackswan.
- Singh, Yogendra. (2018). Modernization of Indian Tradition. Jaipur: Rawat Publications.
- Census of India. (2011). Primary Census Abstract. New Delhi: Registrar General and Census Commissioner of India.
- Government of India. (2024). Economic Survey of India 2023–24. Ministry of Finance, New Delhi.
- Ministry of Agriculture and Farmers Welfare, Government of India. (2024). Annual Report 2023–24. New Delhi: Government of India.
- NITI Aayog. (2023). Vision for Viksit Bharat @2047. New Delhi: Government of India.
- National Statistical Office (NSO). (2023). Situation Assessment Survey of Agricultural Households in India. New Delhi: Ministry of Statistics and Programme Implementation.
- United Nations Development Programme (UNDP). (2023). Human Development Report. New York: United Nations.
- World Bank. (2024). World Development Report. Washington D.C.: World Bank.

Chapter- 16

Education as a Catalyst for Skill Development: Opportunities and Challenges in the Journey Towards Viksit Bharat

Poonam Kumari
Assistant Professor
Motherhood University, Roorkee, Uttarakhand

Abstract:

The vision of Viksit Bharat (Developed India) aims to transform India into a prosperous, inclusive, innovative, and globally competitive nation by 2047. Achieving this vision requires a skilled workforce capable of adapting to technological advancements and changing economic demands. Education serves as a catalyst in this process by equipping individuals with knowledge, competencies, and employability skills. The integration of education and skill development has become increasingly important in preparing youth for the modern labor market. This paper examines the role of education in fostering skill development, explores the opportunities created by educational reforms and technological progress, and highlights the challenges that hinder effective skill acquisition. The study emphasizes the need for a collaborative approach involving educational institutions, industry, government, and society to achieve the goals of Viksit Bharat.

Keywords: Education, Skill Development, Viksit Bharat, Employability, Human Capital, Innovation, National Education Policy.

1. Introduction

India is one of the youngest nations in the world, with a significant proportion of its population belonging to the working-age group. This demographic advantage presents a unique opportunity for economic growth and social transformation. However, the benefits of this demographic dividend can only be realized if the workforce possesses the skills required for productive employment and entrepreneurship.

Education plays a central role in developing human capabilities and preparing individuals for participation in economic and social activities. Traditionally, education focused primarily on academic learning and theoretical knowledge. In recent years, however, there has been increasing recognition of the need to integrate skill development into educational systems. The emergence of advanced technologies, globalization, digitalization, and changing labor market demands has intensified the importance of practical skills, critical thinking, creativity, communication, and problem-solving abilities.

The vision of Viksit Bharat 2047 seeks to create a developed nation characterized by economic prosperity, social equity, technological leadership, and sustainable growth. Education serves as a catalyst in achieving this vision by nurturing a skilled, innovative, and adaptable workforce. This paper explores how education contributes to skill development and examines the opportunities and challenges associated with this process.

2. Objectives of the study

To examine the role of education in promoting skill development among learners in India.

To analyze the significance of skill development in achieving the vision of Viksit Bharat 2047.

To identify the opportunities created by educational reforms, technological advancements, and government initiatives for skill development.

To investigate the major challenges affecting effective skill development through the education system.

To assess the gap between educational outcomes and industry skill requirements.

To explore the role of vocational, technical, and digital education in enhancing employability and entrepreneurship.

To suggest strategies for strengthening the integration of education and skill development for sustainable national development.

3. Conceptual Framework

3.1 Education

Education is a lifelong process through which individuals acquire knowledge, values, attitudes, and competencies. It contributes to personal development, social progress, and economic advancement. Education not only imparts academic knowledge but also develops cognitive, emotional, and practical skills required for effective participation in society.

2.2 Skill Development

Skill development refers to the process of enhancing an individual's abilities and competencies to perform specific tasks efficiently. Skills may be categorized into:

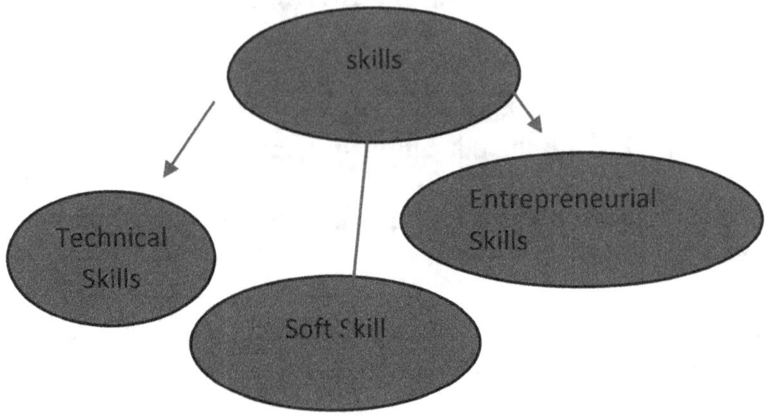

Technical Skills

These are occupation-specific skills such as coding, engineering, manufacturing, healthcare practices, and digital technologies.it is essential for productivity, innovation, employability and global competitiveness

Soft Skills

These include communication, teamwork, leadership, emotional intelligence, adaptability, and problem-solving. Soft skills are not job-specific but are essential for success in almost every profession and workplace

Entrepreneurial Skills

Entrepreneurial skills refer to the abilities and competencies that individual to identify business opportunities, develop innovative ideas, manage resources and take risk. These skills are essentials for generating employment opportunities. Entrepreneurial skills play vital role in transferring India into self-reliant and innovation driven economy by promoting startups, small business and sustainable development.

Digital Skills

In the context of Viksit Bharat 2047, digital skills are extremely important for building a dignity empowered society and knowledge-based economy. Digital literacy, data analysis, artificial intelligence awareness, and cybersecurity competencies have become essential in the modern economy.

3. Education as a Catalyst for Skill Development

Education acts as a catalyst because it accelerates the process of skill acquisition and prepares learners for real-world challenges. Several dimensions demonstrate this catalytic role.

3.1 Building Foundational Skills

Primary and secondary education provide foundational literacy and numeracy skills. These basic competencies are essential for further learning and professional development. Without strong foundations, advanced skill acquisition becomes difficult.

3.2 Enhancing Employability

Educational institutions increasingly incorporate vocational training, internships, project-based learning, and industry exposure into curricula. Such initiatives improve employability by bridging the gap between classroom learning and workplace requirements.

3.3 Promoting Critical Thinking and Innovation

Modern economies require workers who can think creatively and solve complex problems. Education develops analytical reasoning, innovation, and adaptability, enabling individuals to respond effectively to changing circumstances.

3.4 Supporting Lifelong Learning

Technological changes continuously transform job roles and skill requirements. Education encourages lifelong learning, allowing individuals to upgrade their competencies throughout their careers.

3.5 Encouraging Entrepreneurship

Educational programs that focus on entrepreneurship foster risk-taking abilities, business management skills, and innovation. These capabilities contribute to job creation and economic growth.

4. Opportunities for Skill Development in the Journey Towards Viksit Bharat

India's development aspirations provide numerous opportunities for integrating education and skill development.

34. National Education Policy (NEP) 2020

The National Education Policy 2020 emphasizes holistic, multidisciplinary, and skill-oriented education. It seeks to reduce the distinction between academic and vocational streams and promotes experiential learning. The policy encourages students to acquire practical skills from an early stage, thereby enhancing employability.

35. Digital Transformation

Digital technologies have revolutionized learning opportunities. Online education platforms, virtual classrooms, artificial intelligence-based learning systems, and digital resources provide access to skill development programs across geographical boundaries.

Digital transformation allows learners in remote areas to acquire knowledge and competencies that were previously inaccessible.

36. Industry-Academia Collaboration

Partnerships between educational institutions and industries create opportunities for internships, apprenticeships, live projects, and practical training. Such collaborations ensure that educational programs remain relevant to labor market needs.

37. Growth of Emerging Sectors

Several emerging sectors are creating demand for skilled professionals, including:

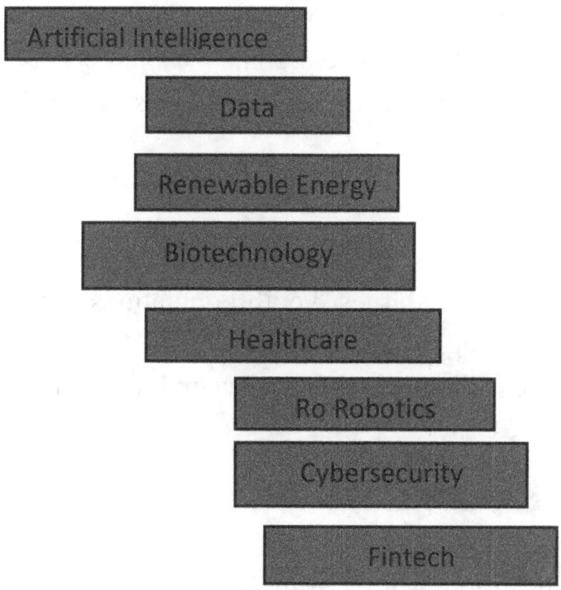

Educational institutions can prepare students for these sectors through specialized skill development programs.

38. Government Skill Development Initiatives

Various government initiatives support skill development and employment generation. These programs aim to enhance workforce readiness, promote entrepreneurship, and improve access to vocational training.

39. Expansion of Vocational Education

Vocational education provides practical competencies required for specific occupations. Integrating vocational training into mainstream education enables students to acquire market-relevant skills while pursuing academic studies.

40. Global Employment Opportunities

Globalization has expanded employment opportunities beyond national borders. Skilled professionals can contribute to international industries, increasing income levels and enhancing India's global competitiveness.

41. Demographic Dividend

India has one of the world's largest youth populations. This young workforce provides a significant opportunity to develop skilled human resources capable of driving economic growth and innovation.

42. Implementation of NEP 2020

The National Education Policy promotes experiential learning, vocational education, multidisciplinary approaches, and competency-based education, creating a favorable environment for skill development.

43. Expansion of Digital Learning Platforms

Online learning platforms, MOOCs, virtual classrooms, and mobile learning applications have increased access to skill-based education, particularly in remote areas.

44. Growth of Artificial Intelligence and Emerging Technologies

The increasing adoption of Artificial Intelligence, Machine Learning, Robotics, Data Analytics, and Cybersecurity has created demand for new skill sets and specialized training.

45. Industry 4.0 and Smart Manufacturing

Automation and advanced manufacturing technologies require a highly skilled workforce, creating opportunities for technical and vocational education.

46. Startup Ecosystem Development

India's growing startup ecosystem encourages innovation, entrepreneurship, and self-employment among educated youth.

47. Expansion of Vocational Education

The integration of vocational courses into schools and higher education institutions provides students with practical skills and employment opportunities.

48. Government Skill Development Missions

Various national programs support skill training, entrepreneurship, and workforce development across sectors.

49. Increasing Industry-Academia Collaboration

Partnerships between educational institutions and industries provide internships, apprenticeships, practical training, and exposure to workplace requirements.

50. Global Employment Opportunities

The international demand for skilled professionals in healthcare, information technology, engineering, and other sectors creates opportunities for Indian youthRise of the Gig and Freelance Economy

Digital platforms enable individuals to work independently as freelancers, consultants, content creators, designers, and software developers.

51. Growth of Green Economy and Sustainable Jobs

Renewable energy, environmental management, climate technology, and sustainable development sectors are generating new employment opportunities.

52. Increased Focus on Entrepreneurship Education

Educational institutions are establishing incubation centers, innovation hubs, and startup support programs that encourage entrepreneurial skills.

53. Women Empowerment Through Skill Development

Skill-based education is enhancing women's participation in the workforce, entrepreneurship, and leadership roles.

54. Rural Skill Development Initiatives

Targeted programs are helping rural populations acquire employable skills, reducing regional disparities and improving livelihoods.

55. International Collaborations and Knowledge Exchange

Partnerships with foreign universities, industries, and training organizations provide access to global best practices and advanced skills.

56. Expansion of Digital Infrastructure

Improved internet connectivity and digital services are facilitating access to online education and skill development programs.

57. Promotion of Research and Innovation

Educational institutions are increasingly focusing on research, innovation, and technology development, fostering higher-order skills.

58. Multidisciplinary and Flexible Learning Pathways

Modern educational reforms allow students to combine academic and vocational subjects, enhancing adaptability and career readiness.

59. Expansion of Healthcare and Allied Sectors

The growing healthcare sector requires trained professionals in nursing, healthcare management, diagnostics, and telemedicine.

5. Challenges in Skill Development

Despite significant progress, several challenges continue to hinder effective skill development in India.

60. Skill Gap

One of the most pressing challenges is the mismatch between educational outcomes and industry requirements. Many graduates possess theoretical knowledge but lack practical skills needed by employers.

61. Quality of Education

Variations in educational quality across institutions affect skill acquisition. Inadequate infrastructure, outdated curricula, and insufficient practical exposure limit learning outcomes.

62. Limited Industry Exposure

Many educational institutions have weak connections with industry. As a result, students receive limited practical experience and struggle to adapt to workplace environments.

63. Digital Divide

Although digital learning offers numerous opportunities, unequal access to technology remains a major challenge. Students in rural and economically disadvantaged areas often lack internet connectivity and digital devices.

64. Shortage of Skilled Trainers

Effective skill development requires qualified instructors who possess both theoretical knowledge and practical expertise. The shortage of skilled trainers affects the quality of vocational and technical education.

65. Social Perception of Vocational Education

In many communities, vocational education is viewed as less prestigious than traditional academic education. This perception discourages students from pursuing skill-based pathways.

66. Rapid Technological Changes

Technological advancements continuously alter skill requirements. Educational institutions often struggle to update curricula quickly enough to keep pace with industry developments.

67. Regional Disparities

Significant disparities exist between urban and rural regions regarding educational infrastructure, training facilities, and employment opportunities. These inequalities affect access to quality skill development programs.

68. Lack of practical Exposure
69. Students often receive theoretical knowledge but limited hands on training, internship or real world experiences.

6. Role of Stakeholders in Promoting Skill Development

The successful integration of education and skill development requires active participation from multiple stakeholders.

6.1 Government

The government plays a crucial role in policy formulation, funding, infrastructure development, and implementation of skill development programs. Effective governance can facilitate equitable access to quality education and training.

6.2 Educational Institutions

Schools, colleges, and universities must redesign curricula to include practical learning experiences, vocational education, internships, and industry-relevant competencies.

6.3 Industry

Industries can support skill development through apprenticeships, mentorship programs, collaborative research projects, and curriculum design. Their participation ensures alignment between education and labor market needs.

6.4 Teachers and Trainers

Educators serve as facilitators of skill development. Continuous professional development programs can help teachers adopt innovative teaching methods and remain updated on industry trends.

6.5 Students

Students must actively engage in learning opportunities, pursue continuous skill enhancement, and embrace lifelong learning practices to remain competitive in dynamic labor markets.

7.Present Status of Skill Development in India

Indicator
Latest Data

Employability Rate of Indian Youth Report 2026)	56.35% (India Skills
Employability Rate (2024)	51.25%
Formally Skilled Youth	4.4% of youth population
Informally Trained Youth	16.6%
Graduates Working in Qualification	
Matched Jobs	Only 8.25%
Graduates in Low-Skill Jobs	More than 50%
Postgraduates in Low-Skill Jobs	44%
Individuals with Vocational/ (2017-18) to 34.7% Technical Training (2023-24)	Increased from 8.1%
Schools Offering Skill Courses	
(Class IX and Above)	47% of schools
Female Participation in (2016-17) to 22.8%	Increased from 7.7%
Apprenticeships (2024-25)	
Candidates Trained under PMKVY 4.0 candidates	27.08 lakh

Future Skill Job Roles Developed 102 job roles in AI, Industry 4.0, Green Jobs, etc.

Trainers Certified under PMKVY 4.0 34,505 trainers

7.1 Key Findings

India's employability rate has improved significantly, indicating positive progress toward a skill-based economy. Despite improvements, a large gap remains between educational qualifications and industry requirements, with only 8.25% of graduates employed in jobs matching their qualifications. More than half of graduates are engaged in low-skill occupations, highlighting the need for stronger integration of education and skill development. Government initiatives such as PMKVY 4.0, apprenticeship programs, and NEP 2020 are expanding access to vocational and future-oriented skills. Emerging sectors such as Artificial Intelligence, Data Science, Cybersecurity, Renewable Energy, and Green Jobs are creating new opportunities for skilled youth.

The statistics reveal both progress and challenges in India's skill development ecosystem. According to the India Skills Report 2026, the employability rate of Indian youth has reached 56.35%, reflecting gradual improvement in workforce readiness. However, only 4.4% of youth possess formal vocational training, and merely 8.25% of graduates are employed in jobs aligned with their educational qualifications. More than half of graduates continue to work in low-skill occupations, indicating a persistent mismatch between education and labor market demands. Government initiatives such as PMKVY 4.0 have trained over 27 lakh candidates and introduced more than 100 future-skill job roles in emerging sectors including Artificial Intelligence, Industry 4.0, and Green Technologies. These developments demonstrate that while significant opportunities exist, achieving the vision of Viksit Bharat requires stronger collaboration between educational institutions, industry, and policymakers to bridge existing skill gaps.

8. Strategies for Strengthening Skill Development in Viksit Bharat

Several strategies can enhance the effectiveness of education as a catalyst for skill development.

8.1 Curriculum Reforms

Curricula should emphasize competency-based learning, practical applications, problem-solving, creativity, and innovation. Regular updates are necessary to align educational content with industry requirements.

8.2 Integration of Vocational Education

Vocational education should be integrated into mainstream schooling and higher education to provide multiple learning pathways and career opportunities.

8.3 Promotion of Digital Literacy

Digital literacy programs should be expanded to ensure that all learners can participate effectively in the digital economy.

8.4 Strengthening Industry Partnerships

Educational institutions should establish long-term partnerships with industries for internships, apprenticeships, faculty training, and curriculum development.

8.5 Teacher Capacity Building

Continuous professional development initiatives can equip teachers with modern pedagogical skills and technological competencies.

8.6 Encouraging Entrepreneurship Education

Entrepreneurship should be promoted through innovation labs, incubation centers, startup support systems, and practical business training.

8.7 Inclusive Skill Development

Special attention should be given to marginalized communities, women, rural populations, and economically disadvantaged groups to ensure equitable access to skill development opportunities.

9. Education, Skill Development, and Sustainable Development

Skill development contributes not only to economic growth but also to sustainable development. Skilled individuals are better equipped to address social, environmental, and technological challenges.

Education promotes responsible citizenship, environmental awareness, ethical decision-making, and social inclusion. By developing human capital, education strengthens national productivity while supporting sustainable and inclusive growth.

The achievement of Viksit Bharat requires a balance between economic advancement and social well-being. Skill development through education can help create a workforce capable of driving innovation, sustainability, and social progress.

10. Conclusion

Education serves as a powerful catalyst for skill development and plays a pivotal role in India's journey towards Viksit Bharat. By equipping individuals with knowledge, competencies, and employability skills, education contributes significantly to economic growth, innovation, entrepreneurship, and social transformation.The opportunities created by educational reforms, digital technologies, industry collaboration, and emerging economic sectors provide a strong foundation for building a skilled workforce. However, challenges such as skill gaps, quality disparities, inadequate infrastructure, digital inequality, and limited industry exposure must be addressed through coordinated efforts.Achieving the vision of Viksit Bharat by 2047 requires a comprehensive approach that integrates education and skill development at all levels. Governments, educational institutions, industries, teachers, and learners must work together to create an inclusive, future-ready, and skill-oriented ecosystem. Through sustained commitment and strategic reforms, education can become the driving force behind a skilled, innovative, and developed India.

The study highlights that initiatives such as the National Education Policy 2020, digital learning platforms, vocational education, industry-academia collaboration, and government skill development programs have created significant opportunities for developing future-ready skills. Emerging sectors such as Artificial Intelligence, Green Technologies, Data Analytics, Healthcare, and Industry 4.0 further expand employment prospects for skilled individuals.However, several challenges continue to hinder effective skill development, including the skill gap between education and industry requirements, inadequate infrastructure, regional disparities, the digital divide, limited practical exposure, and social perceptions regarding vocational education. Addressing these issues requires coordinated efforts from policymakers, educational institutions, industries, and society.

To realize the vision of Viksit Bharat 2047, India must strengthen the linkage between education and skill development through curriculum reforms, technology integration, industry partnerships, teacher capacity building, and inclusive learning opportunities. A skill-oriented and future-focused education system will not only improve employability but also promote innovation, entrepreneurship, and sustainable national development. Therefore, education must be recognized as a strategic driver for creating a skilled workforce capable of contributing to a prosperous, self-reliant, and globally competitive Viksit Bharat.

References

- Government of India. National Education Policy (NEP) 2020.
- Ministry of Skill Development and Entrepreneurship, Government of India.
- UNESCO. Education for Sustainable Development Reports.
- World Bank. World Development Report on Education and Skills.
- International Labour Organization (ILO) Reports on Skills and Employability.
- OECD Reports on Future Skills and Workforce Development.
- United Nations Sustainable Development Goals (SDG 4: Quality Education).
- Various scholarly articles on education, employability, and skill development in India.

- The Times of India
- Drishti IAS

Chapter- 17

ग्रामीण विकास एवं शहरीकरणः विकसित भारत 2047 के परिप्रेक्ष्य में

धर्मेन्द्र सिंह सिंह शोधार्थी, समाजशास्त्र विभाग

बरेली कॉलेज, बरेली

सारांश

भारत एक विशाल विविधताओं वाला देश है जहाँ आज भी लगभग 65 प्रतिशत जनसंख्या ग्रामीण क्षेत्रों में निवास करती है। एक ओर जहाँ ग्रामीण भारत अपनी पारम्परिक संस्कृति, कृषि–निर्भरता और सामुदायिक जीवन को सँजोए हुए है, वहीं दूसरी ओर शहरीकरण की प्रक्रिया तीव्र गति से आगे बढ़ रही है। वर्ष 2047 तक विकसित भारतश की संकल्पना को साकार करने के लिए यह आवश्यक है कि ग्रामीण विकास और शहरीकरण दोनों की प्रक्रियाएँ समन्वित एवं समावेशी हों। प्रस्तुत शोध पत्र में ग्रामीण–शहरी संबंधों, प्रवासन की प्रवृत्तियों, बुनियादी अवसंरचना की स्थिति, सरकारी नीतियों और सामाजिक–आर्थिक चुनौतियों का समाजशास्त्रीय विश्लेषण किया गया है। साथ ही यह भी रेखांकित किया गया है कि विकसित भारत की राह में ग्रामीण–शहरी द्विभाजन को समाप्त कर एक समग्र विकास दृष्टि अपनाना किस प्रकार अनिवार्य है।

मुख्य शब्दः ग्रामीण विकास, शहरीकरण, विकसित भारत 2047 प्रवासन, समावेशी विकास, ग्रामीण–शहरी द्विभाजन

प्रस्तावना

भारत की आत्मा उसके गाँवों में बसती है। यह महात्मा गाँधी का वह कथन है जो आज भी उतना ही प्रासंगिक है जितना स्वतंत्रता संग्राम के दिनों में था। किन्तु यह भी उतना ही सत्य है कि इक्कीसवीं सदी का भारत महानगरों, मेट्रो स्टेशनों और डिजिटल बुनियादी ढाँचे की ओर अग्रसर है। इन दोनों वास्तविकताओं के बीच एक गहरा तनाव है, एक ऐसा तनाव जो न केवल भौगोलिक है, बल्कि सामाजिक, आर्थिक और सांस्कृतिक भी है।

भारत सरकार ने वर्ष 2047 तक, अर्थात् स्वतंत्रता की शताब्दी पर, भारत को एक विकसित राष्ट्र बनाने का लक्ष्य निर्धारित किया है। विकसित भारत 2047 की इस संकल्पना में प्रति व्यक्ति आय में वृद्धि, मानव विकास सूचकांक में सुधार, तकनीकी नवाचार, और सामाजिक न्याय कृ सभी को एक साथ साधने की आकांक्षा है। परन्तु यह लक्ष्य तब तक अधूरा रहेगा जब तक ग्रामीण भारत की कोटि–कोटि जनता इस विकास यात्रा में सहभागी नहीं बनती।

एक समाजशास्त्री की दृष्टि से यह प्रश्न केन्द्रीय महत्त्व का हैरू क्या शहरीकरण की प्रक्रिया ग्रामीण विकास को गति दे रही है अथवा उसे खोखला कर रही है\ क्या ग्रामीण प्रवासी शहरों में उचित अवसर पा रहे हैं, या वे शहरी हाशिये पर धकेले जा रहे हैं? इन्हीं प्रश्नों के उत्तर खोजने का प्रयास इस शोध पत्र में किया गया है।

ग्रामीण भारत की समाजशास्त्रीय स्थिति

जनसांख्यिकीय परिदृश्य–

2011 की जनगणना के अनुसार भारत की कुल जनसंख्या का 68-8 प्रतिशत भाग ग्रामीण क्षेत्रों में निवास करता था। यद्यपि 2011 के बाद की जनगणना के आँकड़े अभी तक पूर्णतः प्रकाशित नहीं हुए हैं, किन्तु विभिन्न सर्वेक्षणों और अनुमानों के आधार पर यह स्पष्ट है कि भारत का एक बड़ा हिस्सा अभी भी ग्रामीण है। देश में लगभग 64 लाख गाँव हैं जिनमें बहुधा कृषि ही जीवन–यापन का प्रमुख साधन है।

राष्ट्रीय नमूना सर्वेक्षण NSSO के आँकड़े बताते हैं कि ग्रामीण परिवारों की औसत मासिक आय शहरी परिवारों की तुलना में अभी भी काफी कम है। यह आर्थिक असमानता ही ग्रामीण–शहरी प्रवासन का मूल कारण बनती है।

ग्रामीण जीवन की चुनौतियाँ

ग्रामीण भारत की समस्याएँ केवल आर्थिक नहीं हैं। सामाजिक स्तर पर जाति–आधारित भेदभाव, महिलाओं की सीमित स्वायत्तता, शिक्षा की गुणवत्ता में कमी और स्वास्थ्य सेवाओं तक पहुँच का अभाव, ये सभी ऐसे कारक हैं जो ग्रामीण समाज को पिछड़ेपन के चक्र में बनाए रखते हैं। प्रो. एम. एन. श्रीनिवास ने अपने श्रामपुराश अध्ययन में दिखाया था कि किस प्रकार परम्परागत सामाजिक संरचनाएँ परिवर्तन की प्रक्रिया को प्रभावित करती हैं (श्रीनिवास, 1955)।

इस सन्दर्भ में यह उल्लेखनीय है कि आज भी भारत के अनेक ग्रामीण क्षेत्रों में पक्की सड़क, बिजली की निर्बाध आपूर्ति, पेयजल और स्वच्छता की बुनियादी सुविधाएँ अपर्याप्त हैं। श्स्वच्छ भारत मिशनश और श्जल जीवन मिशनश जैसी योजनाओं से सुधार हो रहा है, परन्तु लक्ष्य और यथार्थ के बीच अभी भी पर्याप्त दूरी है।

भारत में शहरीकरण प्रवृत्तियाँ और स्वरूप–

शहरीकरण की गति और विस्तार

भारत में शहरीकरण की प्रक्रिया पिछले तीन दशकों में उल्लेखनीय रूप से तीव्र हुई है। 1951 में जहाँ केवल 17-3 प्रतिशत जनसंख्या शहरी थी, वहीं 2011 तक यह अनुपात 31-2 प्रतिशत हो गया। संयुक्त राष्ट्र के अनुमानों के अनुसार 2047 तक भारत की लगभग 50 प्रतिशत जनसंख्या शहरों में होगी (United Nations] 2018)।

परन्तु भारतीय शहरीकरण की एक विशिष्टता यह है कि यह मुख्यतः महानगरों और बड़े शहरों की ओर केन्द्रित है। मुम्बई, दिल्ली, बेंगलूरु, हैदराबाद जैसे महानगर असाधारण गति से विस्तार पा रहे हैं जबकि मध्यम श्रेणी के शहर और कस्बे पर्याप्त विकास से वंचित हैं। इसे समाजशास्त्री श्प्रधान शहर प्रभावश (च्तपउंजम ब्पजल म्मिबज) कहते हैं।

शहरीकरण के सामाजिक आयाम

शहरीकरण केवल एक जनसांख्यिकीय घटना नहीं है, बल्कि यह एक गहरी सामाजिक–सांस्कृतिक प्रक्रिया है। शहरों में आकर व्यक्ति की पहचान, उसके सामाजिक सम्बन्ध, उसकी मूल्य–प्रणाली कृ सभी में बदलाव आता है। लुई वर्थ ने 'Urbanism as a Way of Life' (1938) में इसी बात को विस्तार से स्पष्ट किया था, शहरी जीवन व्यक्तिवाद को बढ़ावा देता है, सामुदायिक बंधन शिथिल पड़ते हैं और सामाजिक अलगाव बढ़ता है।

भारतीय सन्दर्भ में यह प्रक्रिया और जटिल है। यहाँ जाति, धर्म और क्षेत्रीय पहचान शहरी वातावरण में भी बनी रहती है। झुग्गी–झोपड़ी बस्तियों (slums) में रहने वाले प्रवासी अपनी ग्रामीण पहचान को सामूहिक रूप से सहेजते हैं, त्योहार मनाते हैं, गाँव के देवता की पूजा करते हैं, और सामाजिक आयोजनों में सम्मिलित होते हैं। यह श्सांस्कृतिक निरन्तरताश शहरी एकीकरण की जटिलता को दर्शाती है।

ग्रामीण–शहरी प्रवासनः कारण, प्रक्रिया और परिणाम–

प्रवासन के प्रेरक कारक

प्रवासन के विश्लेषण के लिए E- G- रेवेन्स्टीन का श्प्रवासन के नियम और एवरेट ली का 'Push&Pull सिद्धान्त आज भी उतने ही प्रासंगिक हैं। ग्रामीण क्षेत्रों से धकेलने वाले (push) कारकों में कृषि में कम आय, भूमि की अपर्याप्तता, सूखा–बाढ़ जैसी प्राकृतिक आपदाएँ, रोजगार के सीमित अवसर और सामाजिक भेदभाव प्रमुख हैं। वहीं शहरों में खींचने वाले (चनसस) कारकों में बेहतर आजीविका की सम्भावना, उच्च शिक्षा के अवसर, स्वास्थ्य सुविधाएँ और सामाजिक गतिशीलता की उम्मीद शामिल हैं।

2020 की कोविड–19 महामारी ने इस प्रवासन की भेद्यता को उजागर किया। जब अचानक लॉकडाउन लगाया गया तो लाखों प्रवासी मजदूर पैदल ही सैकड़ों किलोमीटर दूर अपने गाँवों की ओर लौटने लगे। इस श्रिवर्स माइग्रेशनश ने यह स्पष्ट कर दिया कि शहरी व्यवस्था में इन श्रमिकों का समावेश कितना उथला और अनिश्चित है।

महिला प्रवासन और सामाजिक परिवर्तन

प्रवासन में महिलाओं की भूमिका पर विशेष ध्यान दिया जाना चाहिए। परम्परागत रूप से पुरुष प्रवासी होते थे और महिलाएँ गाँव में रहती थीं। किन्तु अब यह चित्र बदल रहा है। वस्त्र उद्योग, घरेलू कार्य और नर्सिंग जैसे क्षेत्रों में महिला प्रवासन बढ़ा है। शहर आकर महिलाओं में एक ओर आर्थिक स्वावलम्बन आता है, तो दूसरी ओर नई सामाजिक चुनौतियाँ भी उत्पन्न होती हैं कृ कार्यस्थल पर असुरक्षा, किफायती आवास का अभाव और सामाजिक समर्थन नेटवर्क का कमजोर होना।

सरकारी नीतियाँ और कार्यक्रमः एक समालोचनात्मक आकलन–

ग्रामीण विकास की प्रमुख योजनाएँ

स्वतंत्रता के बाद से भारत सरकार ने ग्रामीण विकास के लिए अनेक कार्यक्रम चलाए हैं। महात्मा गाँधी राष्ट्रीय ग्रामीण रोजगार गारंटी अधिनियम (मनरेगा, 2005) इस दिशा में एक मील का पत्थर साबित हुआ है। इस योजना ने न केवल ग्रामीण परिवारों को रोजगार की गारंटी दी बल्कि महिलाओं की कार्यबल में भागीदारी को भी बढ़ाया। अध्ययनों से ज्ञात होता है कि मनरेगा ने ग्रामीण मजदूरी दरों में सुधार और प्रवासन की दर को कम करने में सकारात्मक भूमिका निभाई है

शहरी नियोजन और स्मार्ट सिटी मिशन

शहरी विकास के क्षेत्र में श्स्मार्ट सिटी मिशन (2015) ने एक नया आयाम जोड़ा। 100 शहरों को डिजिटल–सक्षम, कुशल और टिकाऊ बनाने का लक्ष्य निर्धारित किया गया। परन्तु इस मिशन की आलोचना इस आधार पर की गई है कि यह मुख्यतः मध्य और उच्च–मध्य वर्ग की आवश्यकताओं को केन्द्र में रखता है। शहरी गरीबों, झुग्गी–बस्ती निवासियों और असंगठित मजदूरों के लिए इस योजना में पर्याप्त स्थान नहीं है (Datta 2015)।

अमृत मिशन (AMRUT — Atal Mission for Rejuvenation and Urban Transformation) के अन्तर्गत जल आपूर्ति, सीवरेज और हरित क्षेत्रों के

विकास पर ध्यान दिया जा रहा है। यह योजना अपेक्षाकृत अधिक समावेशी है किन्तु इसके क्रियान्वयन में राज्यों के बीच असमानता स्पष्ट दिखती है।

ग्रामीण–शहरी द्विभाजनः समाजशास्त्रीय विमर्श

असमान विकास का ढाँचा–

रॉबर्ट रेडफील्ड ने 'Great Tradition' और 'Little Tradition' के माध्यम से शहरी और ग्रामीण सांस्कृतिक ध्रुवों को समझाया था (Redfield 1955)। भारतीय परिप्रेक्ष्य में एम. एन. श्रीनिवास का श्संस्कृतिकरणश का सिद्धान्त और योगेन्द्र सिंह का श्आधुनिकीकरणश का विश्लेषण इस संदर्भ में प्रासंगिक है। ये सिद्धान्त यह समझने में मदद करते हैं कि ग्रामीण और शहरी भारत के बीच सांस्कृतिक अन्तर महज जीवनशैली का नहीं, बल्कि अवसरों की संरचनागत असमानता का भी प्रतिबिम्ब है।

भारत में विकास का प्रवाह परम्परागत रूप से शहरों से गाँवों की ओर सोचा गया। परन्तु व्यवहार में यह 'trickle' बहुत धीमी रही। ग्रामीण क्षेत्रों में प्रतिभा और परिश्रम की कमी नहीं है, कमी है तो अवसरों, संसाधनों और सम्मानजनक जीवन की।

डिजिटल विभाजन और नई असमानताएँ

डिजिटल इण्डिया अभियान के बावजूद ग्रामीण और शहरी क्षेत्रों के बीच इंटरनेट पहुँच, डिजिटल साक्षरता और स्मार्टफोन के उपयोग में भारी असमानता है। TRAI (2023) के आँकड़ों के अनुसार शहरी क्षेत्रों में इंटरनेट घनत्व ग्रामीण क्षेत्रों की तुलना में लगभग दोगुना है। यह डिजिटल विभाजन (Digital Divide) नई प्रकार की असमानता उत्पन्न कर रहा है जो विकसित भारत के स्वप्न की राह में एक बड़ा अवरोध है।

विकसित भारत की संकल्पना में यदि डिजिटल सेवाएँ — बैंकिंग, स्वास्थ्य, शिक्षा, सरकारी सेवाएँ — केवल डिजिटल माध्यम से उपलब्ध होंगी, तो ग्रामीण और डिजिटल रूप से वंचित आबादी इससे बाहर रह जाएगी। इसलिए तकनीकी विकास को सामाजिक समावेश के साथ जोड़ना अनिवार्य है।

2047 के लिए रणनीतियाँ: एक समाजशास्त्रीय दृष्टिकोण–

समावेशी ग्रामीण विकास

विकसित भारत की राह में पहली आवश्यकता यह है कि ग्रामीण विकास को केवल कृषि तक सीमित न रखकर उसे बहुआयामी बनाया जाए। ग्रामीण क्षेत्रों में लघु उद्योग, हस्तशिल्प, पर्यटन, और सेवा क्षेत्र के विकास पर ध्यान देना होगा। श्एक जिला एक उत्पाद (ODOP) जैसी पहल इसी दिशा में सकारात्मक कदम है।

इसके साथ ही पंचायती राज संस्थाओं को वास्तविक अर्थों में सशक्त करना होगा। संविधान के 73वें संशोधन (1992) ने विकेन्द्रीकरण का जो ढाँचा दिया था, उसे जमीनी स्तर पर प्रभावी बनाने की आवश्यकता है। जब तक ग्राम पंचायतें अपने बजट, नियोजन और क्रियान्वयन में वास्तविक स्वायत्तता नहीं पाएँगी, तब तक श्नीचे से ऊपरश का विकास सम्भव नहीं होगा।

नियोजित और मानवीय शहरीकरण

शहरीकरण को रोकना न सम्भव है, न वांछनीय। किन्तु इसे नियोजित, न्यायसंगत और मानवीय बनाया जा सकता है। इसके लिए मध्यम आकार के शहरों, जिनकी जनसंख्या एक से पाँच लाख के बीच हो, को विकास के केन्द्र के रूप में विकसित करना होगा। यह रणनीति न केवल महानगरों पर दबाव कम करेगी बल्कि छोटे शहरों और उनके आसपास के ग्रामीण क्षेत्रों को भी लाभान्वित करेगी।

शहरी गरीबों के लिए किफायती आवास, सुरक्षित पेयजल, स्वच्छता और सार्वजनिक परिवहन की सुलभता — ये मूलभूत आवश्यकताएँ हैं। झुग्गी–बस्तियों के पुनर्विकास में वहाँ रहने वालों की सहभागिता और उनकी सहमति अनिवार्य होनी चाहिए। विस्थापन के बिना पुनर्विकास ही सच्चे अर्थों में 'स्मार्ट' है।

ग्रामीण–शहरी सातत्य की अवधारणा

आधुनिक नगर–नियोजन में ग्रामीण और शहरी को अलग–अलग देखने की परम्परागत सोच को बदलने की आवश्यकता है। श्ग्रामीण–शहरी सातत्य (Rural&Urban Continuum) की अवधारणा यह सुझाती है कि दोनों के बीच कोई स्पष्ट रेखा नहीं है, बल्कि एक क्रमिक परिवर्तन की श्रृंखला है। इसी आधार पर पेरी–अर्बन क्षेत्रों (शहर के आसपास के अर्ध–ग्रामीण क्षेत्रों) के विकास पर विशेष ध्यान देने की जरूरत है, जो न शहर हैं और न पूरी तरह गाँव, और इसी कारण विकास की दृष्टि से अक्सर उपेक्षित रहते हैं।

सामाजिक न्याय और समावेश

विकसित भारत की अवधारणा में यदि दलित, आदिवासी, महिला और दिव्यांगजन पीछे छूट जाते हैं तो वह वास्तविक विकास नहीं होगा। बी. आर. अम्बेडकर ने कहा था, जब तक जाति और लिंग के आधार पर भेदभाव है, भारत एक सच्चे लोकतन्त्र का दावा नहीं कर सकता। इसलिए ग्रामीण विकास और शहरीकरण की नीतियों में श्समावेशी विकास को केवल नारा नहीं, बल्कि एक ठोस क्रियाशील सिद्धान्त बनाना होगा।

निष्कर्ष

विकसित भारत 2047 का सपना तभी साकार हो सकता है जब हम ग्रामीण और शहरी भारत को प्रतिस्पर्धी नहीं बल्कि परस्पर पूरक मानें। ग्रामीण विकास और शहरीकरण एक–दूसरे के विरोधी नहीं हैं, यदि इन्हें सही नीतिगत ढाँचे में संचालित किया जाए तो ये एक–दूसरे को पुष्ट कर सकते हैं।

समाजशास्त्रीय दृष्टि से यह स्पष्ट है कि भारत का विकास महज आँकड़ों की वृद्धि से नहीं मापा जा सकता, उसे सामाजिक न्याय, सांस्कृतिक गरिमा और व्यक्तिगत स्वतंत्रता के मानकों पर भी परखना होगा। जब हर गाँव का युवक यह महसूस करे कि उसे अपना गाँव छोड़ने की मजबूरी नहीं है, जब हर प्रवासी मजदूर शहर में इज्जत की जिंदगी जी सके, तब हम कह सकते हैं कि भारत वास्तव में विकसित हो रहा है।

अन्ततः, विकसित भारत की असली परीक्षा यही होगी कि उसकी समृद्धि उसके अंतिम आदमी तक पहुँची या नहीं, और यह अंतिम आदमी आज भी अपने गाँव की पगडंडियों पर, अपने खेत में, अपनी झुग्गी में खड़ा है और उम्मीद की नजरों से देख रहा है।

संदर्भ–सूची

- अम्बेडकर, बी. आर. (1936). जाति का विनाश (Annihilation of Caste). मूल भाषण, पुनर्प्रकाशनः नवयान, 2014
- Census of India. (2011). Primary Census Abstract. Office of the Registrar General & Census Commissioner, India. Government of India.
- Datta, A. (2015). New urban utopias of postcolonial India: 'Entrepreneurial urbanization' in Dholera smart city, Gujarat. Dialogues in Human Geography, 5(1), 3-22.
- Dréze, J., & Khera, R. (2017). Recent social security initiatives in India. World Development, 98, 555-572.
- Government of India. (2022). Viksit Bharat @2047: Voice of Youth. NITI Aayog. https://www.niti.gov.in
- Lee, E. S. (1966). A theory of migration. Demography, 3(1), 47-57.
- Ministry of Rural Development. (2023). Annual Report 2022-23. Government of India.
- National Sample Survey Office. (2019). Situation Assessment of Agricultural Households and Land and Livestock Holdings of Households in Rural India, 2019. MOSPI, Government of India.
- Ravenstein, E. G. (1885). The laws of migration. Journal of the Statistical Society of London, 48(2), 167-235.
- Redfield, R. (1955). The Little Community and Peasant Society and Culture. University of Chicago Press.

- Srinivas, M. N. (1955). The social system of a Mysore village. In M. Marriott (Ed.), Village India (pp. 1-35). University of Chicago Press.
- TRAI. (2023). Telecom Subscription Data. Telecom Regulatory Authority of India. https://www.trai.gov.in
- United Nations. (2018). World Urbanization Prospects: The 2018 Revision. Department of Economic and Social Affairs, Population Division. United Nations.
- Wirth, L. (1938). Urbanism as a way of life. American Journal of Sociology, 44(1), 1-24.
- Yadav, Y., & Palshikar, S. (2009). Between Fortuna and Virtu: Explaining the Congress' ambiguous victory in 2009. Economic and Political Weekly, 44(39), 33-46.
- Singh, Y. (1973). Modernization of Indian Tradition. Thomson Press.

www.ingramcontent.com/pod-product-compliance
Lightning Source LLC
LaVergne TN
LVHW052305200926
848481LV00002B/474